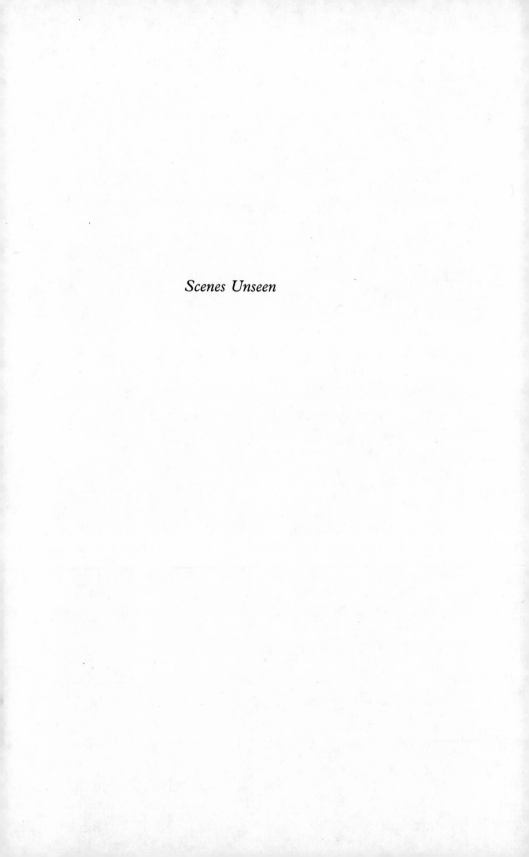

Scenes Unseen

Scenes Unseen

*Unreleased and Uncompleted Films
from the World's Master Filmmakers,
1912–1990*

by

Harry Waldman

McFarland & Company, Inc., Publishers
Jefferson, North Carolina, and London

Photos courtesy of: Museum of Modern Art (New York),
British Film Institute (London), Central Office of Informa-
tion (UK), Euro-London Films, Lilly Library (Indiana
University), Cinémathèque Française, DEFA (Berlin),
Staatliches Filmarchiv (Berlin), Stiftung Deutsche
Kinemathek (Berlin), Filmoteca Española (Madrid),
Academy of Motion Picture Arts and Sciences (Hollywood),
and Museo Nazionale del Cinema (Turin).

British Library Cataloguing-in-Publication data are available

Library of Congress Cataloguing-in-Publication Data

Waldman, Harry.
   Scenes unseen : unreleased and uncompleted films from the world's
master filmmakers, 1912–1990 / Harry Waldman.
     p. cm.
   Includes bibliographical references (p. 259) and index. ∞
   ISBN 0-89950-601-1 (lib. bdg. : 50# alk paper)
   1. Motion pictures—Production and direction. 2. Motion picture
producers and directors. I. Title.
PN1995.9.P7W34 1991
791.43'75—dc20   90-53611
                                                       CIP

Manufactured in the United States of America

McFarland & Company, Inc., Publishers
  Box 611, Jefferson, North Carolina 28640

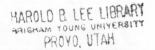

To Susan L. Morse

Table of Contents

Introduction

When the last scene will have been written and filmed ... and the film will have turned brittle and the emulsion dried to cracking ... I will be thinking of the grim long grind of the years of my life ... and of my work ... that I have built up, reel by reel ... I shall be able to say: "I never bargained ... I never took off my hat to convention ... I have always told the truth as I saw it ... They liked it or they did not."

Erich von Stroheim, 1950

It's hard not to admire von Stroheim's sentiment: In a world prey to the seductions of money and power, uncompromised artistry is a rare commodity, demanding great personal sacrifice and courage.

The great American director paid for his pigheadedness, but never budged. The irony is that we, his audience, are paying as well. Lost to us, because of his refusal to compromise, are three of his nine films. Filmgoers never got a chance to judge for themselves *The Honeymoon* (part II of *The Wedding March*, 1926–31), a sweeping end-of-an-era tale of love's conflict with class barriers, carnality, and decadence. Producers halted production when von Stroheim wouldn't curb costs. Edited by others into a mutilated version, it was never released in the United States.

Similarly, audiences were deprived of the great scenes from von Stroheim's next two works because the director insisted on presenting material of an unprecedented candor. When Gloria Swanson, the lead actress and producer of *Queen Kelly* (1928) couldn't stop him from compiling material she found objectionable, she had the director dismissed and tacked on her own ending. She released *Queen Kelly* outside the United States. Then when von Stroheim was ousted as director from *Walking Down Broadway* (1933), the ignominy of failing to complete three films in a row finished his career in Hollywood. Only the footage from *Queen Kelly* survives today.

Unfortunately, von Stroheim's fate wasn't unique. In the 100-year history of filmmaking dozens of other potentially great films by master directors and actors were either never completed or not released. Many of these films are gone for good. But the little-known stories behind the lost films and documentaries by cinema's greatest names illustrate what fiction

1

writers have known all along: People's failures often contain stories more compelling than their successes.

Behind the unseen films of the great directors lie stories of love spurned (*L'École des Femmes*, 1941, Max Ophuls); conflicts between producers and directors (*La Fleur de l'Âge*, 1947, Marcel Carné); unmanageable stars (*I Loved a Soldier*, 1936, Henry Hathaway); and freak accidents (untitled footage by Robert Flaherty, 1914 and 1915). War and economic upheaval also intruded (*Air Pur*, 1939, René Clair; *Le Corsaire*, 1939, Marc Allégret; *The Molander Affair*, 1944, G. W. Pabst; and many others).

Government suppression has prevented many a film from coming to the screen. Examples abound in the career of Russian director Sergei Eisenstein, who fought losing battles with the Soviet government on films like *Bezhin Meadow* (1935), *The Great Ferghana Canal* (1939), and *Ivan the Terrible, Part III (The Battles of Ivan)* (1946). Plagued by difficulties with the authorities, the director accepted suppression of some of his work. In response to government censorship of *Ivan the Terrible*, he said contritely in October 1946, "We artists temporarily forget those sublime ideas to whose service our art is dedicated"—that is, the ideas of whoever happened to be in power, in this case Josef Stalin.

Inexperience, too much work, or a director's declining capabilities also shelved potentially major works. Financial misunderstandings, conflicts of artistic vision, and sentimental rivalry—all have gotten in the way of the creation of a new film or documentary. Then again, sometimes well-known directors were their own worst enemies. Hans Richter spoke his mind in 1929 when he said, "The value of an actor in film is relatively not greater than that of any other object." Should it have come as any surprise that actors would give authoritarian directors trouble on the set? Charles Laughton's role in bringing to an end Josef von Sternberg's lush *I, Claudius* (1937) is memorable for just that. Surviving footage of von Sternberg's last try at recovering his reputation remains stirring for what might have been. Laughton is self-conscious and masochistic, but he is really acting. He can't complete the film because he is wrestling with his own emotional turmoil—and the haughty director is too unsympathetic or unaware to help.

At other times, fear killed films. Fear doomed Hans Richter's film *Metall* (1931–33) about a heroic anti–Nazi strike. Despite shooting a great deal of footage, Richter could not complete the film after Hitler came to power in January 1933. Similarly, unfettered artistic expression was suspect in Spain under Franco, where one victim was Alberto Cavalcanti's 1962 filmed version of Garcia Lorca's play, *Yerma*. And the Soviet Union under Stalin was no place to try to release Sergei Yutkevich's pro–Lenin film *Light Over Russia* (1947) or Lev Kuleshov's epic revolutionary tale and love story, *Dodunda* (1936).

Within recent years, fear has brought to a halt the showing or making of several works. In London in 1989, the British Board of Film Classification banned the short *Visions of Ecstasy* because of blasphemy. In the words of director Nigel Wingrove, the film depicts "the erotic imaginings" of St. Theresa of Avila, a 16th-century Spanish nun. In the same year in India, the state government of West Bengal withdrew permission for director Roland Jaffe to film *The City of Joy*. Based on the book by Dominique Lapierre, the documentary aimed to recount the work of a Catholic priest in the slums of Calcutta.

The United States has not remained immune. In April 1989, after the Iranian leader Ayatollah Khomeini issued a public death threat against British author Salmon Rushdie for his writing of *The Satanic Verses*, the American film *Veiled Threat* (directed by newcomer Cyrus Nowrasteh and starring Paul Le Mat) was dropped from the Los Angeles Film Festival. Critical of the Ayatollah, the thriller about an Iranian journalist murdered in southern California failed to secure an American distributor and also lost its distribution in a number of countries.

It's not yet too late for *Veiled Threat,* nor for the footage of certain once-lost films that have lately been undergoing restoration attempts. Belatedly, people are recognizing the genius behind even the unfinished films of master filmmakers. But for most of these films and many of the unreleased films of years ago, it is too late.

Jean Renoir once said that every work of art which is known to the public influences public opinion. What a loss it is that these works by master filmmakers, begun in earnest and high hopes, were stillborn.

I owe a special debt to a number of people who helped see me through this project. Henry Okun did a marvelous job translating material in German and French. Linda Okun and Elaine Pedreira were of further assistance in translating. Kevin Hagopian of the Film and Television Center, SUNY Albany, and the staff of the Library of Congress were always cordial and professional in directing me to film sources.

In researching for stills, I must thank the individuals who went out of their way to help me: Mary Corliss and Teri Geeskin, Museum of Modern Art; Janet Lorenz, National Film Information Service, Los Angeles; Rebecca Cape, Lilly Library, Indiana University, Bloomington; Raymond Soto, UCLA Theatre Arts Library; Jane Byrne, British Film Institute; Christine Petiteau, Cinémathèque Française; Roberto Radicati, Museo Nazionale del Cinema, Turin; and M. D. Devesa, Filmoteca Española, Madrid.

Finally, Jeff Colin and agent Julian Bach were generous in their praise of the project, while Mike Zamm was unfailingly supportive during the 18 months of research and writing. Throughout this period, my wife Susan added editorial comments—words of encouragement—without which this book (and its author) would be the poorer.

I. THE PRODUCER'S VETO

The horrible thing is when the producer interferes and wants to turn the director into a mere shop foreman, carrying out his orders. The talent that's discouraged, the great pictures that aren't made.

William Wyler, 1947

Given the natural tension between director and producer—the two dominant egos behind every film—it's not surprising that clashes of will jeopardized so many films. Rather it's a wonder any were finished and released at all.

Personalities aside, two more diametrically opposed forces would be hard to imagine. The director is the dreamer, the producer the pragmatist, answerable to his investors. One is preoccupied with conveying his artistic vision to the screen. Artistry be damned, says the producer, if the product fails to return a profit on his investors' money or is a threat to any future production.

Since the first film, directors and producers have had to deal with the issue of who is in charge. Some of the earliest producers, whether working for a large studio or not, saw themselves as persons of influence shaping the design of a film. They conceived the pictures, nursed the writers, pampered and promoted the stars, and hired the directors.

Other producers were mere executors on their own or followers of their studios' rules. They were mostly business managers who oversaw the budget and made sure the investors were happy.

Of course, producers have also been actors, writers, and directors. As hyphenated producers, they rarely surrendered control of their pictures to a studio or other producing organization. One reason, according to Hollywood's Directors Guild in 1938, was the big studios' "army of the inept [producers], who have been promoted to positions of authority for which they are unqualified, inexperienced, and utterly lacking in creative ability."

Even artists like Upton Sinclair got their usual priorities turned around when they played the heady role of producer. In 1932 when the well-known writer cabled the great Russian director Sergei Eisenstein on location in Mexico, it wasn't to plumb the director's excitement about his sweeping view of that vibrant culture being compiled in *Que Viva Mexico!*

5

Why, Sinclair wanted to know, had the man he was bankrolling gone $28,000 over budget in shooting the epic? A little power, Oscar Wilde might have said, is a dangerous thing.

One filmmaker ran into real production trouble after 20 years in the industry. In 1947, French director Marcel Carné began filming *In the Prime of Life (La Fleur de l'Âge)*. As soon as he began, it seemed clear that the fates were aligned against the film. He was working with a relatively unknown producer named Nicolas Vondas.

What happened to Vondas—and therefore to his movie—was what often happens to producers with more ambition than means. Nine times out of ten, Carné stressed, they decide to produce a movie whose theme they like without having come to any arrangement with a distributor. Then when a distributor is found, he has his own ideas of what he likes, and he lays down new conditions. In Carné's case, one such condition turned out to be the element of an "entertaining" setting for the picture. This was the coup de grace for *La Fleur de l'Âge*.

Kirk Douglas is another example of an artist switching roles and going for the sure crowd pleaser over art. In 1957, in the position of actor-producer, Douglas was overseeing Lewis Milestone's *King Kelly*. In the end he made the decision to shelve the picture.

Frank Capra once said, "It can't be just a typographical error that the names of top directors are consistently associated with top pictures." In what follows, five top directors came into conflict with producers. The outcome was a crop of unfinished and unreleased films.

1. Marcel Carné (1909–)

La Fleur de l'Âge (In the Prime of Life). 1947, 1 reel. Produced by Nicolas Vondas. Script by Jacques Prévert and Marcel Carné. Songs by Prévert and Joseph Kosma. Photographed by Roger Hubert. Design by Alexandre Trauner. With Arletty (Florence), Anouk Aimee, Martine Carol, Julien Carette, Paul Meurisse (warden), Claude Romain, Serge Reggiani (escapee), Jean Tissier, Margo Lion, and Maurice Teynac. Unfinished.

The failure to finish *La Fleur de l'Âge* in 1947 signaled the end of Marcel Carné's major contributions to cinema. Carné was forced by circumstances beyond his control to drop the project a quarter of the way through after three months of shooting. The incomplete film also represents another watershed in Carné's career: It was his last film with his longtime collaborator, the screenwriter Jacques Prévert.

For the film *Jenny* (1936) until *La Fleur de l'Âge* (1947), Carné and Prévert created some of the best European cinema of the period: *Bizarre Bizarre* (1937); *Port of Shadows* (1938); *Daybreak* (1939); *The Devil's Envoys* (1942); *Children of Paradise* (1945). The writer-director team brought eight films to the screen.

La Fleur de l'Âge followed Carné's and Prévert's *Gates of the Night* (1946). It was an expansion of a scenario Prévert had written in 1936, called *L'Île des Enfants Perdus (Island of Lost Children)*, which had been inspired by the revolt of 200 young prisoners in a penitentiary on Belle-Île in 1934. It caused a huge uproar and a governmental inquiry. Corniglon-Molinier was slated as producer, but the industry banned the 1936 project because it made mention of the fact that tourists collaborated spontaneously in the police action to recapture the escapees.

In 1947, when a fairly unknown producer named Nicolas Vondas asked Carné to make a movie—subject to some conditions—the abandoned *L'Île* came to mind. As Carné wrote in his autobiography, "I had never really gotten over not being able to shoot *L'Île des Enfants Perdus*." Further, Prévert valued the idea, which might allow their colleague Arletty to make a comeback. Her reputation after the Liberation was at a low because of accusations of collaboration. Because of a longstanding affair with German officer Hans Soehring during the Occupation, she was imprisoned and then placed under house arrest for 18 months. Still, in 1947

7

producer Vondas wanted Arletty, then nearly 50 years old, preferring her to Danielle Darrieux, 30, who had been cast for the aborted 1936 project.

Carné and Prévert renamed the film *La Fleur de l'Âge* to distinguish it from a 1943 release entitled *Le Carrefour des Enfants Perdus (Crossroads of Lost Children)*. It became an allegory of a youngster on the run on an island-prison, branded bandit, hooligan, and thief ("bandit! Voyou! Voleur!") by the tourists.

The new film enjoyed a top-quality cast and financing from Vondas and two coproducers. Carné made modifications to the script to introduce the character played by Arletty. The film now rested on a double romance: a young escapee (Reggiani) with an older married woman (Arletty), and a sick young inmate (Claude Romain) with a girl from the island (15-year-old Anouk Aimee). The death of the sick inmate at the hands of the guards precipitates a mass escape and the recapture of the fugitives.

Carné and Prévert added the "entertaining" element demanded by the producer and the distributor. It came in the form of a yacht, which had to be leased for three months. *La Fleur de l'Âge* was supposed to end with Reggiani, behind bars, looking at the splendid yacht—Arletty aboard—disappearing over the horizon.

Filming began in May aboard the yacht at Belle-Île de Mer off the coast of Brittany, a region known for its unpredictable weather. During the developing of the scenario, in fact, Carné had told Prévert in no uncertain terms that exteriors should be kept to a minimum, and that shooting in cloudy or rainy weather would often not be possible. But Prévert ignored Carné's warnings, causing what Carné calls "the first heated discussions between us." The upshot was that, according to Carné, for nearly a month "the sun seemed to play hide and seek with us." The filmmakers tried to shoot when they could, and thought of waiting out the weather, but that didn't work, said Carné, because it failed to take into account "the irritation, the anxiety that gets hold of you thinking of all the lost hours, spoiled, irretrievable."

Other factors also came into play. The housing accommodations on the island were poor, making it difficult for the crew to rest after hours. Then there was the yacht, which Carné had hoped would be skippered by "an old salt, capable of coping with all situations." When the yacht finally arrived—eight days late—it was instead under the command of a "captain who ranted against everything." A second game of hide and seek ensued for Carné, this time not with the sun, but with the yacht. At any threat of wind or swell, the yacht's captain refused to leave the port.

In Paris, rumors about the film were flying. One publication asked, "When will they entrust large sums of money to normal people?" In a panic, thinking that Carné had lost his mind, Prévert visited the director on location. The director showed the screenwriter the rocks breaking against the waves, and asked what significance the charges against him held in comparison to that grand sight.

Despite little actual filming, the costs of renting the yacht quickly mounted, so that forty-five million francs wound up being spent on only one reel of film, nearly five times the allowed budget. In mid–July, producer Vondas abruptly went abroad. One of the other backers, named Pierre O'Connell, was supposed to have relayed this message to Carné: "It's high time that Carné learned that you do not start a film with a budget of sixty million that you double or triple in the course of shooting; it's finished."

The final straw came when the yacht suddenly left Belle-Île en route to its next film assignment for the Gaumont company. Although Carné had managed to shoot a couple of yacht scenes of Arletty and Serge Reggiani, and Arletty showering, he still had more to go.

In a last desperate meeting with his backers (Pierre O'Connell and Arys Nissotti) back in Paris, Carné was told that the movie might yet be completed if certain scenes were eliminated—at least a dozen, as Carné recalls. Carné refused point blank, and the project was shelved.

In the words of Gerard Guillot, who has written extensively about Jacques Prévert, "The sequences shot are Carné's most beautiful, with some of the most beautiful passages by Prévert." Georges Sadoul, the film historian, called Prévert's script "remarkable." While Carné attributed the film's demise to fate, others saw conspiracy. One film observer intimated the producers had second thoughts about making a film with the controversial Arletty. They also might have found the subject matter too hot.

La Fleur de l'Âge was soon forgotten. A private showing of the single reel was given in 1954 in Paris, but the unfinished film was then reportedly mislaid. It is still lost.

The following excerpt from the script of *Le Fleur de l'Âge* appeared in the November 1960 issue (number 14) of *Premier Plan*, which was devoted to the work of Jacques Prévert.

La Fleur de l'Âge

(The Prime of Life)

FLORENCE'S CABIN

Florence, from the front, naked under the shower.

In front of her, through the partly open door of a wardrobe, the young man from the penitentiary, half-hidden by the hanging clothes, is watching her, dazzled, fascinated.

The yacht sways lightly. The door of the wardrobe creaks and opens further. Surprised, Florence turns her head and notices the young man, who is looking at her, eyes shining, a smile on his lips.

With a quick gesture, the young woman covers herself with her bathrobe.

THE YOUNG MAN. — Too late, I've seen everything.

FLORENCE (shrugging and suppressing a smile). — What are you doing here?

THE YOUNG MAN (continuing, without hearing her). — And earlier too, I saw you... And you were awfully beautiful, even from far, and you swim well too.

FLORENCE. — You ran away?

THE YOUNG MAN (smiling). — Looks like it... (then, delighted): Hey, you recognized me, didn't you?

FLORENCE (very naturally). — Yes, of course.

THE YOUNG MAN. — Funny... When I stashed myself here, I knew it was your cabin... I don't regret the move... You remember what you told me, this morning?

FLORENCE (smiling and intrigued at once). — No... nothing much, no doubt...

THE YOUNG MAN (indignant). — Nothing much!... (then very serious) For you, maybe... You said I was nice... It's important, you know... It's been a long time since somebody told me that... specially somebody like you!... (suddenly): You're married?

FLORENCE. — Yes.

THE YOUNG MAN. — Pity...

Florence can't help laughing, but worried for the young man, she questions him.

FLORENCE. — You're being chased?

THE YOUNG MAN. — Sure... (suddenly bitter) Didn't you hear the music?

FLORENCE. — The sirens?

THE YOUNG MAN. — The sirens... the bells... and also the dogs!

FLORENCE (sad, revolted). — The dogs...

THE YOUNG MAN. — Yeah, the dogs...

At that moment, there's a knock at the door.

FLORENCE (raising her voice). — What is it?

THE YOUNG MAN (in a low voice).—I'm not nosey... I don't want to know... (he closes the door of the wardrobe while a voice from the corridor can be heard, and this muffled voice, which wants to sound self-assured, is Olivier Pavane's).

OLIVIER.—It's me, Florence... Olivier.

FLORENCE.—You can't come in, I'm completely naked...

OLIVIER.—So what?... I'm not prejudiced... (and turning the door handle, he enters. He looks at Florence, both amazed and delighted...)

FLORENCE (furious).—Get out!

OLIVIER (insinuatingly).—Why didn't you lock the door?... Simple absentmindedness, no doubt...

FLORENCE.—No, of course not, let me see, I'm waiting for you... (suddenly scornfully). I don't believe it. You are drunk.

OLIVIER (without listening to her).—I came to make my apologies. Florence... (he comes near her) I was being vulgar a while ago... (suddenly bursting out in a little cynical laughter) Vulgar! Really, between us, do women dislike it so much, vulgarity?

As Florence only looks at him while shaking her head with a smile full of irony and contempt, Olivier puts a hand on her shoulder.

OLIVIER.—And what if I tore this bathrobe off you... like this... because you appeal to me... to see... really, would you start shouting... calling?

FLORENCE.—You should be writing it in a book... huge comic success guaranteed... (changing her tone) You are pitiful, my poor Olivier ...

OLIVIER (hurt, withdrawing his hand)—You know, I've had women who are more beautiful than you, more beautiful and...

FLORENCE (still smiling).—...younger even! You couldn't be more gallant!... (suddenly)... You're pathetic, go away!

OLIVIER.—Ultimately, my dear, I risk compromising you... you're afraid somebody might come in... Michel, for instance... Don't worry. I know how to behave, the customs, the traditions, and in such a situation, what is required? The wardrobe!... speed, discretion (still looking at Florence, he opens the wardrobe) ... disappearance!
    Amazed, he finds himself facing the young man, who is looking at him, his face somber, tense.

OLIVIER (ironic, recovering his self-assurance).—Oh! Excuse me, Florence, but I think I opened the door of the nursery...

Other Lost Films

La Rue des Vertus. 1938. Produced by J. P. Frogerais. Script by Jacques
Prévert. Photographed by Eugen Schufftan. Design by Alexandre Trauner. Music
by Maurice Jaubert. With Jean Gabin (Valentin), Arletty, Jules Berry, and Jac-
queline Laurent (Françoise). Unfinished.

Ten years before *La Fleur de l'Âge* Carné had left unfinished *La Rue
des Vertus*, another film scripted (with accompanying dialogue) by Prévert,
also called *L'Auberge des Quatre Couteaux* and *L'Eau Fraîche*. The idea for
the film had followed on the heels of *Hotel du Nord* (1938). Carné re-
assembled the team that had put together *Port of Shadows* (also 1938) to
make a film about American gangsters, but that year there were many
gangster films flooding the market. In addition, with three days left to go
in the shooting schedule, Prévert had not quite worked out the dialogue for
the crucial scene in the film, the murder of Valentin by Françoise. By common agreement director, screenwriter, and producer abandoned it for
something better: Prévert's script of *Le Jour Se Lève (Daybreak)*.

Following *La Fleur de l'Âge*, Carné's career went into a tailspin. His
postwar films, critics noted, threatened the "auteur" theory of cinema. Instead of the unusual and poetic naturalist films for which he'd become
known, his work following the breakup with Prévert was viewed as out of
step with changing French and European tastes. Critics panned the films
as "old-fashioned." Five of these, as a result, have not been released in the
United States. He scripted all but the last. The five are:

The Country I Come From (Le Pays d'ou Je Viens), 1955.
Chicken Feed for Little Birds (Du Mouron pour les Petites Oiseaux), 1963.
Three Rooms in Manhattan (Trois Chambres à Manhattan), 1965.
The Young Wolves (Les Jeunes Loups), 1968.
La Bible, 1976.

In Carné's films, the heroes are often honest, courageous, and hard-
working men, driven into crime by society. Likewise his lovers seek happiness in each other's arms but are thwarted by the environment. *The Country I Come From* was Carné's first color film, and starred the singer Gilbert
Becaud. In this "diverting," "beguiling" poetic fantasy, a stranger arrives
in a small town on Christmas day, sets right some romantic intrigues which
were keeping two lovers apart, then leaves singing.

Carné took up the theme of alienation in the 1968 film *The Young
Wolves*, which was screened at the Oberhausen Festival. The protagonists
were based on characters from old French literature.

In his 1963 *Chicken Feed for Little Birds* Carné made a ribald comedy-thriller, starring Paul Meurisse, that tried to bring back the feel of prewar French films. "Technically excellent," the film displayed "the kind of ruthless comedy that could get some foreign play." His 1965 film, *Three Rooms in Manhattan,* was shown at the Venice Film Festival. A story of two people (Annie Girardot and Maurice Ronet) trying to overcome their fears of commitment, Carné's film met with still unfavorable critical review. One critic wrote that it "displays an old-fashioned flat technique and melancholia not in keeping with the more incisive probings into the difficulties of the sexes" (*Variety,* 9/22/65).

Carné ended his film career with *La Bible,* 1976, a 90-minute oratorio film according to the mosaics of the Basilica of Monreale-Sicily. Made for theatrical and television release, the film had a special screening in Cannes in 1977.

In 1975 Carné published his autobiography, *Marcel Carné: La Vie à Belles Dents.* In subsequent years he bequeathed to the Archives du Film a large number of documents on *La Fleur de l'Âge.* Included are Prévert's scenario, Carné's modifications, cost estimates for the film, a shooting script, and stills. In 1979 he donated additional papers and a film collection to the French Library in Boston. The film archive includes 50 years' worth of his films, manuscripts, photographs, and correspondence with such collaborators as Jacques Prévert, Jean Anouilh, Jean Gabin, Simone Signoret, and Arletty.

Arletty remembers Marcel Carné as the "Herbert von Karajan of film. He treats his shooting scripts like musical scores. All the images . . . are prerecorded in his head. . . . Carné also has a gift for creating a good ambiance among his actors. We felt secure with him. . . . He and Jacques Prévert knew how to bring together a cast and crew."

In 1988, the script for *La Fleur de l'Âge* was published by Flammarion in Paris.

2. James Cruze (1884–1942)

Gasoline Gus. 1921, 5 reels. Produced by Famous Players–Lasky. Screenplay by Walter Woods. Photographed by Karl Brown. With Roscoe "Fatty" Arbuckle (Augustus "Gasoline Gus" Peeler), Lila Lee, Charles Ogle, Theodore Lorch, Wilton Taylor, Knute Erickson, and Fred W. Huntley. Unreleased.

Freight Prepaid (Via Fast Freight). 1921, 5 reels. Produced by Famous Players–Lasky. Screenplay by Curtis Benton. With Roscoe Arbuckle (Erastus Berry), Lila Lee, Nigel Barrie, Herbert Standing, and Raymond Hatton. Unreleased.

In 1921, the efficient and prolific director James Cruze used the actor Fatty Arbuckle in five films. One, *Gasoline Gus*, was, according to the film studio, a "roaring farce about a poor boob who made a million with a fake oil well." Three of the films were later banned after comedian Arbuckle was embroiled in a scandal. *Gasoline Gus* and *Freight Prepaid* have still not been released in the United States.

The trouble began in mid–August 1921, when the model Virginia Rappé collapsed at a hotel party in San Francisco. After several days of poor medical care, she was transferred to the maternity ward of a hospital. There she died of peritonitis from a ruptured bladder. A postmortem reportedly revealed that her uterus, ovaries, and Fallopian tubes had been removed in an attempt to cover up an illegal abortion.

A week after her collapse, the comedian Fatty Arbuckle, who had thrown the party to celebrate a $3 million film contract, was charged with manslaughter. By September 11, the Hearst papers had picked up the story and run with it. The news spread worldwide. Arbuckle underwent three trials (two produced hung juries) in seven months before being found innocent on April 12, 1922. The jury even apologized to the defendant.

But it didn't matter. Arbuckle's career was ruined. On April 18, Will Hays, the official Hollywood censor, banned Arbuckle from movies. Three Arbuckle comedies had already been shelved by Paramount production company (the new name for Famous Players–Lasky) the previous September: *Gasoline Gus*, after a one-week run in New York, and *Leap Year* and *Freight Prepaid*, which were released in Europe only in 1922. Concerned that the scandal not hurt their careers, Adolph Zukor, head of Famous

14

Actress Lila Lee in Freight Prepaid, *1921 (other actors unidentified). Released only in Europe, James Cruze's comedy, starring the ill-fated Fatty Arbuckle (center), became a victim of one of the most famous scandals ever to hit Hollywood.*

Players–Lasky Company, and colleagues took preventive measures. They removed these Arbuckle films from distribution so that public censure would not jeopardize their future films. The actions represented a tacit recognition of moviegoers' growing clout. In 1921, 35 million people went to the theatre each week, so a lot of money was at stake. The tipoff to how the industry viewed Arbuckle's future came when *Gasoline Gus*, despite a record-breaking first week and profit projections of $1 million or more, was pulled from Grauman's Chinese Theatre in New York before anybody asked the distributors, theatre owners, or studios to do so.

Associates tried to help Arbuckle—Charles Chaplin said, "I know Roscoe to be a genial, easygoing type who wouldn't hurt a fly"—but little of what they said was picked up by the press or heard by the film studios. Even when the ban was lifted in 1923, his films were not released. Paramount's rival studios helped their cause by agitating against him—and keeping Arbuckle out of competition.

Arbuckle managed to take up directing two-reelers until 1932, the year before he died. This was in line with Hays's view that "every man in the right way and at the right time is entitled to his chance to make good.... There will be no suggestion now that he should not have his opportunity to go back to work in his own profession." His life as the actor "Fatty" is best remembered by director James Cruze's public protest to his treatment. In 1923 Cruze put the following scene into his movie *Hollywood*: An unemployed actor, looking for an assignment, approaches the casting director. The fellow immediately puts up the sign: "No Work Today." The actor turns to face the camera: It's Fatty Arbuckle.

3. Sergei Mikhailovich Eisenstein (1898–1948)

Que Viva Mexico! 1930–31. 285,000 ft. (40 hrs) of unedited footage. Script by Eisenstein. Photographed by Edward Tissé. Production assistant, Grigori Alexandrov. Four parts: "Conquest." "Sandunga." "Fiesta." "Maguey": plus a prologue and epilogue. "Soldadera" episode unfinished.

In October 1930, a discouraged Sergei Eisenstein was about to return to Moscow emptyhanded after a year's travel in Europe and the United States in search of an elusive Hollywood contract. Then in California he met Robert Flaherty, whom he and his colleagues held in high esteem; Eisenstein claimed that Flaherty's *Nanook of the North* had taught Russian filmmakers more than any other foreign film. Flaherty listened enthusiastically to Eisenstein's conception for a film about Mexico and urged him to begin work. Backing, he promised, could be obtained from socialist writer Upton Sinclair.

In December, Eisenstein and his colleagues, Alexandrov and Tissé, reached Mexico. Traveling through the country, Eisenstein began to formulate the epic *Que Viva Mexico!* It was to be a sweeping look at the contrasts of life—past and present—in this ancient and violent land. By April of 1931, he'd developed a "sales script" for his backers in Pasadena, California.

The prologue traces "the sources and primitive manifestations of Mexican culture" in the country's native Indian population. It is based on the mural "The Worker's Burial" by the Mexican painter David Alfaro Siqueiros. The first episode or "novella," called "Conquest," is the dramatic synthesis of two Indian penitent rituals at the time of the Spanish arrival in Mexico. It serves as a kind of transition between the "Spanish tone" of "Fiesta" and a later episode. The next episode, "Sandunga," photographed in soft image by Tissé, is a sensual and passionate retelling of a wedding in a matriarchal Indian society in Tehaunatepec. It includes the well-known shot of the young nude couple resting. "Fiesta" follows, and its subject is the modern Spanish elements in Mexican culture, particularly the bullfight. Dedicated to Goya, the episode, begun in Mexico, was to have had its picador scenes completed in Moscow. "Maguey," the fourth

17

Que Viva Mexico! *1931–32. Sergei Eisenstein's 4-part epic tale.* Top: *In the "Maguey"* *episode, Maria discovers the body of her betrothed, Sebastian.* Bottom: *From the* *epilogue: "Day of the Dead."*

episode, recounts, according to Eisenstein's notes, "the cruelty to the peons in the days of the tyranny of Porfirio Díaz." "Soldadera," the last sequence, meant to tie together the earlier scenes, was to have been the heroic account of the hundreds of women who followed the fighters of the Mexican Revolution, nursing the wounded and burying the dead. Its basis was the fresco "Las Soldaderas" (1926) by Orozco, the great Mexican painter, and this sequence was to have been dedicated to him. Finally, the epilogue contained a look at "modern" Mexico and the holiday called "Day of the Dead," a "time of rejoicing and renewal ... the mainstay of the Mexican people who have coped with misery and death."

Eisenstein failed to film *Soldadera*. This sequence, which in Eisenstein's plan would comprise "the best material, story and effects, which have not been exploited before," was to have shown the birth of a new country. Without it, *Que Viva Mexico!* remains unfinished, it "loses its meaning, unity, and final dramatic impact: it becomes a display of unintegrated episodes," wrote Eisenstein. Eisenstein's inability to film this last sequence ultimately caused the collapse of the entire project.

What stopped him was money—and his backers' growing impatience with his disregard for costs. Instead of the projected four months the project stretched to more than 13. As Eisenstein repeatedly reshot scenes and changed emphasis from the mystical and religious in some scenes to the mathematical and physical form of others, language differences, site relocations, and the three-month-long rainy season further added to delays. "We have a great film and have expanded the original idea," wrote the director in January 1932. But he'd gone way over budget—$53,000 instead of $25,000—and had to plead with his backers in California for more money.

Sinclair agreed, but his wife attached a condition. She insisted that Eisenstein be controlled by her brother, Hunter Kimbrough. The director reluctantly accepted. Film negatives shot thus far were sent to Eastman Labs in Los Angeles for developing since Mexico lacked modern film facilities. Mexican officials were assured that "nothing detrimental to Mexico had been filmed." Authorities, headed by General Callas, agreed to assist Eisenstein in the filming of the all-important next segment, "Soldadera," by providing 500 soldiers, 10,000 guns, and 50 cannons for 30 days so that Eisenstein could film a battle on a scale that no other studio at that time could hope to match.

But Kimbrough's arrival soon ended Eisenstein's hopes for seeing the film completed to his satisfaction. Eisenstein rebelled at Kimbrough's assignment as his supervisor with the right to make all the cuts. Kimbrough, Eisenstein protested, was "an ambitious man [who] poisons our existence and creates an atmosphere in which it is impossible to work."

Sinclair wavered, seemed inclined to support Eisenstein, but not so his wife. Her view held sway. Early in 1932, Eisenstein lost his California backers.

Eisenstein's friends, desperately seeking help—but at the same time sending Eisenstein no money themselves—contacted David O. Selznick of MGM. Selznick, sympathetic, wanted to buy out Sinclair and finance Eisenstein himself. But Mrs. Sinclair was unmoved: She notified Eisenstein that the project was stopped, that the film "can be neither . . . sold nor financed by anybody."

In March 1932, Eisenstein returned to Moscow—without a film to show for his three years abroad. On sailing, he had received the following cable from Sinclair: "Bon voyage. All film will follow on next ship." But in the Soviet Union, Eisenstein's fellow filmmakers, now guided by Boris Shumayatsky, head of the union of cinematographers, attacked him for his association with foreigners. In the West, Upton Sinclair vacillated over what to do with the unfinished *Que Viva Mexico!* He sent the film as far as Hamburg, then had it recalled. In August, he gave some of the film to Selznick at MGM, and additional footage to the Hollywood producer Sol Lesser "to recover our investment."

Selznick incorporated footage into the 1934 film *Viva Villa*, which he produced. From the footage of "Maguey," Sol Lesser made the full-length film *Thunder Over Mexico* (1933, 7000 ft./7 reels, edited by Harry Chadlee); from the episode "Fiesta" he made the 2-reeler *Death Day* (1933); and from additional footage came the short *Eisenstein in Mexico* (1933). Eisenstein, who eventually saw these bits of his handiwork, branded them "cinematic discordances cobbled together by the filthy hands of moneymakers."

Eisenstein grieved over the mutilation of *Que Viva Mexico!*, comparing it with the death of a child. Six months after his return to Moscow he suffered a nervous breakdown.

In the West, the controversy over the film raged for years. Eisenstein had his backers in Lincoln Kirstein (*Arts Weekly*, 1932), Seymour Stern (*Modern Monthly*, 1933; *Experimental Cinema*, 1934), Vivian B. Braun (*Film Art*, 1933), Ivor Montagu (*New Statesman* and *Nation*, 1934), Paul Rotha (*Cinema Quarterly*, 1934), Marie Seton (*Film Art*, 1934; *Sight and Sound*, 1939), and Herman G. Weinberg (*Little Theatres of the South*, 1934). The editors of *Experimental Cinema* condemned the "vulgarization" of the film in 1933 while deploring the failure of Eisenstein's followers to raise the money he needed to finish the project. In a "Manifesto" they implored Eisenstein's backers "to realize the gravity of the situation and give the film to Eisenstein." One more supporter, the Workers' Film and Photo League of Detroit, passed a resolution expressing its opposition to the Sinclair-Lesser version of *Que Viva Mexico!*

But Eisenstein also had his detractors. Upton Sinclair defended his actions (*New Republic*, 1933; *New Statesman* and *Nation*, 1934); the writer

Edmond Wilson argued in the *New Republic* that Eisenstein wasn't used to the freedom he'd had in Mexico to make a film; Adolfo Best-Maugard (*Close Up*, 1933), head of Mexico's Department of Fine Arts, disclaimed responsibility for the project; and one observer (*Sociology and Social Research*, 1934) regarded the "film's propagandistic technique of direct representation as inept" compared to the "methods of indirect suggestion employed in *Cavalcade* (1933)."

In 1939, Roger Bunford and Marie Seton, Eisenstein's biographer, obtained the original footage not used in *Thunder Over Mexico* and tried to edit it according to Eisenstein's conception and script. Their 56-minute (6000-ft.) film was called *Time in the Sun*. In the mid–1950s, Upton Sinclair turned over more unedited footage to the Museum of Modern Art. From this material, Jay Leyda, a student of Eisenstein's, compiled (from the 25,000 feet of footage) the study-film *Eisenstein's Mexican Project* (1958). Eventually, Upton Sinclair's estate returned the original footage of *Que Viva Mexico!* to the Soviet Union, where Grigori Alexandrov, who had accompanied Eisenstein to Mexico, edited five hours of film and stills into the "official" 90-minute, subtitled *Que Viva Mexico!* (1979). In the film, Alexandrov discusses the shooting and the script, and relates how the sketches and stills now form a definitive version of the film.

Other Lost Films

Bezhin Meadow (Bezhin Lug). 1935–37. Produced by Mosfilm. Script by Eisenstein and Alexander Rzheshevsky, from Turgenenev's *Leaves from a Huntsman's Notebook*. Dialogue by Isaac Babel. Photographed by Edward Tissé. Music by Gavril Popov. Casting adviser, Elizaveta Telesheva. With Vitya Kartashov (Stepok), Boris Zakhava (the father), Elizaveta Telesheva (the mother), Nikolai Khmelyov, and Pavel Ardzhanov. Unfinished.

By the spring of 1935, Eisenstein was back at work. He had accepted the censure of his colleagues at the All Union Conference of Cinematographic Workers in January of that year. Only Lev Kuleshov had supported him. He was then allowed to begin work on *Bezhin Meadow*, his first sound film, which would treat sound "as a new montage element."

Bezhin Meadow is based on a Turgenev short story about Stepok, an 11-year-old member of the Young Pioneers, who becomes a martyr at the hands of his father in defense of collectivization. Eisenstein would attempt to make "a film about children and adults for adults and children." His design followed in the footsteps of Turgenev's impressionism and subjectivity: The film would be "expressive of a specific artistic form and of a psychological interpretation" of the father-son conflict. The director envisioned making two versions of the film, one for adults, one for children.

Bezhin Meadow, *1935. This still is from the first portion of Eisenstein's* Bezhin Meadow, *filmed in Moscow: Stepok's dead mother, Stepok, his father.*

For the film, Eisenstein created countless sketches illustrating every aspect of the project. He selected 200 children out of 2,000, and then picked 11-year-old Vitya Kartashov as Stepok. Yet the director also wished to prove that a good film could be made speedily and efficiently with nothing lost in artistic merit. He began shooting on June 15 on location (70 percent of the film required location scenes) at one of the largest state farms in the country, near the Azov Sea. The photographer Tissé was taking 45 different shots a day, but compared to *Potemkin*'s 75 in one day, Eisenstein exclaimed, "Not good enough, not good enough. Don't let the old battleship shame us."

The film begins with a prologue, a kind of poetic summoning up of Turgenev. In the crucial "highway" scene, shot first but taking place halfway into the film, Stepok, who in one scene appears haloed in light, is standing guard over the harvest, knowing that his father and others are plotting to sabotage the crop. Guards are supposed to watch his father, but he escapes and shoots and kills his son. Eisenstein then filmed the funeral scene in a church, the director and photographer making use of different lenses to "produce different tensions": The flat, 150mm lens produced no emotion, while the less-corrected, 25mm lens gave a "rounded image, producing a positive sense of strain in the spectator." These scenes were to come near the end of the film. Eisenstein envisioned the sound as being "less and less realistic . . . climax[ing] in a volume of boat-whistles and factory sirens." Eisenstein's first sound film, he wrote, "would be a visual-sound counterpoint—the highest plan for the realization of conflict between optical and acoustical impulses."

In the fall of 1935 Eisenstein was back at the Mosfilm studio to shoot the start of the film—the burial of Stepok's mother—and to add the sound sequences. This would include the important "family scene" in which the crazed father confronts a calm son who is about to leave home forever. But with three-fifths of the work complete, the project came to a sudden halt because Eisenstein developed smallpox—Moscow's only case in two years. After completing a three-week quarantine, Eisenstein planned to resume filming in December and complete the film on schedule by May 1936. But the smallpox was followed by the flu. While he was recovering, his film came under official scrutiny by the Soviet censor Boris Shumayatsky, chief of the GUKF (State Directorate for the Cinema and Photographic Industry), whose job it was to "resolutely uproot the harmful remnants of Formalism." The film was determined to be unsuitable because it was neither antireligious nor propagandistic, so the writer Isaac Babel was brought in in August to revise the dialogue. Further illness (another bout of influenza, then ptomaine poisoning) on the part of Eisenstein and more revisions did little to ease the concerns of the Party Central Committee, which "after analyzing a significant number of filmed sequences, declared the film antiartistic and politically quite unsound."

On March 17, 1937, Shumayatsky declared a halt in the production. He spelled out the reasons two days later in *Pravda*: The film "lacked the guiding principle that gives a work the correct ideological and artistic direction. . . . Eisenstein gave no thought to reality when depicting the Soviet countryside. Among the characters he has filmed we find biblical and mythological types rather than the images of collective farm workers." In addition, Eisenstein "not only failed to prevent, he clearly promoted the constant hullaballoo of publicity around his name."

Eisenstein "confessed" to the charges of "harmful Formalistic exercises . . . and consciously reduced ideological content." In his last statement on the film, "The Mistakes of *Bezhin Meadow*," he accepted the fact that the work had to be discontinued; "additional shots and retakes could not save it." The unfinished film had cost 2 million rubles ($400,000), the most expensive in Soviet annals.

During World War II, the unfinished negative of *Bezhin Meadow*, never released, was officially said to have been destroyed when the facility where it was housed was flooded. It is just as likely that the film was destroyed on ministry orders in 1937.

In 1967, Eisenstein's colleague, the director Sergei Yutkevich, and V. Kleiman supervised the production of a "static," 70-minute film of *Bezhin Meadow*, with music by Prokofiev. Made up of two parts, one 25 minutes long, the other 45 minutes, this "bit essay" of stills of the film is all that remains of Eisenstein's first work of sound.

The Great Ferghana Canal. 1939. Script by Eisenstein and Piotr Pavlenko. Photographed by Edward Tissé. Music by Prokofiev. Design by Eisenstein. Unfinished.

By the summer of 1939, Eisenstein had made *Alexander Nevsky* and been reprieved by the authorities. He now sought to make *The Great Ferghana Canal*, an epic on the scale of *Que Viva Mexico!*

This one would be a three-part film about the fertilization of the deserts of Uzbekistan from antiquity to the prerevolutionary days to the present period. Eisenstein wrote: "The film will be a big machine—no "khronika" or documentary—but a big film about Uzbekistan starting with—Tamerlane on the wonderful background of Samarkand, Bokhara, Hiva etc.—which are fantastically beautiful. . . . It will be a great tragedy of the struggle of human beings. . . . The hundreds of years' struggle which could become victorious now. It is highly dramatic and very pictorial."

Eisenstein left for Tashkent to get to the "very heart of the theme"— water versus the desert. Following a historical introduction that showed Tamerlane's forces invading the land and diverting the water, thus condemning the country to drought, part one of the film would end with victory by nature and the desert sand. Part two would continue with the "advance" of the desert and the death of a young girl. The finale would be a demonstration of the victory over nature because of the canal.

On location, Eisenstein and Pavlenko wrote the script, which contained 657 shots. The script was published in *Iskusstvo Kino* in September. Tissé shot some preliminary footage, Prokofiev prepared the music, Eisenstein designed the sets and costumes in October, actors were cast—then the film was shelved. According to Pavlenko, "It didn't come off, and couldn't come off—we knew too little," referring perhaps to the fact that World War II had just started.

The only footage of this unfinished film—test shots by Tissé—was edited into a short documentary about the building of the canal; the fact that this, along with the script and Eisenstein's sketches of the film's design, represented the only tangible remnants of the project brought Eisenstein to the brink of suicide.

Ivan the Terrible, Part III (The Battles of Ivan). 1946, 4 reels. Script by Eisenstein. Color photography by Edward Tissé. With Nicolai Cherkassov (Ivan), Alexander Mgebrov (Pimene), Vladimir Balachov (Piotr), Ambroise Boutchma (Alexey Basmanov), and Mikhail Nazvanok (Kourbsky). Unfinished.

Shortly thereafter, Eisenstein was asked by Mosfilm, which had produced *Alexander Nevsky*, to direct *Ivan the Terrible*. The film studio was responding to the growing trend for historical films apparent in Soviet filmmaking for the years 1940–41. In his last great effort Eisenstein planned to tell the full story of "this image—fearful and wonderful, attracting and repelling, utterly tragic."

After the release of part one in 1945, Eisenstein—awarded the Stalin Prize—began the very lengthy part two. It was edited by February 1946, when the director suffered a heart attack.

Stalin saw the film as the director was recovering in the Kremlin Hospital and at Barvikha. In September, the Central Committee of the Communist Party attacked Eisenstein because he "betrayed his ignorance of the historical fact by showing the progressive bodyguard of Ivan the Terrible ["Oprichniks"] as a degenerate band rather like the Ku Klux Klan, and Ivan the Terrible himself . . . as weak and indecisive . . . like Hamlet."

Part two was suppressed, but Eisenstein, never actually told of the banning, apparently tried to work out a compromise with Stalin for completing the story of Ivan the Terrible. As soon as he recovered, he would incorporate, according to Marie Seton, the "least offensive" portions of part two into the final episode of the czar, called *The Battles of Ivan*. Eisenstein had four edited reels of unused footage from part two and planned to shoot additional material outside the studio in Alma-Ata. Because of its length, Eisenstein had earlier decided to break up part two into two parts—part three containing the battle scenes and the great mass movements.

In this final episode of a projected trilogy, Ivan is no longer "indecisive." Whereas Ivan had been too hesitant in attacking his enemies in part two, in part three he takes stern measures against them. The film would emphasize Ivan's use of purges to rid himself of "traitors."

The assassin Piotr of part two sides with Ivan in part three, but becomes one of his few backers. Others turn against Ivan. His former supporters, the Basmanovs, betray him, as does Kourbsky. But it is the treachery of Bishop Pimene of Novgorod that causes Ivan to take terrible measures against the population. The Bishop planned to lead his city over to Livonia.

It appears Eisenstein had taken the criticisms of part two seriously. In the *Battles of Ivan*, the czar, even while he had moments of doubt, was given sufficient grounds now for slaughtering thousands from Novgorod.

In deciding to make a film that indirectly supported Stalin, it is ironic that Eisenstein never recovered to complete the last episode in the trilogy. Part two remained banned (until 1958) and with it the unfinished part three—the *Battles of Ivan*—was destroyed.

The following excerpt from the script of *Ivan the Terrible, Part III* was printed in the book *Ivan the Terrible*, by Sergei Eisenstein.*

Ivan the Terrible—Part III

Twilight. A patrol. A man on a tree. Another under the tree on horseback. And the same thing happens as before, with the difference that here the commandant is Prince BYCHKOV-ROSTOVSKY. *And that the* OPRICHNIKS *who arrest him are led by* ALEXEY BASMANOV.
The Strelitz regiments advance through the darkness.
At an outpost near the Bitch's Bridge the same scene repeats itself. But the commandant who is seized is Prince KHOKHOLKOV-ROSTOVSKY, *and the* OPRICHNIKS *are headed by* FYODOR BASMANOV.
The Strelitz regiments advance through the darkness.
Fade out.

Fade in to the TSAR's *hall in the village of Alexandrov. It is All-Souls'-Day. The* TSAR *and the* OPRICHNIKS *wear monks' habits. Above the* TSAR *and the* OPRICHNIKS *is a fresco of forty martyred saints painted against a background of sky. They direct their gaze downwards. Their golden halos shine brightly.* FYODOR *sings. He is standing beside the lectern: the psalm book has been turned upside down; he is taking part in* IVAN's *favourite game. He sings the profane hymn to the executed in a high falsetto. The* CHOIR *sings the second part.*
FYODOR: 'Peace to their souls, Jesus,
            Now with the saints,
            Peace to the souls of the boyars, of the commandants,
            Of the traitors who hand over the Tsar's frontiers,
            In return for gold, silver and flattery...
Six pairs of brimming goblets clang dully together; the noise is like the tolling of bells.
FYODOR: '...In order to build up fortunes...' *The goblets clang together...* 'and give joy to the devil.'
Once again the goblets come together. Then twice more.
FYODOR: '...Eternal repose to those who have sold the kingdom for a few pieces of silver.' *Still more clanging of goblets.* 'Who have opened the frontier to the Germans.'
All the goblets come together.
FYODOR: '...And who today dwell in heaven.'
OPRICHNIK CHOIR: 'They no longer know illness, grief, sighs, but rejoice in the life eternal...'
They dance accompanied by the CHOIR *and by the rapid clanging of the goblets.*
CHOIR: '...The weeping over their tombs turns to joyous singing...
Have pity on me, Lord, have pity!...'
FYODOR BASMANOV *sings louder than anyone; nevertheless he pointedly*

avoids the gaze both of his father and of the German STADEN. BASMANOV's
gaze does not wander from his son. TSAR IVAN *sits in the middle of the table.
A celestial, paradisal town is painted on the wall behind him. But the* TSAR
*gazes absently, morosely, reflectively before him—— The wild singing
continues.*

CHORUS: 'Peace to their souls, Jesus,
>To the souls of the boyars, the commandants,
>The traitors
>Who burn in the flames
>Of hell,
>Who stew in pots
>Like shrimps...'

*Dully six pairs of goblets clang against each other, ringing out like
bells.*

CHORUS: '...Those who have had their heads cut off...'
Two goblets clang together.

CHORUS: '...Those who died on the scaffold...'
Two more goblets clang together.

CHORUS: '...Those who rot on gibbets...'
Two more goblets clang together.

CHROUS: '...Those whose carrion made Moscow stink...'
All the goblets clang together.

FYODOR: '...Those who are going to present themselves before God...'

CHORUS: '...No longer shall they know sickness,
>Nor grief, nor lamentation,
>But taste life eternal...'

The OPRICHNIKS *dance, accompanied by the* CHORUS...

CHORUS: '...The weeping over their tombs turns to joyous singing...'
*...and by the rapid clanging of the goblets.
As the song gets wilder, the* TSAR's *expression becomes grimmer. The more
outrageous the words, the gloomier he becomes.
And suddenly the* TSAR *interrupts the song and says.*

IVAN: The cause of the oprichniks is not a subject for laughter.

Everone stops. The silence is scarcely broken by the clink of a solitary goblet.

IVAN: *But there are some amongst us who have traded the cause of the
oprichniks for gold——*

The OPRICHNIKS *huddle close together.*

IVAN *continuing*: There are some who betray the Tsar's confidence, who
batter the oprichniks' holy oath ... who turn it into coin...

The emotion increases with the gathering surge of the indictment. Each
OPRICHNIK, *sitting, pale with fear, asks himself whether it is he who is being accused.* FYODOR *gazes fixedly at* STADEN. STADEN *betrays his
uneasiness. He grips his sword tightly and murmurs between his teeth.*

STADEN: Have mercy, Herr Gott.

IVAN *continuing remorselessly*: There is amongst you one who is both
venerable and who enjoys the highest confidence...

IVAN looks before him, but the OPRICHNIKS *gaze first at each other then, little by little, they all look in the same direction.*

IVAN: And this wretch has betrayed my confidence. He has betrayed the
Tsar. Till the end of time he has dishonoured the cause of the
OPRICHNIKS by his greed...

All eyes come to rest on the same place. All eyes gaze at ALEXEY BASMANOV.
BASMANOV *does not see the glances fixed on him. He looks stonily down at
his goblet. The* TSAR *also looks at* BASMANOV, *then turns away.* BASMANOV
gets up suddenly FYODOR *turns.* BASMANOV *looks at his son.*

BASMANOV *murmuring:* Can it be . . . my son?

FYODOR *says nothing and does not look at his father.* BASMANOV *turns to
the* TSAR *with the intention of justifying himself, but suddenly he perceives
that there is a tray by the* TSAR's *elbow. There are grapes on the tray. The*
TSAR *takes a grape and puts it in his mouth. But the tray is held by the
former serf of the Staritskys.* BASMANOV's *one-time assistant,* DEMYAN
TESHATA. DEMYAN *smiles cunningly.* BASMANOV *stops short and sighs.*

BASMANOV: It's not my son. . . . Thank God!

*Quietly he leaves the table, stops in the middle of the hall and bows his
head. For the first time the son looks at his father. His features are grief-
stricken. His father does not observe this fact; he stays where he is standing,
head lowered. The* TSAR's *glance passes interrogatively across those present.*

IVAN: Who is worthy enough to cut off so wise a head?

Every gaze remains lowered. Only MALYUTA *looks at* IVAN. IVAN's *scrutiny
passes sadly across the faces of the* OPRICHNIKS.

IVAN: You do not hold to your oath.

His eyes rest on FYODOR *whose head is lowered . . .* FYODOR *feels the* TSAR's
gaze on him. Despite himself he raises his head to look the TSAR *right in the
eyes. The* TSAR *subjects* FYODOR *to a bitter test: with a scarcely perceptible
movement, he nods his head . . .* FYODOR *leaves the table, goes up to his
father and leads him off. In passing he glances at* STADEN *who realizes that
his own life is worth no more than that of* BASMANOV, *and that that life is
coming to an end. Under* FYODOR's *gaze* STADEN *loses his composure.*
FYODOR *turns and takes out his father. They leave.* DEMYAN *follows them,
his eyes smiling . . .*

IVAN *spits out between his teeth:* The traitor must be thrown to the dogs.

Darkness. The BASMANOVS *stand in the dark. Father and son.*

They are silent, then the father speaks.

BASMANOV: Don't be distressed. I was tempted. I am guilty. I've been
caught. So much the worse for me. Let it be a lesson to you.

4. Lewis Milestone (1895–1980)

King Kelly. 1957. Produced by Jerry Bressler. A Bryna-MGM production. Script by Daniel Mainwaring and Edna Anhalt, from an original story by R. Wright Campbell. With Kirk Douglas and Elsa Martinelli. Unfinished.

In the mid–1950s, Lewis Milestone, director of *All Quiet on the Western Front* (1930), tackled three films which are little known in the United States. Two of these films were made in Europe and not released in any first-run houses in the United States. The third, an unfinished work called *King Kelly*, represented Milestone's attempt to renew his reputation.

In 1956–57, Lewis Milestone was to direct the epic *King Kelly*. The film was being coproduced by Kirk Douglas's production company, Bryna, formed in the mid–1950s. As actor-producer, Douglas set up several projects; *King Kelly* was one of the most ambitious. He asked Milestone, the veteran director of men in battle, to direct, and Daniel Mainwaring, known for his carefully detailed locales and characterizations, to develop a script based an original story by the novelist R. Wright Campbell. Filming was slated for the summer 1956 and then postponed until spring 1957. It was to costar Elsa Martinelli, whom producer Douglas had cast in his first production, *The Indian Fighter* (1955).

Milestone and star hoped to bring to the screen a "*Citizen Kane*–type" tragedy about a little-explored subject. *King Kelly* would investigate the politics of the Southwest as it recounted the life of an ex–Civil War soldier who founds an empire.

Milestone and producer-actor Douglas collaborated for nearly a year on the project. Douglas has said that an enforced collaboration "can give us an asset that the lonely artist sometimes wishes he had—another brain. Two heads are better than one, if each contains a little imagination." Then again, Douglas and Milestone would also be forced to share the credit or the blame. For Douglas, this was all right. He expressed the producer's view that "each of us must care. Making a movie is not turning out an automobile ... It is a creative process, not a mechanical one, and unless it receives the love and attention it deserves, it may result in a film with the inspiration of a sausage."

Then Kirk Douglas, who had gained a reputation as a producer with

They Who Dare, *1953. Lewis Milestone's men in action: Dirk Bogarde and Denholm Elliot.*

an uncanny ability to forecast the future, cancelled the project after signing on a second scriptwriter. Douglas went on to star in *Paths of Glory* (1958). This meant that for the last ten years, Lewis Milestone had not directed a commercially successful film.

Since 1947, when attendance at theatres began to die, Milestone had been out of favor in Hollywood. A craftsman who once drew the best out of a screenplay, Milestone believed in the telling of a story, not in the "revolutions" of filmmaking such as "Vistavision, Superscope, Todescope, and all the rest," he wrote. "The widescreen is a wonderful invention, but it will never be applicable to every story until its inventors can show how to narrow it down during the action to accommodate intimate scenes between two people, or scenes where only one character is on stage."

Other Lost Films

They Who Dare. 1953, 101 min. Produced by Mayflower Pictures/British Lion. Script by Robert Westerby. Photographed by Wilkie Cooper. With Dirk Bogarde, Denholm Elliot, Akim Tamiroff, and Gerard Oury. Unreleased in U.S.

The Widow X (La Vedova X). 1954, 89 min. Produced by Venturini/
Express. Script by Louis Stevens. Photographed by Arturo Gallea. With Patricia
Roc, Massimo Serato, Akim Tamiroff, Leonard Botta, and Anna-Maria Ferrero.
Unreleased in U.S.

In 1953, Milestone was in England to make the action film *They
Who Dare*, based on an actual incident. Like his highly successful *A
Walk in the Sun* (1946), it's about soldiers under great tension: During
World War II, six British commandos and four Greek soldiers are on a
mission to blow up Nazi aircraft on a Greek island, from which Allied
ships are being harassed. The men, armed with explosives, are taken to
the island at night aboard an old Greek submarine. The difficulty in the
operation comes when the men try to get off the island after the attack
starts.

The film starred a young Dirk Bogarde (Lt. Graham) and Denholm
Elliot (Sgt. Corcoran), who teamed up with veteran actor Akim Tamiroff
(Capt. George One). Milestone recounted that the film was based on an
actual incident, the script drawn from the verbatim recollections of the
sergeant.

Despite the director's intention to dramatize the story as the sergeant
told it, he discarded the script along the way and had Bogarde improvise.
Milestone made use of pans to reduce the number of cuts, ad employed
wipes and dissolves to keep distractions to a minimum. In 1954, a British
reviewer said this "gripping and suspenseful effort" contains "full dramatic
content." Milestone's "economical direction" was labeled "a model of
efficient storytelling."

Milestone's other directorial effort in Europe was the Italian production called *La Vedova X*, the story of a beautiful woman who is wrestling
with passion. Diana (Patricia Roc), a widow, seduces Vittorio (Massimo
Serato), who is ten years younger. He loves her to distraction, but she
refuses to marry him because she envisions his abandoning her when she
becomes old. Instead, she literally throws him into the arms of the younger
Adriana (Anna-Maria Ferraro). The two become engaged, but Vittorio,
still rejected by Diana—who yet loves him—commits suicide. Diana then
grows old peacefully, her passions evaporated, her proud, contradictory
soul at peace.

Milestone's "relatively fresh, imaginative treatment" of the book by
Susan York made the impending tragedy and "high-powered romance . . .
compelling," wrote a French publication in 1955. The director manifested
a fidelity to the source of the story, and his film was called "a faultlessly en-
chanting, delicately animated, literal work." One well-executed sequence—
emphasized by Milestone because it had a particular strangeness to it—
involved a telepathic exchange between the two tormented lovers.

The Widow X, *1954. Patricia Roc starred in Lewis Milestone's forgotten European tragedy.*

The film appears to have had very limited showings anywhere. In Europe (except Italy and France), it opened up five years after being made, and the only record of its having been screened in the United States is a single trade review based on a showing in Hartford, Connecticut, in 1957. The Distributor Corporation of America was listed as producer.

In 1959, Melvin Frank's film *The Jayhawkers*, which had been in production since March 1957, was released. It explored a theme similar to that of Milestone's unfinished *King Kelly*. That same year, Milestone directed *Pork Chop Hill*.

5. James Whale (1896–1957)

Hello Out There. 1949, 41 min. Produced by Huntington Hartford. Script by George Tobin, based on William Saroyan's play of the same name. Design by Whale. Photographed by Karl Struss. With Marjorie Steele, Harry Morgan, and Lee Patrick. Unreleased.

James Whale was the veteran director of *Frankenstein* (1931) and the *Invisible Man* (1933). Having retired, after making *They Dare Not Love* in 1941, to take up painting, Whale made a last movie in 1949. His film *Hello Out There* has never been released because the film's wealthy producer, who was married to leading actress Marjorie Steele, disliked the acting.

In 1949, the 53-year-old James Whale was induced to come out of retirement by George Tobin, a screenwriter. He offered Whale a chance to develop his storylines and to experiment within the new medium of television. At station KTTV in Hollywood, the new producer Huntington Hartford, who was heir to the A&P fortune, sought self-promotion by distributing an inexpensive series of adaptations of short stories and plays to a host of stations. At 41 minutes, *Hello Out There* was slated to be the first production—and Marjorie Steele's first film.

Hello Out There was based on William Saroyan's 1942 one-act play. It recounts the last days of a playboy-gambler (Harry Morgan) accused of rape. Whale designed the set and shot the film in a few days. The whole production cost only $40,000. The film, described by a colleague as containing Whale's trademark—a "tremendous influence of German expressionism"—takes place in prison.

Whale's *Hello Out There* was then screened for a preview audience that included Charles Chaplin, Jean Renoir, John Huston, and William Saroyan. They are said to have approved of the film, describing it as somewhat impressionistic. But producer Hartford had another reaction. While he found his wife's performance as the sheriff's spouse passable, he thought Harry Morgan's acting as the gambler was terrible. Yet still worse, he concluded that Whale had allowed the bad performances and done a poor job directing. This could only reflect badly on Hartford's reputation.

Hartford then dropped *Hello Out There* and the idea of distributing films to television. He went on to produce two short stories which RKO released as *Face to Face* in 1952. This two-part, 90-minute film emphasized character interactions. The first story was an adaptation of Joseph Conrad's "The Secret Sharer" (with James Mason); and the second, of Stephen Crane's "The Bride Comes to Yellow Sky" (scripted by and starring James Agee). Marjorie Steele, as "the bashful bride, shows promise," said one reviewer about her role in Crane's story.

In 1957 James Whale drowned "in mysterious circumstances," according to the official record. A suicide note indicated otherwise.

II. THEIR OWN
WORST ENEMIES

The motion picture director is in the position of the leader of the orchestra.
He waves a baton in order to get the right tempo. He sees that the bas-
soon does not come in while the violin is playing its solo. He holds together
all the departments and sees that they all function on time, that every-
thing meets in this little set where he is about to turn the camera for a few
minutes.

Cecil B. DeMille, 1927

Many a great director has conducted himself as his own worst enemy.
As a reviewer once noted, it was almost inevitable for some of them because
too much praise early in their careers made them intolerant of restraints and
criticisms in their later years.

The same year that DeMille, speaking to the Harvard Business School,
defined what he considered the proper role of the director, a film observer
wrote about the kind of director the public is more used to imagining.
"Every studio seems to be full of geniuses of one kind and another, persons
who need only one outstanding success to flash them like a meteor across
the film firmament. And once a . . . director has a taste of this ecstatic and
intoxicating praise, he or she must have genuine strength to resist it and
react in normal manner toward it."

Rather than resisting his reputation, in many cases such a "genius"
directs as if there were no limits to what he can or should do. The pattern
goes something like this: The talented director is at first acclaimed a true
find by the studio or his producer. He is patted on the back and called great;
and everyone is eager to please him. Then when his next few pictures fail
to become box-office hits, he becomes a great problem to manage. The star
director is often in the habit of spending too much, driving his colleagues
too hard, going way overboard in making "his" kind of movie.

Take the case of Erich von Stroheim. In 1925, he was an established
director. He then completed his film *Greed*, but his version never made it
to the screen. In an interview years later, he gave his reaction: "When I saw
how the censors mutilated my picture . . . which I really did with my entire

heart, I abandoned all my ideals to create art pictures and made pictures to order from now on.... When you ask me why I do such pictures I am not ashamed to tell you the true reason: only because I do not want my family to starve."

Yet in 1928, when von Stroheim took on the assignment of *Queen Kelly*—backed by and starring Gloria Swanson—he directed as he always did: in his way. This meant problems for the producers.

Swanson remembered it this way in a newspaper interview in 1961:

> We had a complete script which had been passed by the Hays office, and he [von Stroheim] agreed to stick to this.... But then we got to the scenes in the brothel—well in the script it was a dance hall, but Stroheim had other ideas, and proceeded to spend a fortune—of my money— shooting stuff I knew perfectly well would never get into the finished picture. I don't mind spending money ... provided it all shows on the screen, but this was sheer waste and enraged me, so we halted the picture to see what could be done.

Orson Welles early in his career established a reputation for extravagance. Yet he used to insist he was always cautious about money. He said, "David O. Selznick talks about money and worries about art. I talk about art and worry about money." From the way he undertook to make the film *It's All True* in 1941, it would be hard to tell.

When a temperamental, ambitious, much-praised, and talented director couldn't work within limits, trouble stalked his projects. Nothing was more fascinating than seeing his failings.

6. Paul Fejos (1897–1963)

The Stars of Eger (Egri Csillagok). 1923, Produced by Transylvania Films. Script by Fejos from the novel by Geza Gardonyi. Photographed by Gyula Papp. Design by Istvan Basthy. With Mara Jankowsky (Eva), Zoltan Maklary (Dobo), Ili Takacs, Gyula Stella, Sandor Fulop, Gyula Zilahy, Sandor Bihary, Lajos Rethey, Elemer Balo, and Janos Vaszary. Unfinished.

The Hungarian director Paul Fejos, once considered in the same class as Michael Curtiz and Alexander Korda, had been directing films for more than three years when at age 26 he began his seventh work *The Stars of Eger*, in 1923. He failed to finish *The Stars of Eger* because he was so preoccupied by jealousy of his attractive wife, the actress Mara Jankowsky. Said an obituary writer, "He had the temperament of an artist." But clearly it went beyond that.

In Jankowsky's name Fejos fought half a dozen duels he regarded as necessary to protect his name and honor. He'd married her in 1921, and she starred in five of his first seven films. Giving her a leading role in *The Stars of Eger* put the production in jeopardy from the start. When Jankowsky, exasperated, finally left Fejos, with her went all hope for completing the project. With the collapse of this love affair, Fejos abandoned the film and left Hungary in 1923 for the United States, where he obtained a divorce.

Fejos had taken on *The Stars of Eger* a year after the death of Geza Gardonyi, the Hungarian author of the 1901 novel on which the film was based. Fejos was always interested in themes involving individuals forced to survive in difficult times. He looked at the events of their lives and tried to show an understanding for their plight.

The Stars of Eger contained such a theme. The movie, like the book, dealt with Turkey's brutal rule over Hungary from 1526 until the end of the seventeenth century. In vain Hungary appealed to the Pope for help. Outside help never came. Only the emergence of the great Magyar leader finally saved the nation and crushed the Ottoman tyrants.

In the United States, with *The Stars of Eger* and his marriage behind him, Fejos worked on Broadway, then went to Hollywood in 1926. He wrote a few Westerns, then in 1928 received from Universal a contract to direct the films *The Last Moment* (now lost) and *Lonesome*. The following year, he convinced the studio to obtain the rights to *All Quiet on the Western Front*, a film that could have secured his international reputation. But since he was busy in 1930 filming *King of Jazz*, Universal offered the director's job to Lewis Milestone instead.

Over the next thirty years, Fejos made a number of career shifts. Returning to Europe in 1931, he worked in France for a year. Then in Hungary in 1932 he made the famous film *Marie* (1932), all the while refusing Hollywood's call to return. In the period 1936–1939, when he married again, he embarked upon the making of scientific documentaries in the East Indies (1936), New Guinea (1937–38), and Thailand (1939). These films concentrated on aspects of the inhabitants' daily lives. Beginning in 1939, his work was financed by the Swedish industrialist Axel Wenner-Gren. He expanded his ties with the industrialist at about the time his second marriage was ending by becoming director of the Wenner-Gren Foundation for Anthropological Research in 1941. He became the foundation's president in 1955.

Each career change by Fejos seemed to coincide "with matters of the heart," a pattern first evidenced in 1923. The unfinished film from that year, like all of his early Hungarian works, is now lost.

7. Abel Gance (1889–1981)

Sun and Shade of Manolete (Sol y Sombre de Manolete). 1944, 2 reels
(20 min.). Produced by J. A. Montesinos for Augustus-Film. Script by Abel Gance.
Photographed by Enrique Guerner and Andre Costey. With Manuel Rodriguez
Sanchez (Manolete), Isabel de Pomes, Felix de Pomes, Jose Garcia Nieto, Sylvie
Gance, Juan Calvo, Luciano Diaz, and Manuel Requena. Unfinished.

In a career that spanned 60 years, from 1911 to 1971, it seems that Abel
Gance completed only one movie—*Napoleon* (1927)—or versions of the
same thing. With a reputation for being bombastic, hard-headed, and ego-
tistical, Gance expressed contempt for film studios, and avoided working
for them as long as he could. When finally forced to—after the debacle of
his first sound film, aptly titled *End of the World* (1930)—he did so, he said,
"in order not to die."

Five of his films from the 1930s, two from the 1950s, and one from
1960 have not been released in the United States. His one unfinished effort
was an attempt to capture on film the greatness of a Spanish hero, the famed
bullfighter Manolete.

Gance fled France for Spain in 1943 just ahead of the Gestapo: He was
suspected of being Jewish, and was on a Nazi blacklist for being a member
of the International Committee for the Defense of the Soviet Union, an
organization he'd joined in the early 1930s. In Spain he began work on a
film about the Spanish bullfighter Manolete, starring the great matador
himself.

Under the title "Manolete, el Hombre el Mas Cerca de la Muerte"
("Manolete, the Man Closest to Death"), Gance composed a dramatic
comedy that leaned towards the tragic. The main character would be a
ringmaster similar to those who, in Greek theatre, establish contact with the
spectator. His scenario attracted the bullfighting specialist Jose-Maria de
Cossio, who wrote to the director:

> The bullfighting aspect of the movie ... seems to me as interesting as
> it is original. Its greatest success resides in its managing to avoid what we
> call "espagnolade," something that corresponds to a romantic vision of
> bullfighting, which is a French conception, but which has become a
> commonplace today, artistically without effect.... The ambiance of the

41

Sun and Shade of Manolete, *1944. Abel Gance's unfinished spectacle starred the famed—and, for the director, larger than life—Manolete. These shots are from the filming of the crowd at the bullfight to observe the great matador.*

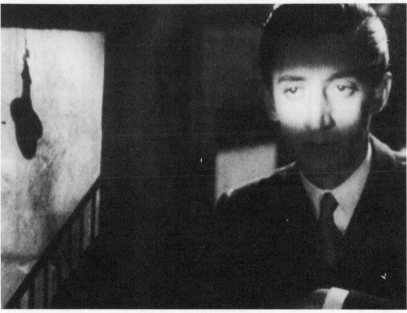

Sun and Shade of Manolete, *1944.* Top: *Manolete in his "suit of lights."* Bottom: *Intimations of the tragic in the hero.*

fields pertaining to the bulls as well as that of the arenas is well captured, with a praiseworthy sobriety, especially so for having been made by a foreigner. Once more . . . the most nuanced and precise vision of things is given us by foreigners.

Having found a producer, obtained credit from Portuguese sources, and had the dialogue written by the poet Eduardo Marquina, Gance began shooting at the studios of Augustus-Film in Madrid in December 1944. Gance and his cameraman followed Manolete's exhibitions throughout the country and filmed the most exalting passes of the great toreador. Observer Carlos Fernandez Cusenca said of the filming: "I stayed in admiration before the natural talent of the genial torero who accomplished with perfection all that was asked of him."

After some screen tests, Manolete had begun working in front of the "monster," as he called the camera. But he didn't seem to have any problems with it. The famous matador, promised 700,000 pesetas, was in a hurry to finish so that he could begin training in the country by mid–February for engagements in South America. Photographer Enrique Guerner shot two reels of film, including bullfighting scenes and scenes of Manolete wearing his famed suit of lights. Gance guarded these reels with his life.

After two weeks, however, Gance was forced to stop work. He complained, in later writing, "They derailed my *Manolete*, which did not have in it even one Spanish centime, the little money invested in it being Portuguese. . . ."

The director had overestimated the amount of money producer J. A. Montesinos was willing to spend on the film, and failed to recognize that Manolete meant to keep his February deadline. Still, up until the time of Manolete's death in 1947, attempts were made to revive the production. Gance finally abandoned the film. Spanish cinema was left without the tribute that filmmaker and subject both deserved.

After the war, Gance had difficulties returning to France because the authorities looked on him unsympathetically for having worked in Spain.

Gance would not complete another full-length film until 1955. In retrospect, the coming of sound had been an obstacle difficult for him to overcome, as we see in the following half-dozen of his films, all of which have been ignored.

End of the World (La Fin du Monde). 1930, 105 min. Ecran d'Art production. Directed by Gance, in collaboration with Jean Epstein, Edmond T. Gréville, and Walter Ruttman. Script by Gance. Photographed by Jules Kruger and Roger Hubert. Design by Lazare Meerson. With Abel Gance (as Jean Novalic), Colette Darfeuill, Sylvie Granade, Jean d'Yd, and Samson Fainsilber. Unreleased in U.S.

The Ironmaster (Le Maître de Forges). 1933, 90 min. Produced by Fernand Rivers. Script by Gance. Photographed by Harry Stradling. Music by Henri Verdun. With Gaby Morlay, Henri Rollan, Paul Andral, Irma Genin, and Jane Marken. Unreleased in U.S.

Poliche. 1934, 90 min. Produced by Films Criterium. Screenplay by Henri Decoin from the work by Henry Batailie. Photographed by Harry Stradling. Music by Henri Verdun. With Marie Bell (Rosine), Constant Remy (Didier Mereuil), Violaine Barry, Pierre Dac, Edith Mera, Catherine Fontenay, and Betty Daussmond. Unreleased in U.S.

The Story of a Poor Young Man (Le Roman d'un Jeune Homme Pauvre). 1935, 120 min. Produced by Maurice Lehmann. Script by Gance and Claude Vermorel. Photographed by Roger Hubert. Design by Robert Gys. With Pierre Fresnay, Marie Bell, Marcelle Prince, Jean Fleur, Saturnin Fabre, and Marthe Mellot. Unreleased in U.S.

Woman Thief (Le Voleur de Femmes). 1936, 90 min. Produced by Films Union. Script by Gance. Photographed by Roger Hubert. With Jules Berry, Annie Ducaux, Jean-Max, Saturnin Fabre, Gilbert Gil, Suzanne Depres, and Blanchette Brunoy. Unreleased in U.S.

The Tower of Nesle (La Tour de Nesle). 1954, 120 min. Produced by Fernand Rivers. Script by Gance. Photographed by Andre Thomas. Design by Rene Bouladoux. Music by Henri Verdun. With Pierre Brasseur, Michel Bouquet, Jacques Toja, Marcel Rain, Nelly Kaplan, and Sylvana Pampanini. Unreleased in U.S.

Magirama. 1956, compilation of shorts. Produced by Gance and Nelly Kaplan. Music by Henri Verdun. Unreleased in U.S.

Austerlitz. 1960, 170 min., color. CFPI-Lyre-Galatea-Dubrava Films production. Script by Gance and Nelly Kaplan. Photographed by Henri Alekan and Robert Juillard. Music by Jean Landru. With Rossano Brazzi (Lucien Bonaparte), Claudia Cardinale (Pauline), Martine Carole (Josephine), Jean Marais (Carnot), Orson Welles, Vittorio de Sica, Michel Simon, Jack Palance, Leslie Caron, Maria Ferraro, Ettore Manni, and Pierre Mondy (Napoleon Bonaparte). Unreleased in U.S.

End of the World was the first French talking feature, a "whale of a production," a "megalomaniac's effort," and a "sand well for those most concerned in its financing," wrote critics in 1931 (*Variety*, 2/11/31). Given free reign, a $600,000 budget, and sophisticated production facilities, Gance created another spectacle to follow *The Wheel* (*La Roue*) and *Napoleon*. The film needed extensive cutting (from 16,000 to 10,000 feet) to make it marketable.

Gance himself stars as a Christ-like figure come to rescue a world facing social and political catastrophe: A comet is heading towards Earth. The film was all Abel Gance, the righter of wrongs. Throughout, Gance "let

Abel Gance's End of the World *(1930), the first French sound spectacle, nearly ended the filmmaker's career. Here the director himself stars as a Christ figure.*

loose his love for personally staging himself," wrote the critics. He overacts, and his voice fails to carry because of the poor quality of the film.

Gance's failure to make artistic use of sound in such an expensive production nearly ended his career. His reputation nose-dived, and for the next 10 years, when French filmmaking hit its peak, Gance's films were seen by few. Until he regained some influence in the early 1940s, he had to settle for smaller, more manageable projects, and the studios called the shots. *End of the World* was last screened only in French in the U.S. in 1934.

"Aimed at the sentimentally unsophisticated, meaning the vast majority" (*Variety*, 12/26/33), Gance's *The Ironmaster* is the story of a well-born woman (Gaby Morlay) who marries a commoner, after she loses her fortune and her lover jilts her. Initially heartbroken at the prospect of life with a man she loathes, she eventually comes to love him. The film was praised for its photography and the acting of Gaby Morlay.

Gance then made *Poliche*, a tearjerker about a beautiful woman, Rosine, who is unable to return the love of Didier Mereuil (nicknamed Poliche). Next came *The Story of a Poor Young Man*, filmed at a cost of 1.6 million francs, and based on a popular novel by Octave Feuillet. In the

Top: *Silvana Pampaniniin in Abel Gance's* Tower of Nesle *(1954). This film contained material too provocative for distributors.* Bottom: *Gance's* Magirama, *1956, in Polyvision.*

novel, a rich man loses his fortune because of a sensational revelation, but gains the love of a young woman instead. Gance's production was the sound version of a story first filmed in 1911, then again in 1927. A year later, he filmed *Woman Thief*, a rare 1930s Gance film. Jules Berry plays a blackmailer. The film, based upon the novel by Pierre Frondaire, is an action-filled suspense thriller that runs only 90 minutes.

Gance's first completed film since *Le Capitaine Fracasse* (1943) was *The Tower of Nesle* which brought him back into prominence. "A scorching piece of filmic bravura," *Variety* called it in 1955. Based on a story by Dumas Père, the color work is a violent, full-blown spectacle of the Middle Ages. The French version, even more than the Italian version, is filled with erotic images that, according to the same trade publication, remind viewers of "a bolder and more virile period of filmmaking."

Still, Gance reminded critics that "if we had had a free hand in terms of eroticism, we would have made the most beautiful films in the world." The director admitted as well that he had "wanted to make a cloak-and-dagger western." The year the film was shown in France a young François Truffaut called the work "extraordinarily sound and youthful. Gance moves *La Tour de Nesle* with hell-for-leather speed. The shots ... recall miniatures in Laurence Olivier's *Henry V*."

The following year Gance, now called by some a "failed genius," turned to experimentation. *Magirama* was Gance's filmic example of "Polyvision" and "triple screen," in contrast to Cinerama. The picture contains six shorts: extracts from Gance's *Napoleon* (1927), *J'Accuse* (1937), and *Quatorze Juillet* (1953); Norman Mclaren's *Begone, Dull Care* (1949); and Nelly Kaplan's two pieces, *Aupres de ma Blonde* (1944) and *Chateau de Nuages*.

Austerlitz, completed in 1960, is Gance's last major film and only his second full-length film since the end of World War II. *Austerlitz* is the sequel to his 1927 film *Napoleon*, which ended with the "Little Corporal" consolidating his powers in Italy in 1797. The latter film, a French-Italian-Yugoslav production, continues the story through Napoleon's greatest victory, Austerlitz, when, in 1805, he defeated the Russian and Austrian armies. Gance's film used a host of actors to explore the long, battle-filled story of aristocratic France in the era of Napoleon. In 1960, 20th Century–Fox accepted the picture for United States distribution, but did not release it at 170 minutes.

In the mid–1960s Gance made two films for French television, never seen in the United States: *Marie Tudor* (1965, 200 min.), and *Valmy* (1967, 70 min.). The former is as adaptation of a Victor Hugo play, while the latter was the dramatization of the Napoleonic battle.

Footage of the unfinished *Sun and Shadow of Manolete* was screened for the first time at the 1963 San Sebastian film festival when Gance's reputation was on the rise in Europe. In 1971 Gance remade his 1927 film *Napoleon* in a sound version, calling it *Napoleon and the Revolution*.

8. Pier Paolo Pasolini (1922–1975)

Frenzy (La Rabbia). 1963, 50 min. Produced by Gastone Ferrante. Script by Pasolini, commentary by Georgio Bassini and Renato Guttuso. Unreleased.

Study of Love (Comizi d'Amore). 1964, 90 min. Produced by Alfredo Bini. Commentary written and spoken by Pasolini. Photographed by Mario Bernardo and Tonino Delli Colli. With Pasolini, Susanna Pasolini, Alberto Moravia, Eugenio Montale, Cesare Musatti, Giuseppe Ungaretti, and Oriana Fallaci. Unreleased in U.S.

Oedipus Rex (Edipo Re). 1967, 110 min. Script by Pasolini. With Franco Citti (Oedipus), Sylvana Mangano (Jocasta), Alida Valie (Merope), Carmelo Bene (Creon), Julian Beck (Tiresias), and Pasolini (High Priest). Unreleased in U.S.

Notes for an African Oresteia (Appunti per una Orestiade Africana). 1969, 70 min. Produced by Jan Vittorio Baldi. Script by Pasolini. Photographed by Giorgio Pelloni. Unreleased in U.S.

Four films that the controversial director Pier Paolo Pasolini made in the 1960s have not been shown commercially in the United States. The director of 20 films, including *Accattone* (1961), *The Gospel According to St. Matthew* (1964), and *Teorema* (1968), has stressed that he made his films "as a poet" with attention for "the little homelands" in specific regions of the world.

Pasolini has called *Frenzy* his third work, "a strange film" because it is composed of documentary material only, none of which he shot, and with commentary in verse which he composed. He chose and organized "extremely banal and sometimes reactionary" news sequences: scenes from the Algerian war, the papacy of John XXIII, returning Italian POWs from the Soviet Union, footage of Marilyn Monroe. The narrative, given by the writer and sometimes actor Giogio Bassani, and by the painter Renato Guttuso, is, according to Pasolini, a "Marxist denunciation of society in our time."

When Pasolini completed his work, the producer added a second episode, directed by Giovanni Guareschi, which was to balance out the political tone of Pasolini's work. Warner Bros., the distributor, found that Guareschi's contribution had "racist overtones." The studio halted release of the film.

A year later, Pasolini, with tape recorder and camera in hand, interviewed fellow Italians for a *Study of Love*. *Variety* summarized Pasolini's film as one in which "all walks of people talk of love, prostitution, homosexuality married and nonmarried love." Subjects in the film include the writer Alberto Moravia and the journalist observer Oriana Fallaci. Pasolini also spoke with people he classified as "subproletariat," poor villagers from southern Italy who display little of the middle class's so-called sexual repression. Pasolini ended the film by reading his poetry at a wedding.

Pasolini made his film with a specifically Italian audience in mind: Italians, he said, would "see their everyday life reflected in this film." Non–Italians, he claimed, would have difficulty understanding the Italian mileu. Having thus narrowed his film's appeal, Pasolini helped seal its demise. The picture failed in Italy and was first shown in the United States in the Pasolini retrospective at the Museum of Modern Art in May 1990.

In the films *Oedipus Rex* and *Notes for an African Oresteia*, Pasolini turned his attention to works of fiction in which, indirectly, he could attack the modern world for its destruction of myth. He again proclaimed the value of "subproletariat" cultures—those that are marginal, preindustrial, and pre–Catholic—over capitalist and communist systems. Despite their being available for viewing (*Notes* can be rented in 35mm from Bauer International Film), neither film has been shown commercially in the United States.

9. Jacques Rivette (1928–)

Out 1: Noli Me Tangere. 1971, 760 min. Produced by Stephane Tchalgad-jieff. Script by Rivette and Suzanne Schiffman. Photographed by Pierre-William Glenn. With Jean-Pierre Leaud, Juliet Berto, Bulle Ogier, Michel Lonsdale, and Eric Rohmer. Unreleased.

Jacques Rivette is a filmmaker whose output of 20 films since 1950 is bound to infuriate, fascinate, or bore viewers. This New Wave director's most accessible work is probably *The Nun (La Religieuse,* 1965). Rivette, who has been quoted as saying "I think the only role of the cinema is to upset people," made *Out 1,* one of the longest films ever.

In early 1970, Rivette began filming an eight-part TV serial. Each episode ran 90 minutes. With a cast of three dozen, he shot 30 hours of improvisation and then pared the material down to produce *Out 1.*

The drawn-out, mysterious story is about Colin (Jean-Pierre Leaud), a man who is first introduced posing as a deaf-mute beggar. He has been receiving "messages" about literary figures from Lewis Carroll's *Hunting of the Snark* and Balzac's *Histoire des Treize.* Further along in the film, Colin is at the point of insanity, found banging his head against the wall. But he recovers sufficiently enough to visit an old friend, whom he lets know he "intends to lead a happy life." Then when he is back on the street, he is seen dancing and playing his harmonica.

Rivette has said that "a film must be, if not an ordeal, at least an experience." Not surprisingly, French television rejected this cryptic picture, and no distributor picked it up for theatrical release.

In nearly 20 years, *Out 1* was shown only once—as an "unprocessed workprint" in September 1971 in Le Havre. Because of the critical reaction to the film, Rivette spent a year cutting the film down to 255 minutes. He titled the shortened version *Out One: Spectre.* It was released in 1974.

Other Lost Films

Northwest Wind (Noroit). 1976, 145 min. Produced by Stephen Tschalgad-jieff. Script by Rivette, Eduardo de Gregorio, and Maria Ludovica Parolini. Photographed by William Lubschansky. With Geraldine Chaplin, Bernadette

Lafont, Kika Markham, Anne-Marie Reynaud, and Georges Gatecloud. Unreleased in U.S.

Paris Goes Away (Paris S'en Va). 1980, 30 min. Script by Rivette and Suzanne Schiffman. With Bulle Ogier, Pascale Ogier, and Pierre Clementi. Unreleased.

Late in 1974, Rivette received backing to make four improvised films. The collected works would be called *Scènes from the Other Side (Scenes de la Vie Parallele)*. Rivette filmed *Duelle*, the second film in the series, first. Released in 1976, *Duelle* is about two women who fight to the death over a man. He then made *Northwest Wind (Noroit)*, the intended third film of the series.

Northwest Wind is based on the play *The Revenger's Tragedy*, by Cyril Tourneur. It takes place during the spring carnival season "when the gods and the mortals come into contact with each other." In the film, the character named Morag (Geraldine Chaplin) is out to avenge her brother, who died at the hands of female pirates. These pirates are lead by Guilia (Bernadette Lafont), "the daughter of the sun." Morag manages to join the pirate gang and, by gaining the allegiance of some members, attempts to have them kill each other off. In the climactic scene, Morag and Guilia battle to the death.

Rivette's allegorical tale was shown at the London Film Festival in 1976 and in Berlin in 1977. Found "unrewarding most of the way" (*Variety*, 9/21/77), the film was not picked up by any distributor in the United States.

After he made *Northwest Wind,* Rivette suffered a nervous breakdown in late 1975. In no shape to make the third film in the tetrology, which was supposed to be part one in the series, Rivette abandoned his project. That film would have starred Leslie Caron and Albert Finney, with dialogue by Michael Graham. Left unmade also was the final film, intended to be a musical with Anna Karina.

In 1978, Rivette returned to filmmaking with the *Merry-Go-Round*. Starring Joe Dellesandro and Maria Schneider, the film was not shown commercially for five years. Rivette faced difficulty getting the film released because Maria Schneider died in the intervening years.

In 1980, Rivette actually considered remaking *Out 1*, but out of the original cast of 36, only Bulle Ogier was available. Instead, the director put her to use in his next improvised short, called *Paris Goes Away (Paris S'en Va)*. Here she plays a woman released from jail who becomes involved in murder.

Rivette's *Paris Goes Away* has not been released, perhaps because Rivette expanded this story into the full-length film *The Northern Bridge (Pont du Nord,* 1982). The latter represented his first commercially released film in six years.

10. Erich von Stroheim (1885–1957)

The Honeymoon (part two of **The Wedding March**). 1926–31, U.S., silent, 70 min. (7,300 ft). Paramount. Screenplay by von Stroheim. Photographed by Hal Mohr and Ben Reynolds. Edited by Josef von Sternberg. With von Stroheim, Fay Wray, ZaSu Pitts, Matthew Betz. Unreleased in U.S.

Queen Kelly. 1928–32, 4 hours. MGM, Joseph P. Kennedy and Gloria Swanson, producers. Screenplay by von Stroheim. Photographed by Ben Reynolds, William Daniels, and Gregg Toland. Edited by Viola Lawrence. With Gloria Swanson, Walter Byron, Seena Owen, Sydney Bracey, and William von Brincken. Unreleased in U.S.

Walking Down Broadway. 1932. 20th Century–Fox. Screenplay by von Stroheim and Leonard Spiegelgass from the novel by Dawn Powell. Photographed by James Wong Howe. With ZaSu Pitts, Boots Mallory, James Dunn, Terence Ray, Minna Gombell, and Will Stanton. Unreleased.

The period 1926–33 was the most volatile in von Stroheim's life. Three unreleased and unfinished films he directed in these years ended his directorial career in Hollywood.

In June 1926, von Stroheim began shooting *The Wedding March*, a film he originally envisioned as a six-hour picture. By January 1927, he had exhausted his budget and was forced by Pat Powers, the producer, to stop shooting. With 50 or more reels on hand (some estimates say as many as 100, equaling 200,000 feet), he and Frank Hull set about editing the film. Faced with a massive amount of footage, von Stroheim decided to make the film a two-part work. The first part would be called *The Wedding March*; the second, *The Honeymoon*. After seven months, during which time von Stroheim had cut the first part down to about 26,000 feet and the second part to about 22,500 feet, B. P. Schulberg, chief of Paramount's production, who had acquired a share of the interest in *The Wedding March* from Pat Powers, lost patience with the project. He asked von Sternberg to take over. Von Sternberg cut von Stroheim's footage of part one down to about 18,000 feet and part two down to about 10,800 feet. Still unsatisfied with the resultant work, Schulberg turned both parts of the film over to Julian Johnston for further editing.

Paramount's chief executive in New York, Jesse Lasky, refused to

Erich von Stroheim and ZaSu Pitts getting married. One of the last scenes from Erich von Stroheim's The Wedding March *(1928), highlighted at the beginning of his film* The Honeymoon *(Part II of* The Wedding March*).*

consider a two-part work, and Pat Powers didn't like Johnston's editing; Johnston had cut part one down to 11,000 feet. Powers was given the right by Lasky to edit the two-part film into one film of twelve reels. As a silent, it was previewed in the winter of 1927–28 in Anaheim and Long Beach, and was found disappointing. Talking pictures were making their debut, so despite the announcement in *the New York Times* that *The Wedding March* would be released in January 1928, it went back to the studios. *The Wedding March*, with a musical track, was released in New York in October 1928. It was 10,400 feet long and ran for 115 minutes.

The fate of *The Honeymoon*—of which von Stroheim filmed only two-thirds (according to the script) and which he never edited entirely—remained in doubt for a number of years while *The Wedding March* was shown in the United States and abroad. In the United States, the film did fairly well in large cities, but elsewhere it was referred to as "a messed-up picture" which might only do well overseas. Since von Stroheim had not completed his edit, he refused to give his permission to let it be shown in the United States. But in all likelihood, since the film was silent, Paramount would only have been able to make money on the film abroad anyway. So in 1931, after *The Wedding March* made the rounds abroad, Paramount edited the film further and then released *The Honeymoon* in Europe and South America. In France, it was called *Mariage de prince*. By the time *The Honeymoon* appeared, two of its leading actors had died.

As a 70-minute silent film, *The Honeymoon* contained a 20-minute condensation (2,000 feet) of *The Wedding March* in order to make it a "separate whole film, complete in itself."

The Wedding March is set evocatively in Vienna in the spring and summer of 1914. It concerns love's conflict with class barriers, carnality, and decadence. It focuses on the love of two women, rich Cecilia (ZaSu Pitts) and impoverished Mitzi (Fay Wray), for a jaded aristocrat, Prince Nicki (von Stroheim). *The Wedding March* ends with two forced marriages: that of the prince to Cecilia, a union that will guarantee the continuation of his family's lavish way of life; and the marriage of Mitzi to a jealous lover, Schani (Matthew Betz), who had threatened to kill Nicki unless Mitzi married him. It is the only von Stroheim film in which the villain, Schani, remains alive.

In *The Honeymoon*, the story begins with the wedding night, and the theme of the picture quickly becomes apparent: Despite his new bride, the prince cannot forget Mitzi, the woman he really cares for. At the same time, Mitzi's jealous husband, Schani, cannot forget the prince. He seeks out Nicki at his Tyrolean hunting lodge and tries to murder him. But the prince is warned by Mitzi. Ironically, Cecilia is murdered; Schani falls to his death. The film ends here, a climax similar to that in von Stroheim's first film, *Blind Husbands* (1919). Von Stroheim had envisioned, according to the script, continuing the story up until the World War, when the prince and Mitzi would reunite, but he was never able to finish the film as he wished it to be.

In the 20-minute condensation of part one, *The Honeymoon* could make only brief reference to von Stroheim's use of soft-focus photography and lavish sets: palace life of the aristocracy, shops, restaurants, parks, hunting lodges. Since surroundings were always central to von Stroheim's work, "Burn-it up-Erich," "the man you love to hate," upheld his reputation for grandiosity. *The Honeymoon* contained essential elements of von Stroheim's filmmaking: a dark and mordant style, deliberate and intense close-ups, scenes that were long and slow.

At the Cinémathèque Française in 1954, von Stroheim was able to reedit *The Wedding March* to his satisfaction. He produced a 16mm film with music and sound effects. He shortened and reordered scenes and eliminated some titles. But he did not work on *The Honeymoon*, the only copy of which was stored at the Cinémathèque. He was said to have considered the unfinished film an embarrassment. He even attempted to stop the Cinémathèque from screening it. In the year von Stroheim died, actually

Queen Kelly, *1928–31. A classic Erich von Stroheim moment: Kelly (Gloria Swanson) is whipped into obedience by Queen Regina (Seena Owen).*

five days after his death, the only print of *The Honeymoon* was destroyed in a fire. Stills survived in the papers of producer Pat Powers.

After *The Honeymoon* came *Queen Kelly*. An unfinished film, it finished von Stroheim's career in Hollywood. The lavish details resulted in such an exorbitant price that, with only a third of the film shot — 4 hours — MGM called it quits. Von Stroheim's intransigence in the face of requests to hold down costs and reconsider some elements in the story didn't help him in the eyes of Gloria Swanson, either. In the end, the 11-reel film was edited down to 2 hours, a musical track was appended, and the ending altered. Because there was no market for a silent von Stroheim/Swanson film in the United States in 1932, the film was released only in France.

The elements of *Queen Kelly* reflect von Stroheim's lifelong fascination with aristocracy, degeneracy, and violent death. In 1928, these elements also attracted Gloria Swanson. While *The Wedding March* was being edited at Paramount, von Stroheim had developed a script (based on the story "The Swamp") for Gloria Swanson and her lover and coproducer, Joseph P. Kennedy.

Shooting began in November 1928 on what was to be a film of seeming dichotomy, but actual similarity, between life in Europe and Africa. Von Stroheim plunged headlong into the project, working long hours, reshooting scenes, paying little heed to cost. Visitors were particularly struck by the efficiency and daring of his work, his brilliant and meticulous observation of detail. At the same time, however, he could not subjugate any part of the film to the whole. In this film, neither he nor any members of his own company were in the cast; Gloria Swanson was in the lead. Within three months, she had second thoughts about the film, particularly about the sleazy elements. (In one scene she became revolted as von Stroheim demonstrated how an actor was to drool tobacco juice onto Swanson's hand as he placed a wedding ring on her finger.) She also found the African sequences, of which she had seen early rushes, unrelated to the European scenes or to characters in them. To her, they were simply more ugliness that stood little chance with the censors. In late January 1929, she called Joseph P. Kennedy and demanded that the director, whom she called a "madman," be fired. He obliged.

Over a three-year period, the producers, having gotten rid of von Stroheim, attempted to alter censorable portions of the film and add dialogue and music to it. They even gave some thought into creating an operetta, with Gloria Swanson singing the lead. In 1931, Swanson hired the photographer Gregg Toland to shoot another ending to the story.

With the Toland ending, the story is as follows: In Kronberg, the capital of Rurirania, Prince Wolfram (Walter Byron) is to be married off by Queen Regina (Seena Owen), his cousin. As was usual in a von Stroheim story, the protagonist falls for a commoner, this time an American orphan, Patricia Kelly (Gloria Swanson). The queen, of course, disapproves. The young woman kills herself, and the prince then commits suicide.

This is the film version that was released in France. In von Stroheim's conception, however, which was never fully filmed, Kelly fails to kill herself and the prince marries another. Kelly enters a convent, then sails for German East Africa to join an aunt. Her life situation quickly sinks in front of her: She inherits a brothel and is forced to marry an alcoholic (in the brothel). After he dies, she meets Prince Wolfram again, this time in Africa. Fortuitously for all, the prince's wife dies and his cousin the queen is assassinated. The new king then takes Patricia for his new Queen Kelly.

Queen Kelly was hailed as a "masterwork" in Europe, but received little circulation. Swanson gave the Museum of Modern Art a print in 1945. In 1950, when she and von Stroheim appeared in Wilder's *Sunset Boulevard*—which contains scenes from *Queen Kelly*—the Museum of Modern Art "previewed" the film. In 1971, the Eastman House acquired production records of the film from Swanson.

Von Stroheim's ninth and last directorial effort was *Walking Down*

Peggy (Boots Mallory, right) comforts Millie (ZaSu Pitts) in the truncated Hello Sister! *(1933), which contained footage of Erich von Stroheim's unfinished* Walking Down Broadway.

Broadway, a modest sound production—Hollywood no longer favored grand projects—written by von Stroheim and a studio writer. This American Depression-era story of jealousy, greed, love, sex, and death was no change for von Stroheim; these elements represent his staples. Uncharacteristically, however, he did complete the film on schedule and within budget (seven weeks, $300,000) by early 1932. When it was shown unedited to preview audiences, the reaction by the producer and employees of the film studio was negative. Von Stroheim's conception of romance included a look at filth and at the less glamorous aspects (unwashed genitals, for instance) of love. Since the director hadn't had a commercially successful film since *Merry Widow* in 1925, the producer, Sol Wurtzel, who found the picture strange and unpleasant, took the film to Alfred Werker and Edwin Burke for reworking. Von Stroheim was off the job. James Wong Howe, the photographer, shot new scenes and Frank E. Hull edited the entire film. The new version of *Walking Down Broadway* was released in May 1933 as *Hello, Sister!*

The released film bears no director credits and makes no reference to von Stroheim because he disassociated himself from it. It's a 55-minute story about Jimmy (James Dunn) and Peggy (Boots Mallory), whose love is nearly destroyed because of the jealousy of rivals, Mac (Terance Ray) and Millie (ZaSu Pitts). The central element in the story is Peggy's pregnancy. *Variety* found that "the picture has little to recommend it. Direction and dialogue are particularly feeble" (May 9, 1933). The main actor, James Dunn, overacts to make up for a weak plot. There is comedy and a "good tenement fire at the finish."

Walking Down Broadway (and *Hello, Sister!*) disappeared. *Cinema Quarterly*'s assessment in 1933 that the whole film had been reshot appeared to settle the question of ever finding any of von Stroheim's original footage. But in 1970 the film historian William K. Everson discovered a print of *Hello, Sister!* in Fox's vaults. By comparing the discovered film to stills of *Walking Down Broadway* made in 1932 and to a surviving script that referred to "new scenes" for *Hello, Sister!* it is clear that *Hello, Sister!* contains enough original footage of *Walking Down Broadway* to mark it as a von Stroheim film. While the editing of *Hello, Sister!* is poor and the ending not von Stroheim's, it still contains enough of von Stroheim's directorial vision, themes, and style. This includes scenes introducing the protagonists and showing their confrontations, a reference to a funeral, Millie being rescued from a sewer, Peggie in a love scene on a balcony, Peggy seeking out medical assistance and then a marriage license, the rainstorm, and the tenement fire and explosion.

Von Stroheim's directorial career, which was second only to D. W. Griffith's in its unity of vision and purpose, was at an end in Hollywood by 1933. He was through at Universal, Paramount, MGM, Fox, United Artists. He saw his plight as serious, for he cabled Sergei Eisenstein that he had reached the "crisis of my life."

11. Orson Welles (1915–1985)

It's All True. 1942, 309 reels. Four parts: "The Story of Jazz"; "My Friend Bonito" (directed by Norman Foster, script by Robert Flaherty); "Carnival"; and "Jangadeiros." Produced by Welles. Script by Welles. With cast of nonprofessionals. Unfinished.

Don Quixote. 1955–75, 45 min. Silent. Produced by Welles and Oscar Dancigers. Script by Welles. Photographed by Jack Draper. With Francisco Reiguera (Quixote), Akim Tamiroff (Sancho Panza), Patty McCormack (Dulcinea), Welles (himself). Unfinished.

The Deep. 1970. Script by Welles. Photographed by Willy Kurant. With Welles, Jeanne Moreau, Laurence Harvey, Olga Palinkas, and Michael Bryant. Unfinished.

The Other Side of the Wind. 1972–84, 90 min. Script by Welles and Oja Kodar. Photographed by Gary Graver. With John Huston, Peter Bogdanovich, Norman Foster, Rich Little, Mercedes McCambridge, Edmond O'Brien, Cameron Mitchell, John Carroll, Lilli Palmer, and Oja Kodar. Unreleased.

The surprising element in Orson Welles's career is not that he failed to finish so many projects but that he finished any at all given the exhausting demands he placed on himself. In 1941–42, for instance, he juggled four projects simultaneously. He'd edited the 148-minute rough cut of *The Magnificent Ambersons* down to about 90 minutes on orders of RKO, turned out the script for *Journey into Fear*, and was overseeing the making of a film entitled *My Friend Bonito* in Mexico. Still, his failure to finish the fourth project, his monumental epic *It's All True*, earned him a reputation as a director who couldn't complete a picture.

Welles became involved in the film after Ourival Fontes, Brazil's minister of propaganda and popular culture, proposed the idea of a documentary about life in the Americas to Walt Disney and other visiting Americans in October 1941. The Brazilian government would provide the movie facilities, RKO would distribute the film, and the Inter-America Affairs Committee, headed by Nelson Rockefeller (a major RKO stockholder), would guarantee 30 percent of the cost, up to $300,000. *It's All True* would contain four episodes: one episode about the carnival in Brazil; the film being made in Mexico called *My Friend Bonito*; and two other episodes, which would be worked out.

Scenes from It's All True, *1941, Orson Welles's unfinished multipart semidocumentary.*
Top: *"Carnival" episode: King Momo announces the opening of the pre–Lenten carnival*
to crowds in Rio. Other actors unknown. Bottom: *The revelers at night.*

From It's All True: *Exhausted party-goers in the "Carnival" episode.*

From It's All True: *The young hero, Jesús Vásquez, at the bullring in the episode "My Friend Bonito."*

From It's All True, *the famous "Jangadeiros" episode: two shots of the suffering people of Northern Brazil.*

It's All True, initially titled *Pan-American,* was supposed to be a standard-length, four-part documentary featuring real people, not actors—a then novel approach. The episode called "Jangadeiros" was Welles's most daring, the story of four Brazilian fisherman ("jangadeiros") from Fortazela Beach (northern Brazil) who sailed to Rio de Janeiro to seek the protection of the dictator, Getulio Vargas, against local authorities who were exploiting them. The four became national heroes, and Welles wanted to tell their story. Over a four-week period, Welles reconstructed their journey and arrival in Rio. But during the fishermen's staged reentry into the port city in May 1942, their leader, Jacare, fell from the raft and, according to reports, was killed and possibly eaten by a shark. A scandal ensued.

Welles's second episode told the story of the samba at carnival time in Brazil. It included film of voodoo practices. The third episode, "My Friend Bonito," was already being filmed by Norman Foster in Mexico; it was based on the true story by Robert Flaherty about a boy and his bull, which had performed so bravely at a bullfight that it was allowed by official decree to live freely. The final episode would be "The Story of Jazz," the basis of which was Louis Armstrong's life.

Welles completed the carnival episode, which he shot in color, and then shot most of the jangadeiros portion, including the unfortunate arrival in Rio that had to be refilmed. When he'd spent $600,000 of RKO's $1 million budget, RKO pulled out, scared by press censure in Brazil and the United States for Jacare's death and, no doubt, annoyed that the Rockefeller money never came through. In addition, Norman Foster stopped shooting his episode in Mexico because he was recalled to Hollywood by Welles himself to direct *Journey into Fear*!

Welles had already shot an enormous amount of footage for such an abortive venture: 309 reels of negative (16mm film, or 200,000-300,000 feet?—15 or more hours. Yet he garnered little sympathy in the early 1940s. Few had heard of the samba, cared about the jangadeiros or Bonito, or could envision a film without stars. One RKO executive quipped about "a lot of colored people playing their drums and jumping up and down in the streets." Welles referred to Rockefeller as cowardly for avoiding the beleaguered project. Back in the United States Welles tried to put the unedited film into some kind of order. Over the years, according to Peter Bogdanovich, he struggled "to make it part of his deal on other pictures that this material be made available to him" for completion. Paramount eventually came into possession of the footage, and in 1985 the studio donated it to the American Film Institute in Washington, D.C.

Don Quixote is the project to which Welles returned for more than 20 years. Begun in 1955, in the Bois de Boulogne, as a 30-minute film for American television, its trials were first shot for producer Louis Dolivet, with Mischa Auer and Akim Tamiroff. The main part of this "purely picaresque thing, a series of sequences," as Welles described it and with which he "fell completely in love," was shot in Mexico in August–October, 1957. By then Francisco Reguera had replaced Auer as Don Quixote and Patty McCormack was playing Dulcinea.

Beginning in the 1960s, Welles continued his film, which blends past and present, in bits and pieces in Italy and Spain. He proceeded carefully, afraid of overdoing the "delicate" story, afraid of succumbing to cliché. During these years he directed *The Trial* (1962) and *Chimes at Midnight* (1966) both critical failures, and acted in more than two dozen movies. Whenever he could muster the money, he filmed the story. In 1964 he claimed that some three weeks' work could finish the picture.

Welles was well aware that much was left undone. Despite the long periods of delay, those who worked with Welles on *Don Quixote* testify to the fact that he pushed the principal players harder than anyone—no human consideration was said to stem Welles's vision. The delays were caused by Welles having to wait for the times when he and his actors were both free to resume filming.

In 1975, years after the principal players had died, Welles resumed the film one last time. In 1982 he declared he would finish *Don Quixote* in two years.

Welles's black and white photography has a simplicity and primitiveness that recalls the great silent images of the Russian director Dovshenko. Over the years the director himself reminded critics that *Don Quixote* has "all kinds of stop action, speeded up motion and so on. They are going to say I stole it from the Nouvelle Vague, but I made it before them." Further, he noted, "it's real improvization: the story, the little incidents, everything is improvised. There are things we found in seconds, in a flash, but after having rehearsed Cervantes for . . . weeks."

A year after Welles died, the unfinished *Don Quixote*—a silent film 45 minutes in length, interrupted only occasionally by Welles's voice playing alternately Quixote and Sancho Panza—was screened at the French Cinemathèque. Thin and emaciated, Don Quixote, with his lance, rides atop Rosinante; at his side is Sancho Panza, pot-bellied and burlesque. The two are seen in deserted landscapes, or surrounded by a herd of sheep, or at a movie theatre. At one point, Akim Tamiroff, giving the performance of his career, is frightened by the moon he is trying to observe; at another he is let loose in period costume on the streets of Pampelune, among today's cars and tourists, yet nobody notices him. The people act as if he's a Spaniard who got lost.

In 1968, off the coast of Yugoslavia, Welles began filming *The Deep*, based on the novel *Dead Calm* by Charles Williams. Welles plays a millionaire on board his yacht with this new bride (Moreau). A psychotic

Top: *A reputed scene from Orson Welles's* Don Quixote, *1956.* Bottom: *In Welles's unfinished film,* Quixote, *Francisco Reiguera does battle again.*

survivor (Harvey) of a violent sea incident comes aboard. Throughout the filming, Welles's juggling of projects continued; Laurence Harvey became ill; photographer Willy Kurant departed in mid-film for another project; Welles ran out of money for the dubbing of the film; he acted in a host of other films; and he agreed to cooperate in an "authorized" biography by Peter Bogdanovich. At the same time, he intensified his six-year relationship with the sculptor Oja Kodar. Welles left the film unfinished before Harvey died in 1973.

Then, even as *Don Quixote* and *The Deep* were in limbo, Welles started making *The Other Side of the Wind*, a "reworking" of his 1963 script *The Sacred Beasts* by, of all people, Oja Kodar. Welles made his film, too, in portions, filming without an actual script, with parts and players joined at the editing stage. On the surface, it's the story of a Hollywood director trying for a comeback. Welles said that Rex Ingram was "more than anybody" the model for the character.

Welles and Kodar put up $750,000 of their own money to make a film that wasn't finished until 1984 because Welles seems not to have known what he wanted: He altered characters and locales, filming in California, Arizona, Spain, and France; he scurried to secure backing from such sources as German television and a Swiss group, Avenel; and digressed by making the film *F for Fake* in 1973. Time, of course, took its toll as the principals aged and some died. The one new element for Welles the director was that the film contained a reference to oral sex.

To obtain more money for this film, Welles appeared in a number of undistinguished roles in the late 1970s and accepted backing from the brother-in-law of the Shah of Iran, Mehdi Mouscheri. He even narrated a film called *The Shah of Iran* in 1978. But the director suffered because of this tie-in to the Shah. After the Ayatollah came to power, *The Other Side of the Wind* was seized in Iran. When the Shah's brother-in-law claimed 80 percent of *The Other Side of the Wind*, the only negative became the subject of a legal dispute in France. The case is unresolved.

Other Lost Films

Too Much Johnson. 1938, 40 min. Produced by Welles and John Houseman. Script by Welles. Photographed by Paul Dunbar. With Joseph Cotton, John Houseman, Virginia Nicholson, Arlene Francis, John Berry, Marc Blitzstein, and Ruth Ford. Unreleased.

Gina Lollobrigida. 1956, 30 min. Narrated by Welles. With Welles, Gina Lollobrigida, Vittorio de Sica, and Rossano Brazzi. Unreleased.

Welles is the creator of two other films that have not been shown. In the summer of 1938, a few months before he would become world famous with his radio broadcast of "War of the Worlds," Welles filmed *Too Much Johnson*, based on the stage play by William Gillett. Welles intended to film the play and then combine it with a stage production. Through this play, which is a parody of the Keystone Kops, Welles wanted to restore to the theater the freshness and innocence of the past by combining live action and film on stage. A 20-minute introduction and two 10-minute episodes comprise his silent film which, in combination with sound effects, resulted in a series of madcap pursuits: a wife spying on her husband; a husband chasing his wife's secret lover; a father keeping his daughter from her boyfriend; etc.

Welles shot *Too Much Johnson* in New York City and Yonkers, New York, in 10 days, producing 25,000 feet of film. According to John Houseman, his actors performed live action, some of it risky, such as John Houseman participating in a staged swordfight on the edge of a two-hundred-foot precipice. Even at this stage in his career, Welles was already creating difficulties for himself by continuing to work on other theatre projects; at the same time he was not paying his performers. When finally pressed by the Actors' Equity, he drained funds from his Mercury Theatre, bringing it to the edge of bankruptcy. Then when Welles was putting the finishing touches on the film, Paramount notified him that the film studio owned the rights to the play. Still, Welles went forward, only to find that the theatre where he planned to unveil the film (Stony Creek Theatre) prohibited the projection of a nitrate film. He performed the stage portion of the play only. According to John Houseman, it was "trivial, tedious, and underrehearsed."

In August 1970, the one copy of the film was destroyed in a fire at Welles's villa in Madrid while actor Robert Shaw was there.

Orson Welles's other unreleased film was apparently left forgotten in a hotel room in Paris for 20 years. The documentary *Gina Lollobrigida* had been intended as a 30-minute exposition for British television. The subjects touched on were Italy, the Italian pin-up, Italian movies of the 1950s, and the actress herself, interviewed by Welles at her home. Welles acts as both narrator and interviewer, thereby appearing during the entire film. When he asks Vittorio de Sica about Lollobrigida, he presents the director as a star in Italy, even though he was then more widely recognized abroad. In talking to Rossano Brazzi about the actress, the inconsistency of the Italians emerges as a theme of the film. The film becomes a kind of meditation on the misfortunes of Welles himself.

It seems that after the film was made and turned down by the television producers, it wound up in the hands of the director of technical services of the hotel, who gave it to a cinema buff in the 1980s. It was shown for the first time at the Venice Film Festival of 1986, and then on French television.

At the same festival, a 22-minute film called *Four Men on a Raft*, put together by Fred Chandler and Richard Wilson, was also screened. This extract from *It's All True* was publicity for a much larger project: a 35mm film that would finally tell the tale of how *It's All True* was made and not made, and how it ended in *Four Men on a Raft*, the one episode of Welles's film that so far has been reconstructed. Besides this extract, the Jangadeiros piece is striking in its momentum and rhythm, its opening and closing shots of a plane flying over a mountain, and the electrifying greeting the heroes receive when they enter the port city. Of the other filmed episodes, "My Friend Bonito" consists of unedited takes, and the carnival sequence remains an assemblage of travelogue shots.

It's All True was Welles's only film made under rudimentary conditions—he used a silenced Mitchell camera, no dolly or cranes. His first film-essay, it presaged a radical change in his style, evidenced ten years later in *Othello*, photographed by George Fanto, photographer of "Jangadeiros," and still later in *F for Fake*. Welles would henceforth achieve by editing what before he obtained by camera movement.

At the end of his life, Welles was still busy. The man who art director Alexandre Trauner said "continually destroys himself" planned to make a film of his 1937 pro union production *The Cradle Will Rock*, with a screenplay by Ring Lardner, Jr., and the British actor Rupert Brook as a young Welles. When the project got bogged down in financial difficulties, he was off to Paris in 1985 to look into the possibility of filming *King Lear*. He died the same year.

III. DIRECTING THE PRIMA DONNAS

The director is the man who paints the dramatic picture. Give him a bigger canvas and recognition and he will do bigger things. But make him paint around the limitations of a certain player and you ... stunt his growth.

Maurice Tourneur, 1918

Producers and directors have rarely talked about "star" troubles. They have rarely criticized stars publicly. The stars might then refuse to work for them.

Nevertheless, few directors will walk away from every confrontation with a star. The honorable director usually takes a stand, even as he knows that if it's a choice of director or star going, the studios usually boot out the director. Any on-going, public confrontation between star and director threatens to halt a production midway.

There were often good reasons for these confrontations. Many stars were just wrong for the parts assigned them, particularly in film's early days. Miscast, misunderstood, fearing failure, some would inevitably misbehave on the set.

One case in point, and one of the most publicized confrontations in screen annals, occurred between Josef von Sternberg and Charles Laughton. The actor was already known as difficult; the director, autocratic. In 1937, they were on the same set in Britain making *I, Claudius*, and they clashed almost from the start. Laughton had wanted his friend William Cameron Menzies to direct. Von Sternberg was directing in order to try to regain lost stature in the industry.

For all his faults, von Sternberg attempted to work with the star, giving him a lot of leeway. But Laughton was battling his own demons. In the end they overpowerd him—and the film.

That same year in Hollywood, von Sternberg's famous discovery, Marlene Dietrich, now a star, was bringing her own film to a halt. She was making *I Loved a Soldier*. Only a few years earlier, she had said of her acting experience: "I didn't know what to do—I just tried to do what [von Sternberg] told me." She was now working with respected producer Ernst Lubitsch. His hand-picked director for the film was Henry Hathaway. Hathaway had just come off a successful production called *Peter Ibbetsen*, "a dream tale." Working with Dietrich he was plunged into his own nightmare.

The peripatetic film director Max Ophuls, having directed films in Germany, France, Holland, and Italy in the years 1930–39, failed to finish his one film in Switzerland during the years of World War II—not because of the international conflict, but because of personal and conceptual conflicts with the film's star Louis Jouvet. The film depended on Jouvet's name and on the reputation of the material, Molière's *School for Wives* (*L'Ecole des Femmes*); in fact, the producers organized the production because of these two factors. When the crunch came, they backed Jouvet, and the production was halted.

One actor tried to avoid conflicts with directors by directing a film with himself as star. That actor was Errol Flynn, remembered by producer Jack Warner as "one of the most charming and tragic men I ever knew." The first time he saw Flynn, he recalled in an interview in 1973, "I didn't know if he could act, but he was handsomer than hell and radiated charm. So I hired him, on impulse, for $250 a week. . . . As soon as I saw Flynn's tests [for *Captain Blood*, 1935], I knew he had it. We gave him $300 for the part, and it made him a star."

By 1950, Flynn was an embarrassment. In Warner's film *Montana* that same year, Flynn was at times too drunk to work. His departure from the studio thereafter was largely unmourned.

Flynn turned to directing *William Tell* in 1953 to recoup his reputation. As actor-director, he was no better able to control himself. His film went unfinished. In 1958, Warner rehired him to play John Barrymore in *Too Much, Too Much*, but it was not a happy experience for anyone.

In March 1962, the Screen Actors Guild was forced to go public. There were an increasing number of Flynn-like experiences taking place, obviously threatening too many films. In response to protests by producers over the behavior of some actors, the guild warned its members that studio executives would no longer "put up with overt, deliberate misbehavior on the sets." The guild stressed that any actor's misconduct "dishonors . . . their own contracts with the producers." It was time, the guild wrote in an editorial, "for actors . . . to decide to give a full day's work for a full day's pay."

But by June, Marilyn Monroe was making headlines for the trouble she brought to George Cukor's unfinished film *Something's Got to Give*.

12. George Cukor (1899–1983)

Something's Got to Give. 1962, 20 min., color. Produced by Aaron Rosenberg and Henry Weinstein. Script by Nunnally Johnson and Hal Kanter. Photographed by Franz Planer, Charles Lang, Jr., William Daniels, and Leo Tover. With Marilyn Monroe, Dean Martin, Cyd Charisse, Wally Cox, and Phil Silvers. Unfinished.

George Cukor has often been called the "actor's director" or the "women's director." He put his skills to the test by trying to make a film with Marilyn Monroe in 1962. The only unfinished film in his career—bearing a title that fate would prove ironic—was doomed from the start.

By 1962, Marilyn Monroe was, at 36, near physical and psychological collapse. Yet by agreeing to star in *Something's Got to Give* for $100,000 she was trying to complete a four-picture deal she had signed with 20th Century–Fox in 1954. George Cukor, who had directed her in *Let's Make Love* (1960), was one of the few directors she would agree to work with. Likewise, the lead male, Dean Martin, had her personal approval.

Something's Got to Give was a remake of a 1940 comedy, *My Favorite Wife*, about a woman (Monroe) long thought dead who reappears just as her "widowed" husband (Dean Martin) is about to remarry. Cukor's film experienced trouble right from the start. Cukor began shooting in May 1962, and after three weeks had gotten one week's worth of work from his troubled star, who was suffering from depression, illness, and dependency on drugs. Cukor, who has said that Monroe "wasn't deliberately heedless, though practically speaking I suppose it came to that," tried to "shoot around her," that is, shoot those scenes with Martin, Charisse, and Wally Cox that didn't require her presence in order to lessen the effects of her absence. In this he had the support of Dean Martin. And further accommodating himself to Monroe's condition, the director built a replica of the set house in the studio in order to maximize the use of Monroe's time when she felt good enough to show up.

Monroe's repeated absences, changes to the script and crew members on the film soon had cost the film company $1 million. In early June, having celebrated her birthday on the set, she flew to New York to attend a birthday rally for President Kennedy. A few days later the columnist Sheila

Something's Got to Give, *1962. Marilyn Monroe in her last film, the only unfinished work by veteran director George Cukor.*

Graham reported the reaction of Henry Weinstein, a coproducer of the film: "The studio does not want her any more." Twentieth Century–Fox, already saddled with huge cost overruns on the film *Cleopatra* (starring Elizabeth Taylor), fired Monroe for breach of contract and slapped her with a $500,000 lawsuit. The studio hired Lee Remick to replace her as the female lead in *Something's Got to Give*, but Martin refused to work with anyone but Monroe. More lawsuits were leveled; then, finally, the studio agreed to rehire Monroe and resume production by the end of the year.

In August 1962, Monroe died. The unfinished color film, contains scenes of Monroe that seemed to belie her physical and emotional condition. They have been called "striking and transcendent." The film received a great deal of attention when photos from scenes in which she swims in the nude surfaced in publications around the world. In 1963, the studio finally filmed the story, renamed *Move Over Darling*, starring Doris Day and James Garner, and directed by Michael Gordon. By this time, George Cukor was committed to filming *My Fair Lady*.

Some footage from *Something's Got to Give* was incorporated into the documentary *Marilyn* (1963, 83 min., narrated by Rock Hudson), which contains clips from the films Monroe made with Fox studio, beginning in 1949 (*Ticket to Tomahawk*) and ending with *Something's Got to Give*. For the unfinished film, she is shown getting a hair test. Her beauty, it is said, was at its peak—tragically near the end of her life.

In December 1990, Fox television broadcast a one-hour documentary entitled *Marilyn: Something's Got to Give*. Shown were the 20-odd minutes of usable color footage from more than 6 hours of film shot in 1962 by George Cukor.

13. Errol Flynn (1909–1959)

William Tell. 1953, 30 min. Directed by Jack Cardiff. Produced by Flynn and Alexander Salkind. Script by Flynn and John Dighton. With Flynn (William Tell), Bruce Cabot (Gesler), Antonella Lualdi (Matilda), Aldo Fabrizi (Arnold), Franco Interlenghi, and Dave Crowly. Unfinished.

The year 1953 found the 44-year-old Errol Flynn in Italy trying to finance a comeback. Fresh from starring in the ill-received Italian production *Il Maestro di Don Giovanni (Crossed Swords)*, he conceived of a project to restore his sagging reputation. He would produce a film version of *William Tell*, based on Schiller's 1804 drama, and cast himself as the patriot and revolutionary hero. His longtime friend Bruce Cabot would play the tyrannical governor; international star Aldo Fabrizi would be the wavering patriot and lover Arnold.

But the film he intended as a vehicle for his comeback would instead prove Flynn's undoing. To his problems of diminished popularity and failing health, it would add financial ruin.

Flynn spent weeks trying to secure backing, without luck. Flynn's continued heavy drinking, despite his recent collapse from hepatitis, kept most financiers away.

Flynn finally had to settle for partial backing from Count Fossataro, a former police chief of Naples, who put up $50,000, and the Italian government, which provided about $150,000. Flynn provided the rest—more than $400,000 plus the film, cameras, and laboratory equipment. He supervised the construction of a finely detailed Alpine village at Courmayeur at the base of Mont Blanc. To direct, Flynn hired the well-known British photographer Jack Cardiff, who had shot *Crossed Swords*. It was Cardiff's first directorial effort. In order to increase its commercial possibilities, Flynn decided to photograph *William Tell* with Cinemascope cameras, making it only the second wide-screen picture after *The Robe* (1953). The Cinemascope cameras came from Darryl F. Zanuck, who at first balked at providing the equipment, but then relented when faced with the threat of a lawsuit under the Monopolies Act.

The movie recounts the famous exploits of the patriot William Tell in the Swiss town of Uri. When Tell refuses to obey the orders of the bullying

William Tell, *1953. Errol Flynn in the production that he hoped would revive his flagging career.*

Austrian governor, Gesler, he is ordered as punishment to shoot an apple off his son's head. In revenge for accidentally killing his son, Tell kills Gesler, and sets off the revolution that ousts the foreign rulers on January 1, 1308.

Cardiff shot about two reels of color film in about two weeks before financing from the Italian backers collapsed. Since most of the government's money had already been spent on construction of the village set, Count Fossataro withdrew his support—together with his initial investment. That left little to fall back on. Desperately, Flynn sought the backing of American and British producers, but the terms of the initial agreements prevented their involvement. Meanwhile, Bruce Cabot refused to work unless he was paid.

At the Venice Film Festival in September, Flynn made a last effort to secure backing. He set out to impress fellow guests, particularly the Italian ministers of finance and education, with his film's cultural significance. It would surely outshine the poorly received production *Guglielmo Tell*, made in Italy in 1949. And he might have succeeded had not his ill health interfered. Suffering from dysentery and diarrhea, the actor was more preoccupied with finding a bathroom at short notice than making polite conversation. Already a fiasco, the evening grew worse. Induced to join a performance of "go-go" dancers, Flynn staged a sham collapse, yelling, "I can't walk.... I'm paralyzed.... This is going to cost the hotel a bundle." The ploy, intended to net insurance money from Lloyds of London, backfired. Once word of Flynn's deception spread, said a friend, any chance of his obtaining support for *William Tell* evaporated.

Flynn—humiliated, ill, and out of pocket half a million dollars—moved to his ocean-going sailboat, *Zaca*, for the next two years in an attempt to recover his losses. In the next six years he managed to act in nine films, but he never regained the popularity he knew in the early 1940s.

The half-hour of Flynn's last epic is now presumed lost. But the village he built as a *William Tell* film set survives. It now draws thousands as a tourist attraction—and nets more money than Flynn once sought.

14. Henry Hathaway (1898–1985)

I Loved a Soldier. 1936, 4 reels. Supervised by Ernst Lubitsch. Produced by Benjamin Glazer. Script by John van Druten. Photographed by Charles Lang. With Marlene Dietrich (Anna), Charles Boyer (Lt. Nemassy), Akim Tamiroff, Lawrence Stander, and Margaret Sullavan. Unfinished.

By 1936 Henry Hathaway was an established director. In four years, he'd already made a dozen films, including the adventure film *The Lives of a Bengal Lancer* (1935) and the surrealist *Peter Ibbetson* (1935). In a career that spanned forty years, he made more than 70 films. He worked with Hollywood's greatest actors. But in trying to complete *I Loved a Soldier*, he was no match for Marlene Dietrich and for fate. Hathaway failed to finish this one film because Dietrich's demands that she appear more attractive in the early scenes of the film than he wanted her to caused filming to be delayed and costs to mount.

The man who came up with the idea for this film was Ernst Lubitsch, who since February 1935 was production chief at Paramount. Lubitsch was producing films and supervising the work of other directors. In early 1936 he proposed that Hathaway direct a sound version of the 1927 silent film *Hotel Imperial* (which had starred Pola Negri). During this period in Hollywood, Lubitsch was that rare director for whom the phrase "you're only as good as your last picture" didn't apply. He made his kind of films his way. And even when they failed at the box office, he continued to make the kind of films he wanted.

Lubitsch had just supervised the direction of Marlene Dietrich in the film *Desire*, and now sought her out again for this new picture despite the fact that she was considered by studio executives to be box-office poison.

I Loved a Soldier was to be an adventure-romance during the Great War. Anna (Dietrich) shelters an Austrian soldier (Charles Boyer) fleeing the Russians in the region of Galicia in Eastern Europe. With this act, her life changes forever.

For the early scenes of the film, Henry Hathaway decided to present Dietrich as an ordinary-looking hausfrau who scrubs floors in the Hotel Imperial. He intended to show how love could literally make Anna feel

79

I Loved a Soldier, *1936. Marlene Dietrich (seated) spoiled Henry Hathaway's effort to complete this Ernst Lubitsch production.*

beautiful—and then *be* beautiful—by showing the transformation that takes place in the woman as she falls in love with the soldier. Lubitsch, according to Hathaway, was very taken with this idea.

Soon after shooting started, trouble began. Dietrich was anxious about her appearance in the film, so she took issue with Hathaway's ideas about the character she was portraying. Rather than having to be ordinary-looking, she decided she would rather project the image viewers would have of Anna.

This kind of creative difference immediately caused filming to be suspended while Lubitsch was asked to mediate. He backed Hathaway, and Dietrich backed down. Then halfway through the film, Paramount executives suddenly removed Lubitsch from his position as head of production. He left for a European vacation, and left *I Loved a Soldier* dangling.

As if set free, Dietrich's persona came to the fore. The Dietrich of these post–von Sternberg years was the actress whose way of doing things left little room for maneuver. According to Hathaway, she insisted that with Lubitsch gone, she now had say over her role. Director and star began to differ more often. When Hathaway, for instance, specified that Dietrich was "not supposed to be beautiful until next Thursday," she pleaded, "Can't it at least be Wednesday?"

Finally, Dietrich said she would not work unless—as stipulated in her contract—Lubitsch produced the film. Hathaway, exasperated, recommended that the studio drop the actress. Paramount now realized it had a problem on its hands, and a legal problem at that. It hired Margaret Sullavan for the lead; Dietrich, who was being eased out, would be used only for the long shots in many scenes. But then came the coup de grace. Only briefly into her role, Sullavan broke an arm tripping over a pile of wires. Paramount executives, not wanting to bring Dietrich back, considered having Sullavan appear in a sling.

Hathaway realized his time as director was over. How could a heroine scrub floors—or get married—with an arm in a sling? Paramount canceled the film. Nearly $1 million had been spent on the unfinished project.

In 1938, Hathaway had the chance to see the four reels of his edited but unfinished *I Loved a Soldier*. A producer named Walter Wanger screened the film, which showed Dietrich's slow transformation from ugly duckling to swan. Hathaway's response was, "We were wrong to let her go." Her acting shone.

Dietrich had also seen the footage. She now appeared to have a change of heart regarding Hathaway. She would complete the film under his direction. But the director still felt humiliated and at first refused to discuss it.

Nevertheless, over the next few months, the idea of reprising the film surfaced. Hathaway himself contacted the studio. The executives balked at any mention of Dietrich. Hathaway contacted Dietrich, who responded with some interest and said she would be back in touch. Finally, Dietrich had an idea. She would complete the film, but only under von Sternberg's direction. Paramount then ended any speculation once and for all. It terminated its contract with her.

In late 1938, William Le Baron, who was Paramount's new production chief, hired Robert Florey, a director with a reputation for finishing films on time and within budget. He directed the 1939 production of *Hotel Imperial*, known in 1936 as *I Loved a Soldier*. Florey completed the film in two months. It starred the Italian actress Isa Miranda and the Welsh actor Ray Milland.

By the time Hathaway retired from filmmaking in 1974, *I Loved a Soldier* was long forgotten. By then he'd established a reputation as the man who always saved the day—the one people called on when they were in a jam. So said actor John Wayne, who characterized him as "a fine craftsman."

15. Max Ophuls (1902–1957)

L'Ecole des Femmes (School for Wives). 1941, TEM Films SA, 300
meters. From the play by Molière. Produced by Pierre Cailler, Jean-Mario Bert-
schy, and François Marthaler. Photographed by Michel Kelber. Design by Christian Berard. With Louis Jouvet (Arnolphe), Madeleine Ozeray (Agnes), Romain
Bouquet (Alain), Maurice Castel (Chrysalde), Raymone Cendras-Sauser
(Georgette), and members of the theatrical company troupe de l'Athenee. Unfinished.

When France fell to the Nazis in June 1940, it became impossible for
director Max Ophuls, a German Jew, and now a French soldier, to work
within the country. His name erased from the credits of his movies and his
visa to the United States delayed, Ophuls was planning to shoot a Franco-
Spanish musical (*Fandango*) either in the south of France or in Spain to
avoid the Nazis. Then a former Berlin theatre colleague (Leopold Lint-
berg), aware of Ophuls' predicament and, as he wrote, his "longing for the
theatre," invited him to Zurich to stage a play. Ophuls seized the life-saving
idea.

At the same time that October, three producers of the Theatre de
Zurich invited famed actor Louis Jouvet and his company to tour Switzerland in Molière's beloved *L'École des Femmes*. Ophuls ran into Jouvet in
Aix-en-Provence, where Madeleine Ozeray, the female star of Jouvet's
troupe and a friend, convinced Jouvet to have *L'École des Femmes* filmed by
Ophuls. The actress found herself attracted to Ophuls because of his
"charm," the danger surrounding him, and his Jewish heritage. (Her great-
grandmother was Jewish.)

Following negotiations, the film team was assembled. Working with
director and star were other French expatriates: the photographer Kelber
and the famous set designer Christian Berard. For them, *School for Wives*
was a quintessential French play, one that stirred their national allegiance.
"Molière restored confidence," said Jouvet, and his performance too was
filled with national pride. No wonder the filmmakers felt a cinematic version of the story of the old Arnolphe in love with the young Agnes would
move audiences to tears. Many had declared that this play, more than any
other, "served France."

While Ophuls was not just anybody, he was as yet only known as the director of the agreeable *Liebelei* (1933). Only a few people knew he was also a man of the theatre. He was in a secondary position to impose his conceptions if Jouvet opposed him. Yet thirty-five years before Bergman's *The Magic Flute*, Ophuls, recalling the experience in 1957, wanted "to show the actor . . . follow him in the wings, backstage, while the dialogue continues; I wanted to take advantage of the play of light in front of and behind the stage, without showing the theatrical technique."

In January 1941, shooting, initially slated for Bessel, was relocated to the Grand-Theatre of Geneva so that Ophuls could erect a moveable crane (a toboggan) in the middle of the opera hall to allow tracking shots. Each afternoon Ophuls improvised, experimented, and reconsidered the lighting. During one session, he fell down a staircase and was almost killed. He continued to work, according to coproducer Pierre Cailler, "as genius dictated." His conception was to alter the play to the requirements of the cinema—to create a true movie. While respecting the theatricality of the material—Ophuls would not introduce any outside scenes nor alter the designer's sets, and retained 1300 of Molière's 1700 verses—the director did want to push the play to its limits. In this he would film the inside of the theatre, the backstage area, and the audience; introduce a prologue in contemporary dress; have tracking shots coming down from the balcony. In the evening, following the filming, Jouvet would play to a full theatre.

Ophuls's ideas were new enough to arouse resistance. His proposals for spectacular and costly shots were suspect to Cailler, a friend of Jouvet's but an amateur in art. Unfamiliar with the cinema, Cailler was, in fact, a publisher making his only feature film. When the female lead, Madeleine Ozeray, appeared to have been persuaded by Ophuls to side with him, Cailler was certain that movie people were irresponsible in trying to create some "fantasy."

It soon became apparent that Ophuls and Louis Jouvet differed on how to film the play. To Jouvet, who had never cared for films, it was only a matter of recording a presentation of the play under the best conditions and using proven staging by theatre designer Berard, whose first film this was. (Before his death in 1949, Berard would design only three films—all for Jean Cocteau.) The famed actor feared that the inventiveness of the camera would affect his preeminence.

But Jouvet, 54, also had a much more personal motive: His life was beginning to imitate his art. He was jealous of Ophuls, 39, because Madeleine Ozeray, Jouvet's young companion, had become Ophuls's mistress. Jouvet got the news from Ozeray. Writing in her autobiography, Ozeray recounts Jouvet's reaction: "But you'll pay for that, my little girl, you'll pay for that." The whole troupe, including his producer friend Cailler, soon found out about the affair. So what Jouvet could not allow himself, according to Ozeray, would be to embody Arnolphe—the betrayed man—in film and in life. As the old Arnolphe, he would be leaving a permanent image of intense pain.

In her memoirs, Ozeray recounts seeing in the film's rushes a staggering authenticity on the part of Jouvet:

> On the screen, in the fifth act, Jouvet appears completely different from what he was on the stage. What else can I say, but that he is admirable. All of Arnolphe's pain snarls, explodes, bursts out, like that of a poor animal that people were torturing. It is impossible to act better. But, seated at my right, I realize that Jouvet is against this interpretation, that the film will not be seen.

In March 1941, *Le Figaro*, which a month earlier had announced, "Soon Molière under the sunlights" (but without mentioning Ophuls), informed its public that "Louis Jouvet has interrupted his movie." Having gotten Pierre Cailler to agree to abandon the project, Jouvet, now homesick, returned to unoccupied France on a new tour. But by rejecting Ophuls, who would have created a filmed version of Molière certain to survive, the star had harmed himself the most.

There remains dispute about how much Ophuls shot in three weeks and where the footage is today. In her 1966 memoirs, Ozeray recalls shooting several hundred meters of film, in fact, much of the play; still-living technicians (assistant director, assistant photographer, soundman, etc.) affirm that the extent of the filmed material is greater than has been thought; but producer Cailler, in a 1986 interview, thought only the prologue of Jouvet in contemporary dress, talking to an empty theatre, was recorded. In these scenes, Ophuls's camera traverses the theatre. Jouvet is seated on the crane, putting on his make-up. The camera then passes through the curtain, disappears, and Jouvet (as Arnolphe) is seen alone on the stage.

It is almost certain that whatever footage was shot was sent in 1941 to the Cinegram laboratory in Geneva, the main film lab in the country, for development. Then again, *L'École des Femmes* may have disappeared with the one coproducer who committed suicide when his involvement in gold smuggling became known. Or, the film may never have been developed and, as writer-researcher Freddy Bauche has asserted, instead have been mislaid or destroyed.

While coproducer Cailler has expressed doubt on its having been destroyed, he also indicated years later that he would have destroyed *L'École des Femmes* if Jouvet had asked him to.

Pierre Cailler never produced another film. After this project came to a halt, he was involved in a lawsuit with the surviving backer. So a kernel of hope remains. Perhaps the unfinished film was seized, held in evidence— and now lies forgotten somewhere. The overlooked and annotated script is preserved in the Cinemathèque Suisse.

The following extract, from the book *Geschichte des schweitzer Films (History of Swiss Films)* by Herve Dumont,* summarizes the prologue of *L'École des Femmes* as scripted and as filmed.

L'École des Femmes

Prologue, first version (according to the script):

> Opening on a camera lens; a whole studio team is gathered around the camera. The camera plunges into a filled theater, passes through it before the amazed spectators (who discover the electrician, the sound man, the spotlight) and stops in front of the apron.
>
> The director (Jouvet), who, until then, had been looking through a range finder, approaches the curtain and disappears through an opening in it. On the other side of the curtain, the production manager, scenic designers, and the cast are getting nervous over the last opening preparations, while Jouvet, in the meantime, dressed as Arnolphe, turns to a fictive public and explains to it the raison d'être of the film. Three knocks are heard...

Second (filmed) version:

> After a show, the actor (Jouvet), dressed in street clothes, remains sitting in the balcony, in an empty, program-strewn theater. He picks up a program, leafs through it, scratches his chin, looks at the stage set, which is still lit up, and says to himself: "Yes, a Molière movie," and in the twinkling of an eye, he is sitting in the stage space on a camera crane. Downward tracking of the camera while Jouvet makes himself up and changes more and more into Arnolphe. As soon as the camera has passed through the curtain, the camera disappears in the air and the actor "lives" the Molière play as if in a trance.

In April 1941, the Swiss police in charge of foreigners refused to extend Ophuls's work permit. Banned from making a film (*Swamp Soldiers*) about a communist actor in a concentration camp, and then having staged *Romeo and Juliet* in Zurich, Ophuls, along with his wife and son, was forced out of the country. However, with the help of Ozeray, who obtained a life-saving visa, Ophuls and family headed first for Lisbon and then the United States. Madeleine Ozeray returned to Jouvet.

*Published 1987 by Schweitzer Filmarchiv.

Other Lost Films

We'd Rather Have Cod Liver Oil (Dann schon lieber Lebertran). 1930, Germany, 30 min. Produced by UFA, Berlin. Script by Ophuls, Emeric Pressburger, and Erich Kastner. Photographed by Eugen Schufftan. With Paul Kemp (St. Michel), Kathe Haack (the mama), Hannelore Schroth (the daughter), and Heinz Gunsdorf (St. Peter). Unreleased in U.S. Now lost.

The Firm in Love (Die Verliebte Firma). 1931, Germany, 72 min. Produced by Deutsche Lichtspiel-Syndicat (DLS), Berlin. Script by Hubert Marischka and Fritz Zeckendorf. Photographed by Karl Puth. Music by Bruno Granichstaden. With Gustaf Frohlich, Anny Ahlers, Leonhard Steckel, Werner Finck, Jose Wedorn. Unreleased in U.S. Now lost.

Man Stolen (On a Volé un Homme). 1934, 90 min. Produced by 20th Century–Fox, Europe. Script by René Pujol and Hans Wilhelm. Music by Bronislav Kapper and Walter Jurman. Photographed by René Colas. With Lilli Damita (Annette), Henry Garat (Jean de Lafaye), Fernand Fabre (Robert), Charles Fallot (servant), Nina Myrol (the lady), and Pierre Labry. Unreleased in U.S.

Divine. 1935, France, 80 min. Produced by Simone Berriau. Script by Ophuls and Jean George Auriol. From the novel *L'Envers du Music-Hall*, by Colette de Jouvenel. Dialogue by Colette. Photographed by Roger Hubert. Music by Albert Wolff. With Simone Berriau (Ludivine Jarisse—Divine), Catherine Fonteney, Yvette Lebon, Georges Rigaud (milkman), and Philippe Heriat (snake charmer). Unreleased in U.S.

In 1930, the 28-year-old Max Ophuls was already an experienced theatre director. Between 1923 and 1930 he directed 200 plays in Austria and Germany before he began directing films. Five films he made—two in Germany, three in France—before fleeing Europe in 1941 have never been released in the United States. But one film made in this period, *Liebelei* (1933), established his international reputation.

Ophuls's first film, translated from the German as *We'd Rather Have Cod Liver Oil*, followed an invitation from the producers of the German film company UFA. The producers had been impressed with Ophuls's work as diaglogue director on the film *No More Love* (directed by Anatole Litvak, released in 1931) and asked him to try his hand on a film of his own.

The film, which pokes fun at revolutions and pretentious idealism, was based on a fantasy by Erich Kastner, the author of *Emil and the Detective*. "If the natural order of things is turned upside down," asks Kastner, "so it's the parents who must obey and the children command, wouldn't life be more pleasant?" Don't bet on it, the film answers. Better the familiar daily spoonful of cod liver oil than a thousand new problems. Beware of change seekers, warns Kastner in Germany of 1930—"They come from the right or the left."

In Ophuls's film, a child takes cod-liver oil and then prays to change roles with his parents. God is "away," so Saint Peter grants the wish. The next day the little boy wakes up with a cigar in his mouth; gets dressed; sends his parents off to school. The parents, having forgotten almost everything, have a miserable time of it, while the boy and his friends, in their new-found roles, cannot make it in the world of work, tax collectors, and strikes. That night, the children take their cod-liver oil again.

The film suited Ophuls's taste. "Without my realizing it [at the time]," he later said, "I have always been attracted to these things." He also discovered his attraction to two other aspects of filmmaking—camera movements and dialogue—that would eventually establish his name. His expertise in handling dialogue, in particular, would enable him to continue his film career outside Germany after fleeing the Nazis in 1933.

Ophuls's second sound film was the musical comedy *The Firm in Love*, a small-scale picture that can be compared to his famous work *La Ronde* (1951) but without the pathos, and, said Ophuls years later, "the first film where I felt myself driven from beginning to end, my first attempt to imprint a rhythm to a film."

The story is simple. A film director and the entire male crew on location fall in love with a beautiful telegraph operator. She is asked to stand in for the star who has deserted the set. Eventually the fog clears from the males' heads, and the young woman is seen to be just an ordinary mortal with ordinary talent. But she does manage to marry the film company's manager and departs happily.

Man Stolen was part of an experiment: In the years 1930–35, Hollywood's studios made some films in France because they feared that English-language films would not appeal to a French audience. This was an unusual experiment, and before it became too prohibitive, the studios produced more than 60 French-language films in Hollywood and Joinville, France. Ophuls's film *Man Stolen* was one of these productions. *Man Stolen* is also one of only two films the German producer Erich Pommer made in France. *Liliom* (1934), by Fritz Lang, is the other.

Man Stolen is a mystery about a kidnapped banker (named Jean de Lafaye) who falls in love with the woman (Annette) who is guarding him. What was unusual about the film was that Ophuls made use of little dialogue. Wrote *Variety* in 1934: "It was done by somebody who knows how to make films. As a production it puts the regular run of local mades to shame.... It contains some marvelous shots taken on the French Riviera, and the photography is worthy of the German origin of its sponsor."

Ophuls's little-seen film *Divine* has been hailed by Truffaut as a "masterpiece of verse and healthiness." Containing dialogue by Colette and inspired by Colette's collection of sketches called *Backstage at the Music Hall, Divine* starred the influential Simone Berriau, a producer and later

Scene from Max Ophuls's Man Stolen *(1934), with Lilli Damita, Henry Garat and unidentified actor.*

director of the Théâtre Antoine. This was her second film, and the exteriors of the film were shot at Berriau's farm of Mauvanne, near Salins d'Hyeres.

Divine concerns itself—as many of Ophuls's later films do—with a woman's emotional life. In this film about the "music hall and nature," antagonistic themes found in Colette's writings, Ophuls introduces the dancer Divine with a 360-degree pan when she arrives at the theatre, and later excitingly captures her rehearsals for a new show. One of his scenes involves that of a showgirl nursing her baby in a dressing room; another demonstrates a method of dining for free at a restaurant; and a third shows Divine with a boa constrictor slithering over her face—"the most disagreeable kiss I have ever known," said the actress afterward.

However, in this environment, Divine's involvement with the snake charmer, debauchery, and drugs soon results in a charge of arson against her. She saves herself in the nick of time and returns "to the nourishing countryside after that great evil, city life." There she marries the milkman.

In 1936, Ophuls collaborated in the anthology film called *Cinephonies,* whose 10-minute pieces about the great musical virtuosos of the time were compiled by the French film critic Emile Vuillermoz for a society of music lovers headed by Jacques Thibaud. Ophuls became involved in the project last, and contributed two works: "Valse Brillante" by Chopin (6 minutes,

500 ft.) and "Ave Maria" by Schubert 5 minutes, 450 ft.). Franz Planer photographed Alexandre Brailowski on the piano and Elizabeth Schumann singing Schubert. One observer wrote that Ophuls's camera "reveals the secrets of their techniques with an extraordinary precision."

The other shorts in the film are Kirsanoff's and L'Herbier's "Les Berceaux" by Fauré: "La Fontaine d'Arethuse" by Szymanowski; "La Jeune Fille au Jardin" by Monpou; and "Children's Corner" by Debussy. Ophuls and his colleagues discovered that there was little commercial interest in *Cinephonies*, produced for Fox Films and supervised by Vuillermoz. It has never been released in the United States. Other films envisioned by the promoters were never made.

16. Josef von Sternberg (1894–1969)

I, Claudius, 1937, 25 minutes (2 reels). Produced by Alexander Korda. Screenplay by Lajos Biro, Carl Zuckmeyer, and Lester Cohen. From the novel *I, Claudius* by Robert Graves. Choreography by Agnes De Mille. Costumes by John Armstrong. Photographed by Georges Perinal. Sets by Vincent Korda. With Charles Laughton, Merle Oberon, Robert Newton, Emlyn Williams, Flora Robson, and John Clements. Unfinished.

Josef von Sternberg, who directed 25 films in his 28-year career, is most famous for the seven beautifully photographed pictures he made starring Marlene Dietrich in the years 1930–35. Dietrich spoke of him not just as a director but as a well-respected teacher. "He taught me alone about camera angles, lighting, costumes, make-up, timing, matching scenes, cutting and editing. He gave me the opportunity for the most creative experience I have ever had."

But not all film people shared Dietrich's enthusiasm for von Sternberg's methodology. Charles Laughton was certainly unable to cooperate with him in von Sternberg's most difficult and ill-fated film.

In 1935, after von Sternberg directed Dietrich for the last time in *The Devil Is a Woman*, Paramount ended his contract. Their films were no longer making money, and Dietrich was labeled as box-office poison. Exhausted, his status slipping following the break-up, von Sternberg escaped to the Far East in 1936. In Indonesia he contracted an intestinal infection that required surgery in Europe. He was recovering in London when Alexander Korda approached him. It seems the well-known producer had acquired the film rights to Robert Graves' book *I, Claudius*. With his new star, Merle Oberon, and actor Charles Laughton under contract, Korda asked von Sternberg to direct.

Alexander Korda had approached von Sternberg to get out of a debt he owed Marlene Dietrich. It seems Korda couldn't pay Dietrich the $100,000 still owed her for her work in his production of *Knight Without Armor*, filmed in 1936. Dietrich said she would forgive him the money if he hired von Sternberg to direct a film.

Korda provided von Sternberg a budget of $500,000 and a chance to explore subjects close to the director's own heart: the ambiguities and contradictions in human nature, the delusions of grandeur. The one person

Scenes from I, Claudius, *1937.* Top: *Charles Laughton as Claudius (right), Emlyn Williams as Caligula (left), and Robert Newton as Cassius (center).* Bottom: *Claudius faces his grandmother, Livia (Flora Robson).*

upset in these proceedings was Laughton, who had wanted his good friend William Cameron Menzies to direct him.

Von Sternberg began shooting in haste in mid–February 1937. He directed in his usual garb: laced-up boots, breeches, and a turban. As for his approach, his exacting methods sometimes had nothing to do with recreating authenticity—he managed, for instance, to call for 60 vestal virgins when the film originally called for six.

Difficulty for von Sternberg lay ahead. This became apparent with Laughton's emotional turmoil. The lead actor was experiencing trouble—he hadn't settled into his character as Claudius. At one point Laughton imagined Claudius to be Edward VIII, making his abdication speech; at another point, Groucho Marx.

To make matters worse, Laughton showed great torment in front of the camera. He would appear on von Sternberg's set, for instance, promptly at nine, look the stage over, then declare it unsuitable for the part he intended to play. In less than a month, the production was behind schedule and over budget. Yet for his own part, von Sternberg offered Laughton little support or sympathy. He referred to Laughton's obvious anxiety as "growing pains."

Then again, von Sternberg persisted because, he declared, he was "opposed to no method he [Laughton] might think valid for impersonating himself." Von Sternberg became ready for any opportunity to roll the cameras. He built a number of sets so that he could film Laughton wherever he was in better shape; and he lit the sets so that the star could be properly filmed, sometimes with his thinking it was only a rehearsal. (The knowledge that the cameras were rolling could also be devastating to Laughton's emotional balance.)

Unable, finally, to come up with anything else that could spur Laughton on, von Sternberg appealed to Korda to direct the actor. Von Sternberg's "peculiar type of wizardry," he admitted, "had come to an end." But to Korda, Laughton was only sabotaging the film.

The final straw for the film came when Merle Oberon, who was playing Messalina, suffered a concussion in an automobile accident a month and a day into the shooting. She was thrown through the windshield, yet was not hurt as much as was first thought. Korda acted quickly when he heard the news. He tried to replace Oberon with Claudette Colbert, then realized that resuming production immediately meant reshooting all those scenes with Laughton. On the other hand, waiting for Oberon to recover meant renegotiating contracts with the stars and basically preparing the sets from scratch. Furthermore, von Sternberg was having his own troubles. He had just been admitted into Charing Cross Hospital Psychiatric Unit. And, he insisted, he "absolutely" did not want to be visited. "I'm sick," he said.

Korda, who was in love with Oberon, seized the opportunity to get out. He first suspended production and then announced he was abandoning the film. This allowed him to pick up $200,000 from the insurance company, which was satisfied that Oberon had really been injured in an accident.

After leaving the hospital a short while later, von Sternberg fled back to the Far East. He then returned to Europe in 1938 to try to film *Germinal*. But, as he described it, in the grip of a "great surge of strength and power . . . something within me snapped." He'd had a breakdown.

Von Sternberg eventually recovered from this episode, yet never regained the one thing he wanted: his reputation.

In 1965, the BBC produced a 73-minute documentary by William Duncalf called *The Epic That Never Was*. It includes the remains of *I, Claudius*. In the two reels of lost footage, one sees von Sternberg in charge of every shot: tour de force scenes of Claudius (Laughton), with tics, a stutter, and all, explaining to the Roman Senate the conditions under which he would become emperor; Emlyn Williams as Caligula; magnificent sets and art direction. The narrator, Dirk Bogarde, characterizes Laughton's performance of a man rejected by the people yet alive emotionally and intellectually as "one of the greatest performances in the history of the cinema." In more footage Laughton appears not so much difficult as masochistic, childish, and very self-conscious. He is also completely unable to work with the authoritarian von Sternberg.

Years after the collapse of *I, Claudius* von Sternberg said, "Actors had truncated my film." In the year he died, the New York Film Festival showed the story of the unfinished *I, Claudius* to Americans for the first time.

Other Lost Films

A Woman of the Sea. 1926, 7 reels. Produced by Charles Chaplin Film Corp. Script by von Sternberg. Photographed by Eddie Gheller and Paul Ivano. With Edna Purviance, Eve Southern, Charles French, Raymond Bloomer, and Gayne Whitman. Unreleased.

Four years before he began his association with Dietrich, von Sternberg directed Edna Purviance. The actress who had starred in Chaplin's films from 1915 to 1923 was making a comeback.

In 1926, while working on his Hollywood film *The Circus*, Chaplin invited von Sternberg to direct *A Woman of the Sea* (working title, *The Sea-Gull*). Chaplin had been impressed with von Sternberg's direction of Georgia Hale in von Sternberg's first film, *The Salvation Hunters* (1925). For one time only, Chaplin would produce another director's work.

Edna Purviance had not made a film for Chaplin in three years. She no longer had a place in his studio. When Chaplin was casting for the *Gold Rush* in 1923, it was clear that Purviance was no longer his leading lady. Chaplin had noted that she had become too "matronly" for comedy. In addition her drinking had caused her to gain weight and make her performances unpredictable. Chaplin put Georgia Hale in the lead in the *Gold Rush* and sought a way to launch Purviance into a career as a dramatic actress.

The vehicle would be *A Woman of the Sea*. The film is Chaplin's drama of two sisters, Joan (Edna Purviance) and Magdalen (Eve Southern). Magdalen leaves her boyfriend, Peter (Raymond Bloomer), and her life in the fishing village (shot in Monterey, California) for life in the big city. There she meets a playboy novelist (Gayne Whitman). In the intervening years Joan marries Peter. When Magdalen returns, the revived interest she shows in Peter threatens her sister's marriage. In the end, Magdalen is forced to pay for her wanton life.

Von Sternberg began shooting *A Woman of the Sea* in January 1926 and continued until June. The film was plagued with problems. In mid-film, for instance, von Sternberg was forced to change photographers. Apparently, the director felt a different cameraman could improve the quality of some scenes. He reshot some scenes with Edna Purviance 10 times. For its time, the seven-reel film contained a great number of titles—more than 160 in all. Von Sternberg edited the film in only three weeks.

Upon completion, von Sternberg claims, the film was shown one time only, at a theatre in Beverly Hills in 1926. "The film," he wrote, "was promptly returned to Mr. Chaplin's vaults and no one has ever seen it again." Von Sternberg goes on to state that he and Chaplin "spent many idle hours with each other ... but not once was this work of mine discussed." Those close to Chaplin have said that he found the story unmarketable. Chaplin said nothing further of the film, and does not discuss it in his memoirs, *My Autobiography* (1964).

Chaplin may have been disturbed by Edna Purviance's performance or felt the vehicle that was to reestablish her film identity lacked depth. John Grierson, the producer, director, and theoretician, claims to have seen the film. He described it as "beautiful and empty." Georgia Hale, who also saw the film, agreed the story wasn't good enough to attract the public.

As for von Sternberg, he is said to have found Edna Purviance anxious in her role. That would account for the many takes the director had to shoot. But von Sternberg also indicated that he managed to put Edna Purviance sufficiently at ease to complete the film. He sounds satisfied with his own efforts. But in his memoirs, *Fun in a Chinese Laundry* (1965), he characterized Chaplin's action as "arbitrary." This, he said, hurt his career for a while, but in the end he "charged it off to experience."

Seven years later, Chaplin added the final mysterious element to all this. In June 1933, the comedian was facing income tax problems. He obtained a tax write-off on the losses incurred in the making of *A Woman of the Sea* by destroying the only negative in front of corporate members of Consolidated Film, Inc.

Neither the film nor any script survives. All that is left are the daily shooting records and the title list from the film. In addition, Edna Purviance saved stills of the film in her private papers.

IV. SHAKY STARTS,
INDIFFERENT FINISHES

There are these great directors, all ready with their best work ahead of
them. Really their best. . . . Because it's only in your twenties and in your
seventies and eighties that you do your greatest work.

Orson Welles, 1972

Who better than Orson Welles to tout the creative abilities of the
very youngest and oldest directors? On the one side, certainly, he spoke
from personal experience. His own *Citizen Kane*, one of the greatest
American classics, was directed by the then little-known filmmaker when
he was only 26.

Of course Welles's experience was not the norm, whatever he says.
Many others who would go on to be acclaimed as great directors recalled
rough, uneven first efforts that they themselves were anxious to disown.
Small wonder that many of these were either never finished or never
released—much as they could probably tell us about the roots of their
masters' methods.

Many final works of accomplished directors deviated in another way
that caused them to be lost to us. Rarely lacking in polish or technique,
unlike the early films, they sometimes represent an indifference to the box-
office appeal that their creators could not have afforded at an earlier stage
in their careers. While the directors themselves often conspire to withold
their early films, it is more often the producers or distributors who block
release of their later ones.

Roberto Rossellini, drawn to filmmaking by his father's building the
Corso Cinema, Rome's biggest movie house, in 1920, began his career in
1934 as a sound effects man helping to dub films into Italian. After making
a series of shorts—all of them now lost—Rossellini started his first feature-
length film in 1940. Called *White Fish*, it was the story of the engine crew
on a destroyer and their reactions to the battles they helped fight but never
witnessed. "People didn't like it," Rossellini noted. "Some officials didn't
either and my name was taken off (the film)."

The American director Franklin Schaffner never intended to become a

97

director. Seeking work after getting out of the army in World War II, he took a job as an assistant director on the film series *March of Time*. Then in 1948 his boss suggested he put his name in for a job opening in television. Interviewed by a CBS official "desperate for anybody," as Schaffner put it, he was hired. Schaffner told the man he'd "never seen a television camera." It didn't matter to the CBS man, who advised, "Go down and look at the studio and hang around for two weeks." Thus the man who would eventually direct *Patton* (1970) worked in television for more than a dozen years before being given a chance in 1961 to direct a feature-length film called *A Summer World*. Before he knew it, however, the film was abandoned by the studio. Schaffner would have to wait two years before breaking in.

French director Eric Rohmer also wasn't especially interested in the cinema as a young man. Yet when he discovered silent movies, he decided to become a filmmaker. This proved difficult without money or equipment, and three early efforts suffered as a result. One of these was a 16-mm film called *La Sonata à Kreutzer* (1956). Employing sound recorded on a tape recorder, this early work has remained invisible these many years, rejected by its creator. Yet Rohmer's longtime colleague François Truffaut called it "wonderful" in 1961. Truffaut compared it "well with the best professional films in 35mm that have been made in the past five years." (Truffaut himself in 1954 made his first film, a 16-mm short called *Une Visite*—rarely shown—that he dismissed as uninteresting. It was photographed by Jacques Rivette and edited by Alain Resnais.)

Then there are the directors Alain Resnais and Jacques Tati, for whom cinema has rarely been box-office. Resnais accounts for his relatively light output in 40 years of filmmaking by the fact that he sometimes began two projects at once, "each taking a year of work, and each of which comes to nothing because no one can raise the money." As he acknowledges, that's a difficult way to make a living.

French director Jacques Tati made only a half-dozen of his hilarious films starring himself as the dour M. Hulot in a 50-year career. His last, called *Parade* (1973), has not been shown in the United States. Tati took his time and never cared much for the reaction of critics to his work: "If I listened to them, I would never make a film. One will write 'I saw M. Hulot. I wanted to laugh but I only smiled.' The other will write 'I saw M. Hulot. I wanted to smile but I only laughed.'"

For these directors, it is, as Tati has expressed, "the spectator who comes out of the cinema full of enthusiasm . . . who does you the most good."

17. Robert Bresson (1907–   )

Les Affaires Publiques. 1934, 4900 ft. Produced by Arc Films. Script by Bresson. Music by Jean Wiener. Art direction by Pierre Charbonnier. With Marcel Dalio, Beby, Gilles Margaritis, Andree Servilanges, Les Clowns du Cirque d'Hiver, Les Girls des Folies-Bergère, Les Girls du Théâtre Pigalle. Unreleased in U.S.

The highly respected and individualistic French painter and director Robert Bresson made his first film in 1934. *Les Affaires Publiques* disappeared during the frantic days of World War II and until 1988, according to Bresson, was thought lost. Screened for the first time at the 1988 San Francisco Film Festival, the film was never released in the United States. It represents, says Bresson, "the opposite of everything I did later."

In 1934, Bresson received backing from an English surrealist to make this somewhat wacky film—the story of a series of ceremonies and events, each of which comes off badly but somehow fails to diminish its officials' prestige.

In the country called "Crogandia," the dictator (Beby the clown) is honoring the head of a fire brigade (Dalio). In order to prove their bravery, the brigade members, dancing a minuet, attempt to set fire to a house, but the house ups and flees from the neighborhood. Still, the head of the brigade is honored for his work. During the ceremony he finds he has to trim his beard to see the medal on his chest.

The dictator then dedicates a statue to himself. During his speech, all the people fall asleep, and it is the statue which suggests the dictator end the talk.

Other events that go absurdly wrong involve a prince who falls from an airplane but remains miraculously uninjured; and an oceanliner which, about to be ceremoniously launched, sinks in front of the invited guests and military brass. (In these scenes Marcel Dalio played an admiral.)

Bresson said he made the film by instinct, but chose never to make another comedy. He went on to work as a scriptwriter or adaptor on *Jumeaux de Brighton* (directed by Claude Heymann, 1936), *Courrier Sud* (directed by Pierre Billon, 1937), and *Air Pur* (directed by René Clair, unfinished, 1939). His first feature-length direction was *Les Anges du Péché* (1943). In 1988, Bresson received the Life Achievement Award from the San Francisco Film Festival.

99

18. Alberto de Almeida Cavalcanti (1897–1982)

Resurrection. 1922. Produced by Cinegraphic. Design by Alberto Cavalcanti, Fernand Leger, Claude Autant-Lara, and Mallet-Stevens. Directed by Marcel L'Herbier. Adapted from the novel by Leo Tolstoy. With Emmy Lynn (Katia), Jori Sarnio, Claire Prelia, and Lily Samuel. Unfinished.

Puntila and His Chauffeur Matti (Herr Puntila und sein Knecht Matti). 1955, 100 min. Produced by Heinrich Baur. Script by Cavalcanti. Bertolt Brecht, Vladimir Pozner, and Ruth Wieden, based on the play by Bertolt Brecht. Photographed by Andre Bac. Music by Hans Eisler. With Curt Bois (Puntila), Heinz Engelmann, Maria Emo, and Edith Prager. Unreleased in U.S.

Carpathian Castle. 1956. A French-Rumanian production. Script by Cavalcanti and Titus Popovici. Based on Jules Verne's novel *Le Château de Carpathes*. Unfinished.

Yerma. 1962. Script by Cavalcanti. Based on the play *Yerma* by Garcia Lorca (1934). With Ana Esmeralda (Yerma). Unfinished.

The versatile Brazilian director Alberto Cavalcanti became famous for his films of "poetic realism" of the 1920s and 1930s. He established his reputation with the French avant-garde film about ordinary life called *Rien que les Heures* (1926). As a director who once said he "believes only in the thematic aspect of film," Cavalcanti was influential in the development of British documentaries in the late 1930s. Always ready to make use of "good technique" in order to express "a great concept," Cavalcanti was attracted to screen adaptations of works by such controversial authors as Brecht. In a 50-year career, his first adaptation went unfinished. More than 30 years later the director faced production problems in adapting works outside of France and Britain; and a fourth film, based on a play by Brecht, has not been shown in the United States.

Cavalcanti began his career designing sets for *Resurrection*, which was being shot in 1922 in the Epinay studios outside of Paris by Marcel L'Herbier. Becoming a member of the avant-garde, which he described as a movement of inward as well as outward dissent and strife with his "masters' art," Cavalcanti found that L'Herbier didn't try to make films "speak their own language. He tried to make films speak literature. . . . We thought there was a language and that it must be searched for, it must be found."

The project went unfinished, Cavalcanti remembered, it spite of everyone's wholehearted effort. Director Marcel L'Herbier, shooting an adaptation of a Tolstoy's novel, became seriously ill because of the cold weather on location. The actors also became ill, there were accidents on the set, and the mounting costs the French branch of Paramount was facing in constructing the exteriors finally brought the film to a halt.

Over the next 40 years, Cavalcanti's scores of films, either directed or produced by him, exhibited a realism and experimentation of picture and sound. The director once commented that he cared little for the fact that he'd gained a lot of "experience" making films: "Experience is not style. When experience bends towards becoming stylistic, it degenerates into mannerism. Realism can encompass all of cinema, while experience cannot pretend to do more than perfect a means of expression."

In Britain after World War II, Cavalcanti made *Dead of Night* (1945), *Nicholas Nickelby* (1945), *They Made Me a Fugitive* (1947), *The First Gentleman* (1948), and *Them That Trespass* (1949). He made his only three Brazilian films in the years 1950–1954, but later declared that going to Brazil was a mistake. Nonetheless, Cavalcanti has been praised by the film historian Georges Sadoul for making the little-seen Brazilian film *Song of the Sea (O Canto do Mar*, 1953), a remake of his lyrical 1927 French silent about youthful life along the coast called *Sea Fever (En Rade)*.

Back in Europe, seemingly able to integrate himself quickly into different cultures, Cavalcanti went on to make films in Austria (*Puntila and His Chauffeur Matti*, 1955), East Germany (*Die Windrose*, 1957), Italy (*La Prima Notte*, 1958), and Britain (*The Monster of Highgate Ponds*, 1960).

Three works during this period stand out. In 1955 Cavalcanti completed *Puntila and His Chauffeur Matti*, a film Bertolt Brecht was said to have called the finest screen adaptation of any of his works. This includes comparison to Brecht's scripts for *Die Dreigroschenoper (The Threepenny Opera*, directed by G. W. Pabst), 1931; *Kuhle Wampe*, 1932; *Murderer Takes to the Road* (adaptation by Pudovkin), 1941; *Hangman Also Die!* (directed by Fritz Lang), 1943; *Song of the Rivers*, 1954, with songs by Paul Robeson; and *Mutter Courage and ihre Kinder*, unfinished, 1955.

Although he had never met Brecht, Cavalcanti greatly admired him. In Austria in 1955 the enterprising screenwriter Ruth Wieden asked Cavalcanti to come up with a script from material Brecht had provided. Cavalcanti developed the story and sent it to Brecht in Berlin. But the exacting playwright rejected Cavalcanti's film treatment and instead sent Cavalcanti his play *Herr Puntila*, which Cavalcanti rejected outright. It seems Brecht had sent Cavalcanti his play, word for word, and expected it to be filmed that way. Recalling that Brecht had once filed lawsuits against such film giants as Fritz Lang and G. W. Pabst, Cavalcanti feared the worst, commenting, "I am in the basket. He's going to annoy me no end."

However, Wieden brought the two men together in Berlin, assuring Cavalcanti that they would understand one another very well. The director recounted in 1975 that Brecht "immediately took me by the arm, as if he knew me all the time. He knew I had refused his script. He knew we were going to try together to make one." Their adaptation for the East German studio DEFA was called *Puntila and His Chauffeur Matti.*

Puntila is a fable, filmed mostly in color and set in Finland, about a Jekyll and Hyde–type landowner who softens under the influence of alcohol and has a very loyal companion in his chauffeur. The film was called "fast-paced" and "folksy" with a title that was "far too long" (Variety, 12/18/57) when it showed in Paris. Cavalcanti made unusual use of a chorus of women—filmed in black and white—who commented on the story. *Puntila and His Chauffeur Matti* has not been released in the United States.

From fall 1956 until early 1957 Cavalcanti was in Rumania making *Carpathian Castle,* which was based on Jules Verne's bizarre and little-known tale *Le Château des Carpathes* (1892) and Villiers de L'Isle-Adam's story about a hero who transplants the soul of a "live" woman into a robot called "L'Eve Future" (1891).

Considered by some to have been a source for Bram Stoker's *Dracula* (1897), Verne's "Chateau des Carpathes" is a gothic countryside tale that employs such supernatural elements as ghosts, werewolves, and vampires. It also makes reference to the then recent inventions of the phonograph and the kinetoscope. The fantastic elements, and the theme that imagination may be more real than reality, bring to mind Cavalcanti's films *Pett and Pott* (1934) and *Dead of Night* (1945). Begun at the Buftea Film Center and on location in the mountains, *Carpathian Castle* gave Cavalcanti a chance to again explore cinematic uses of sound—a specialty of his—to enhance the visual aspects of films.

The story revolves around a castle in Carpathia, where eccentric Baron Rodolphe de Gortz has apparently brought back to life the beautiful opera singer La Stilla, whom he'd admired but never approached until she died singing the finale of *Orlando.* Her lover, Count Franz Telek, has found consolation in his family's castle. Emerging only after several years, he travels to the village of Werst in the Carpathians, where he learns that the villagers are terrified of the goings-on at the nearby ruined castle. The count finds out that not only is the supposedly empty castle owned by Baron Gortz, but Stilla's voice can be heard and she herself can be seen silhouetted against the mountaintop.

When Franz finally confronts the baron, he finds Stilla singing. He rushes to her, but the baron yells, "You'll never take her away from me!" Then when he "stabs" Stilla, broken glass can be heard, and she vanishes.

The baron shouts, "Stilla escapes you yet again, Franz Telek, but her voice is mine and mine alone." He seizes a box and rushes for the door. The seemingly lifelike figure is revealed to be a reflection and her voice a recording.

But Cavalcanti never brought the complete story to the screen. After meeting the film studio's adminstrators, writers and actors, Cavalcanti stressed that everyone believed completely in the movie's future. Yet he nonetheless failed to receive sufficient creative backing. Somewhat sheepishly he had to admit dissatisfaction with the scenario and the actors, and was forced to spend time resolving a host of production problems any associate producer could handle. The upshot was that he found himself unable to concentrate on the creative aspects that should have been his central concern.

The director summed up his failure to complete the film in a 1957 article entitled "Development Problem of the Rumanian Film." He pointed out that his unfinished project underlined major problems within the country's film industry, which would never come of age until, Cavalcanti wrote, four problems were tackled: "the isolation of the filmmaker, the idea of the superiority of the director, the problem of the scenario and of acting."

In early 1961 in Spain, Cavalcanti proclaimed, "I am studying Iberian themes, because I feel cinema should be as international as possible." His unnamed film would star Ana Esmeralda, a ballet dancer and actress. Cavalcanti eventually came up with a script for a film called *Yerma*, based on the tragic play of the same name that 36-year-old Federico García Lorca wrote in 1934. García Lorca, an antifascist, became one of the most famous victims of Franco's rise to power when he was assassinated two years later.

Yerma—which means barren—is a story of contrast between the desire for freedom and the need to conform, expressed in terms of fertility and decay, life and death, inner strength and the striving for "reputation." The story also has a tragic theme running through it, because from the opening scene, the audience realizes something dreadful is going to happen.

Yerma, the main character, is married to Juan. She desires children; he does not, or is at best indifferent to the idea, but wants to live in such a way that his "honor" is not besmirched. Yerma tries to break out of the stifling conformist existence she finds herself in. Married to a man she isn't attracted to, yet desiring the traditional life of a Spanish woman (i.e., as a mother), she fleetingly considers an affair with a man named Victor. Rejecting the idea, she turns to mysterious rites by which she might be able to conceive a child.

Yerma's story ends badly. During a terrible fight with her husband, she kills him. In ending his life, she finds she has "murdered my son ... murdered my son."

Cavalcanti intended to bring this suppressed story to the screen despite the fact that censorship was still the norm in Spain. After Franco had gained control in 1939, all of García Lorca's plays were banned. *Yerma* itself was not performed again in Spain until 1960.

Then in early 1961, when Cavalcanti was deciding what "Iberian theme" to film, the world of Spanish cinema was rocked by a huge scandal. Luis Buñuel, who had come over from Mexico, had just completed filming *Viridiana* in Madrid—Franco's censors had even approved its being made in Spain—when the true nature of the blasphemous film became apparent to the regime. After *Viridiana* won the Palme d'Or at Cannes in May that year, Franco's censors suppressed the work in Spain. Certain individuals involved in the film's dissemination faced retribution. Spain's director of cinema and theatre was dismissed and 20 members of the country's delegation to Cannes were "punished," according to one notice. Journalists and critics were forbidden to mention the existence of Buñuel's film. Finally, UNINCI, *Viridiana*'s Spanish coproduction company, was liquidated by the regime. This Spanish version of United Artists counted among its liberal members Luis García Berlanga, Pío Caro Baroja, and Guillermo Zúñiga.

Under Franco, native Spanish directors in the years 1939–75 produced only three or four films a year. This total of 151 films in 36 years shows most directors were not willing to take the risks of making films. A film could be suppressed in several ways. "At best," said Buñuel when referring to what might happen, "they will ban it or put it on for half a week in an out-of-the-way fleapit where it will achieve neither glory nor blame." A film might lose its right to be shown at a quality theatre or to be exported. Franco's censors were said to have reacted in this fashion to films of unusual content and those disagreeable to the regime.

Faced with this kind of climate, Cavalcanti, it appears, had little choice but to abandon the filming of *Yerma* in early 1962. The Spanish observer for the British publication *Films and Filming* wrote in March 1962, "Buñuel's daring movie had also a fatal effect.... Censorship has become so angry and mistrustful since *Viridiana* escaped them."

Cavalcanti did manage to present *Yerma* on stage, based on his script. In doing so he turned to the theatre for the first time since his youth.

In 1967, Cavalcanti, realizing that for the last decade he'd been considered "a bit out of fashion," managed to return to filmmaking. In Haifa he directed *The Story of Israel: Thus Spake Theodor Herzl* for television, an area for which he was "interested in finding the right kind of technique."

At the age of 72 Cavalcanti wrote his autobiography, *Memorias*, which remains unpublished. It sheds more light on events surrounding his unfinished films.

Six years before Cavalcanti died, a filmed version of *Carpathian Castle* was made for television, the medium in which Cavalcanti worked until the end of his life. That successful retelling of the Jules Verne tale was directed by Jean-Christophe Averty for French television.

Fewer than half of the nearly 100 films Cavalcanti directed or produced have been shown in the United States.

19. Gaston Modot (1887–1970)

Sardonic Tale (Conte Cruel). 1930. Produced by Natan. Script by Modot and Charles Spaak. With Gaston Modot. Unreleased in U.S.

The French actor Gaston Modot entered films in 1908. Over the next 50 years, he worked for some of the greatest directors. The list is long, and includes Gance, Dulac, Clair, Renoir, Pabst, Duvivier, Becker, and Buñuel. For many of these he worked more than once. In 1930, Modot — for the only time in his life — directed a film. A producer warned him: "Before anything else, Modot, no Cubism." Although Modot admitted he "did not have the commercial qualities" to realize movies, his one directorial effort was acclaimed as a highly original sound film. It has never been shown in the United States.

Modot's *Sardonic Tale* is an adaptation of a 1700-word story called "La Torture par l'Esperance," published in 1888 in the novel *Nouveaux Contes Cruels* by Villiers de l'Isle-Adam (1838–1889). (Villiers's full name was Jean-Marie Mathias Philippe Auguste de Villiers de l'Isle-Adam.) Working with Modot on the script was Charles Spaak. This was Spaak's first script. He would go on to write a host of noteworthy films of "poetic realism" in France in the 1930s.

Sardonic Tale, a psychological story of terror, takes place during the Inquisition. Modot stars as Rabbi Aser Abarbanel. The Jewish leader has been branded a criminal by the authorities because he is "without faith." The Spanish Grand Inquisitor Pedro Arbuez sentences the rabbi to the *auto-da-fé*. On the night before his execution, the rabbi believes he can avoid the terrible punishment. He notices that the door to his cell is ajar. Immediately, he heads down the corridor towards what he hopes is freedom. The sense of hope that rises within him is almost too much. But suddenly the rabbi senses that "all stages of this fatal evening were only an arranged torture, that of hope."

In the morning the rabbi is taken before the Grand Inquisitor to meet his terrible fate. The hope that he glimpsed hours earlier disappears forever.

Modot's medium-length film is mentioned in a number of anthologies, but there appear to be no records of it having been screened in the United States. *Sardonic Tale* is now lost.

20. *Alain Resnais (1922–   )*

Les Jardins de Paris. 1948, 1500 meters. Produced by Christiane and Paul Renty. Production company: Les Films de la Roue. Assistant director, Colette Renty. Photographed and edited by Resnais. Script by Roland Dubillard. Unfinished.

Les Statues Meurent Aussi (Statues Die Also). 1953, 3 reels (30 min.). Produced by Prèsence Africaine/Tadie Cinéma. Script by Resnais and Chris Marker. Photographed by Ghislain Cloquet. Music by Guy Bernard. Narration by Resnais. Unreleased.

In the late 1940s, the French director Alain Resnais, today best known for the haunting *Hiroshima Mon Amour* (1959), began his career by making 16mm silent documentaries about artists and creativity. These were *Portrait d'Henri Goetz* (1947), *Visite à Max Ernst* (1947), *La Bague* (performance by Marcel Marceau, 1947), *Van Gogh* (1948), and *Les Jardins de Paris* (1948).

For *Les Jardins de Paris*, Resnais shot about 1500 meters of documentary footage of the gardens in Paris. He filmed such public parks as le Caroussel and le Vert Galant, and shot scenes from the roof of the Louvre. A sequence entitled "Jardin des Plantes" was directed by the film critic André Bazin.

This semiprivate work was commissioned by the producers Christiane Renty and Paul Renty, for whom Resnais had made the 16mm shorts *L'Alcool Tue* and *Campagne Première* in 1947. But Resnais never finished *Les Jardins de Paris*, for he turned to making *Châteaux de France* (1948), the first film he financed himself. This 16mm film of the tourist attractions in the country was Resnais's last before he began making 35mm films and started his "official" work as a filmmaker.

In 1950, Resnais accepted an assignment from the production company Prèsence Africaine to make a 35mm documentary about the breakdown of African culture under French rule. Resnais's narration sets the theme of the film, entitled *Les Statues Meurent Aussi*: "When men have died they enter history. When statues have died they enter art. This botany of death is what we call culture." Chris Marker, who coauthored the script, wrote: "We want to see their suffering, serenity, humor, even though we

107

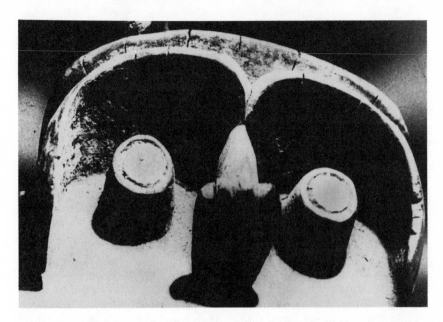

A shot from Les Statues Meurent Aussi, *1953, directed by Alain Resnais.*

don't know anything about them. Colonizers of the world, we want everything to talk to us: animals, the dead, statues."

Completed in 1953, *Les Statues Meurent Aussi* presaged Resnais's 1963 film *Muriel,* which also compared African and French culture. *Les Statues* indicted France for its destruction of African beliefs, the decline of native art and artists. Winner of the Prix Vigo in 1954, the film was banned in France by order of La Commission de Contrôle. In 1963, two reels of the film were put together. In 1965, the ban was lifted, but differences between Resnais and the producers left the third reel unedited.

21. Eric Rohmer (1920–)

Les Petites Filles Modèles. 1952, 60 min. Produced by Guy de Ray and Joseph Keke. Script by Rohmer and P. Guilbaud. With Josette Sinclair (Mme de Fleurville), Josee Doucet, Olga de Poliakoff, and three children. Unfinished.

La Sonata à Kreutzer. 1956, 50 min. Produced by Jean-Luc Godard. Script by Rohmer. With Rohmer (Toukhatchevsky), Jean-Claude Brialy (Pozdnycheff), and Françoise Martinelli (Hélène). Unfinished.

La Signe du Lion (The Sign of the Lion). 1959, 100 min. AJYM production. Photographed by Nicolas Hayer. Script by Rohmer. With Jess Hahn, Van Doude, Michele Girardon, Christian Alers, Jean Le Poulain, and Gilbert Edard. Unreleased in U.S.

The New Wave director Eric Rohmer claims he was "unusually unfortunate in the early years" of his career. His first film, a silent short from about 1950, is now lost. Two subsequent films went unfinished. A full-length feature he made in 1959 has never been fully released. These unseen films, according to an interviewer, represented the French director's first attempts to bring literary techniques to the cinematic medium.

In 1950, while he was a writer and film critic, Rohmer made *Journal of a Scoundrel*, a 16mm silent short influenced by Erich von Stroheim's *Foolish Wives* (1921). In 1952, Rohmer began *Les Petites Filles Modèles*, a full-length feature. This 35mm "children's" film, with overtones of sadism and perversion, was based on the story of the same name by Comtesse de Segur. Rohmer was forced to abandon the film when the producer's money ran out. Not even the negative of *Les Petites Filles Modèles* exists.

In 1956, Rohmer began making a film based on a short story Tolstoy wrote in 1889. Called *La Sonata à Kreutzer*, the film was backed financially by Jean-Luc Godard.

Rohmer's try at filming Tolstoy's story was not the first. Before his effort, nine separate versions made it to the screen, beginning with a Russian interpretation in 1911 (starring Ivan Mozjoukhine). Other adaptations include an American one in 1915 (starring Theda Bara), Machaty's film in 1926, Veidt Harlan's version of 1937, Jean Dreville's French adaptation of 1938 (starring Gaby Morlay and Pierre Renoir), and Gianni Franciolini's Italian production in 1947.

La Sonata à Kreutzer tells the story of Pozdnycheff, a 30-year-old man with a tarnished past. Previous to his marriage to a beautiful woman (Hélène) about five years before, he had seduced the wife of his best friend. The friend then committed suicide.

Pozdyncheff's indifferent relationship with his wife undergoes a change when they have children: She falls passionately in love with the violinist Toukhatchevsky, renowned for his playing of Beethoven's "Sonata à Kreutzer." Pozdyncheff becomes insanely jealous. Crazed, he sees in the violinist a reflection of himself as seducer and in his wife the image of the faithless women he has known. He kills Hélène—and then ponders his life in prison.

La Sonata à Kreutzer lent itself to being the perfect Rohmerian tragedy of lust, jealousy, and murder. Here was a story in which Rohmer could examine a favorite theme: the strains of marriage and the repressed sexual feelings of the partners. But Rohmer never edited the film because he considered it "unscreenable."

In 1959 Rohmer completed his first full-length film, *La Signe du Lion*. The title refers to the sign of the Zodiac that rules midsummer. This early New Wave film was produced by French director Claude Chabrol's company, AJYM. *La Signe du Lion* was released overseas in 1962, but was not shown in the United States.

In *La Signe du Lion* a foreigner, Pierre (played by Jess Hahn), is studying music in Paris. The young man comes into some money by mistake and quickly spends it. When it's gone, he must pay it back to the rightful owners. Consequently, the man winds up penniless and alone.

Rohmer's treatment is an uncompromising picture of a man finding himself degraded and homeless, criss-crossing an authentic and cold city, until he is saved by friends and an inheritance some months after his slow decline. While the director was praised by the critics for capturing the man's plight "with insistence but insight" and warmth, the film attracted little attention.

The film's production company had been sold before the film's release, and the new producer cut the film and replaced Louis Sageur's score with music by Brahms. Rohmer objected. He finally agreed to let the shortened version be shown in the provinces of France and the full version in the art houses and abroad. But in the period 1958–60 there was a glut of New Wave films on the market. *La Signe du Lion* had to wait three years to be released. Then the film flopped everywhere except in Africa, where viewers assumed the title implied a jungle epic.

Haunted by his commercial failure, Rohmer returned to writing criticism and making 16mm shorts. He worked at the French publication *Cahiers du Cinéma* and was as highly regarded as Andre Bazin. It was not until 1969 that he gained an international audience with the first of his moral tales: *My Night at Maud's*.

22. Roberto Rossellini (1906–1977)

Prelude à l'Après-midi d'un Faune. 1938. Script by Rossellini. With music from Debussy. Unreleased.

The great Italian director Roberto Rossellini is remembered for his neorealist films *Open City* (1945), *Paisan* (1946), and *Germany Year Zero* (1947). He began his film career by making short, personal documentaries.

Between 1936 and 1941, using his own money, Rossellini made six films. One of them—his second—was, he recalled when he'd achieved international acclaim, "a documentary about nature" not in the mold of the ordinary tourist-nature film common then. The director demonstrated a youthful "sensitivity" in his episodes of "childhood daydreams, the discovery of life." Essentially autobiographical, the work was judged indecent by the censors. It was never released.

Rossellini has indicated that his short film *Prelude à l'Après-midi d'un Faune* was inspired by Debussy's music. Debussy's music, which premiered in 1894, in turn had been inspired by a poem by Stéphane Mallarmé in 1876. In 1912, the Russian ballet star Nijinsky danced in a 12-minute work entitled "L'Après-midi d'un Faune" which was inspired by Debussy—and not by Mallarmé.

In Nijinsky's famous ballet, a faun meets seven nymphs (in the poem he meets two). Fleeing, one of the nymphs loses her veil. The faun becomes aroused, lies on the veil and masturbates. When Nijinsky danced his ballet, he created a scandal by making concrete what had only been a dream in Mallarmé's poem.

Rossellini's work was a visual, nonballet interpretation of the music and the ballet. In it the young Rossellini displayed a "revolutionary" vision of life, a man deeply impressed "by the water with the serpent slithering about in it and the dragonfly overhead."

In an interview, Rossellini characterized his early work this way: "At that time, I had the reputation of being a mad man full of dangerous ideas, and for this reason I was taken as a drop of vinegar in a salad."

Prelude à l'Après-midi d'un Faune, like all the other early works, is now lost.

111

23. Franklin J. Schaffner (1920–1989)

A Summer World. 1961. Henry T. Weinstein, producer. Script by Howard Koch and Steven Gether. With Fabian, Susan Hampshire, Suzi Parker, and Gig Young. Unfinished.

The Entebbe Project/Operation Jonathan. 1976. Produced by Stanley O'Toole. Warner Bros. studio. Script by Kenneth Ross. With Steve McQueen (Gen. Dan Shomron). Unfinished.

Franklin J. Schaffner was the director of *Patton* (1970), *Papillon* (1973), and other films of men in action. A veteran television director of serious drama of the 1950s, Schaffner failed to make the jump to commercial films in his first try. His breezy tale of life in southern California, called *A Summer World*, was suddenly cancelled without his having a word to say about it.

Fifteen years later, when Schaffner tried to bring his television experience to bear on a fast-breaking story, he found himself too constrained by outside forces to complete *The Entebbe Project*.

Franklin Schaffner had gleaned his skills directing in the early days of television. After signing a three-film contract with 20th Century–Fox in 1961. Schaffner was assigned a film based on a novel by Richard Dougherty, scripted by veteran screenwriter Howard Koch, and rewritten by another writer. Schaffner deduced that he was not being tested much in this commercial effort, *A Summer World*. In fact, he admitted that in the early 1960s he was "most comfortable with simple situations—four walls . . . two men in confrontation, or a love story." Further, he said, "I am also comfortable with an adult-child relationship."

A Summer World would contain a great deal of dialogue, which a television director such as Schaffner would know how to handle. But it would also be dealing with a thornier subject for 1961: teen-age sex. The new generation would have to discover as well that "you have to stop blaming everything on your parents . . . even if they're to ʿame."

To the producer of *A Summer World*, the film was "about the human heart, a very fragile piece for a motion picture." Centering on the unexamined

112

and very middle-class lives of three teen-age couples—Alex (Fabian) and Kate (Susan Hampshire); Peter (Gig Young) and Evelyn; and Edward and Ellen—Schaffner's film can be described as an early version of *Bob and Carol and Ted and Alice* (1965). The highlight of their lives was to be in a sports car rally through the state.

Before Schaffner knew what happened, 20th Century–Fox shelved the film. Director Schaffner got the news from his barber. He would have to wait two years before making his first commercial film, *Woman of Summer* (also titled *The Stripper*).

In the summer of 1976, Hollywood studios scrambled to quickly bring to the screen a thrilling story from the days' headlines: Israel's daring rescue of 104 Jews from Uganda. Warner Bros. asked Franklin Schaffner, whose television experience had taught him how to organize a production on short notice, to direct their $10 million picture, *The Entebbe Project* (also tentatively titled *Operation Jonathan* in honor of the American-born commander who led the raid).

Competing against proposed productions by Paramount (*90 Minutes to Entebbe,* direction by Sidney Lumet, script by Paddy Chayefsky) and Universal Studios (*Rescue at Entebbe,* direction by George Roy Hill, script by Loring Mandel), Warner Bros. sought the cooperation of Israeli officials and the services of Steve McQueen. Said Ted Ashley, who was the head of Warner Bros., "*Entebbe* will be a movie Israel and I will be proud of."

In Israel, Schaffner found himself working under severe constraints, to which his film studio had agreed. Shooting of *The Entebbe Project*—with or without an as yet unwritten script—had to begin by the end of February 1977 and be completed in six months, in time for the Israeli elections in the fall. In addition, *The Entebbe Project* had to be shot in Israel.

Schaffner went to work. He sought verisimilitude. He and his scriptwriter looked into the highly sensitive activities of Israel's secret service (Mosad) and the highly complex military details of the resuce. They also sought to examine the role of Kenya in the rescue. In examining these details of the rescue, Schaffner and company ran afoul of Israel's military censors—who were said to fear, surprisingly, a romanticized retelling of the mission—and were unable to come up with what the censors wanted. Israel's minister of commerce (Chaim Bar-Lev), on the other hand, stated that "Warner Brothers did not want to film just a well-documented drama.... They wanted to reconstruct exactly what happened. That violated our security."

In mid–October 1976, Schaffner was forced to abandon *The Entebbe Project* after Ashley concluded that Israel was not going to provide the necessary information for the film. The other film studios abandoned their projects as well.

In an ironic note, television beat Schaffner to the story: Both ABC and

NBC produced films on the daring operation by the end of the year. ABC made *Victory at Entebbe* (directed by Marvin Chomsky), and NBC made *Raid on Entebbe* (directed by Irvin Kirchner). One observer pointed out that lack of information didn't stop the television studios, since what was important to the story was not the details of the raid—already well known by the public—but the character of the operation. With his background in television, Franklin Schaffner ought to have known that.

The scripts of Schaffner's two aborted films can be found in the Franklin J. Schaffner Film Library at Franklin and Marshall College, Lancaster, Pennsylvania.

24. Jacques Tati (1980–1982)

Parade. 1973, 85 min., color. Produced by Gray-Film, Sveriges Radio, and CEPEC. Script by Tati. Photographed by Jean Badel and Yunnar Fisher. Music by Charles Dumont. With Jacques Tati (Monsieur Loyal), Norman and Ladd, Carl Kossmayer, the Veterans, the Williams, the Sipoles, Michele Brabo, Pia Colombo, and Pierre Bramma. Unreleased in U.S.

In a film career that lasted 50 years, comedian Jacques Tati directed only six films. His character Monsieur Hulot became world famous. *Parade*, his last film—his fantasy for children and adults—recalls the pantomimes that launched Tati in the music halls. About these beginnings, the novelist and screenwriter Colette remarked that Tati "created at the same time the player, the ball and the racket; the boxer and his opponent; the bicycle and its rider. His powers of suggestion are those of a great artist." *Parade* has not yet been shown in the United States.

Jacques Tati made *Parade* as a videotape for Swedish television. That same year a French producer transferred the videotape to film electronically, added a few scenes, and presented it on French television during the Christmas season. At Cannes the following year it was screened out of competition but attracted enough attention to win the French Grand Prix du Cinema. Then in 1975 *Parade* won the Gold Medal in the Children's Film Competition of the Moscow Film Festival. Tati was, as one critic noted, "in form."

Parade is the story of a circus. In this film, Tati portrays Monsieur Loyal. He brings together the performers and the spectators, the clowns and the children. In the circus world of Monsieur Loyal, the children get what they want. They see Tati's great mime routines of so-called adults— the fisherman, a punch-drunk fighter, an anxious tennis player, an irascible soccer goalie, a horse and its rider.

The character Tati plays in this film is more down to earth and less bitter than Monsieur Hulot ever was; he's even less confused. The atmosphere of the circus is one of comedy, joy, and celebration. The film ends as the circus closes down for the night, a few balloons drifting off on the wind as the crew turns out the lights.

In the mid–1970s, French and American producers asked Tati to

Parade, *1973*. Top: *Jacques Tati performs in front of his favorite audience—children.*
Bottom: *Tati in a solo scene from* Parade.

consider a more ambitious project, this time for Hollywood. Their film was to be called *Confusion*, and it would bring back Monsieur Hulot.

For their film, they envisioned Hulot introducing the "Hulot Color System" to network television; he would "create his brand of havoc or, if you will, confusion in the most varied of locations."

Tati envisioned a daring opening for the film: Monsieur Hulot shows up at a TV studio with his color system. Standing around, Hulot is accidentally shot and killed on the set by a ham actor whose gun somehow contained real bullets. Then with the broadcast of the soap opera or show about to begin, real confusion reigns: Employees and executives frantically try to remove the body as the actors are stepping over it to get to their places.

Tati backed away from this idea, afraid he would be unable to raise sufficient funding for a movie with such a bold opening scene. At the last minute Tati rejected the Hollywood offer and turned to solely European backers—afraid, perhaps, to leave the familiar people and technology of his home continent.

In ill health in his last years, Tati died before shooting any of the film.

25. King Vidor (1894–1982)

Truth and Illusion: An Introduction to Metaphysics. 1966, 25 min. Produced by Vidor. Script by Vidor. Assistant director, Michael Neary. Edited by Fred Y. Smith. Unreleased in U.S.

Metaphor. 1979, 40 min. Produced by Vidor. Script by Vidor. With Andrew Wyeth and King Vidor. Unreleased.

"My first pictures," recalled King Vidor in the early 1970s, "back in Texas were documentaries. I guess you can say the wheel has come full circle. And one thing I've kept all along. My feeling for the soil."

The director of such sensitive and realistic Hollywood productions as *The Crowd* (1928), *The Champ* (1931), *Our Daily Bread* (1934), and *Duel in the Sun* (1947) ended his career making what he called "home movies." His last two films, 16mm documentaries, remain unreleased in the United States.

King Vidor made films for more than 65 years. His first efforts, made on borrowed money in his native Texas, captured small-town life and the effects of nature: documentaries on the Galveston Hurricane (1913), troops on parade (1914), and sugar refining (1915); then westerns in 1917 and the Judge Brown series in 1918. But the score or so of films he shot before departing for Hollywood in 1919 are all but lost.

At MGM, the enterprising filmmaker rose through the ranks and then in 1925 made the antiwar film *The Big Parade*, a work, he recalled 50 years after the event, which "put me on the map as a director." He would feel its influence even at the end of his life.

By 1959, Vidor was a veteran of more than 50 commercial films. That year he filmed *Solomon and Sheba*. This wearying experience—a popular success but a critical failure—forced him finally to try making films closer to his liking. After a half-dozen years, when nothing materialized in Hollywood and Vidor was said to have retired, the director shot the 25-minute documentary *Truth and Illusion: An Introduction to Metaphysics*. Vidor narrates a vision of the place of man in the world and offers images that support his views. As he says in the film: "Nature gets the credit which ... should be reserved to ourselves, the rose for its scent, the nightingale for its song, the sun for its radiance. The poets ... should address their lyrics to themselves and ... turn them into odes for themselves."

118

Released only in France, *Truth and Illusion* received a one-time screening in the United States at the September 1972 retrospective of Vidor's films at the Museum of Modern Art in New York City.

Three years before he died, Vidor made one last film. In 1979, he completed the documentary *Metaphor*, a work instigated by the realist painter Andrew Wyeth. The painter of austere rural landscapes had written to Vidor that he considered *The Big Parade* "the only truly great film ever produced." Vidor and Wyeth met, and in *Metaphor*, director and painter discuss the influence of the 1925 production on Wyeth's career and work. Wyeth recalls that he's seen the silent "180 times, and that's no exaggeration."

Metaphor has not been released commercially anywhere, but it was screened in 1980 at the Directors Guild in Hollywood.

V. "FACT" FILMS AND FREAK ACCIDENTS

Experience has shown that [documentary] production is quite different in
method and purpose from that of entertainment story films . . . different in
that the ends are less glamorous. . . . It asks for people with different aims.
— Paul Rotha, 1938

In the 1930s and 1940s in America, several master documentary film-makers—Flaherty, Lorentz, Ivens—went out to record life. They did not depend on editing and commentary to tell their stories. They shot nature and life for the pleasure of filming it, and their images told the story. They were filming what John Grierson called "creative treatments of actuality."

Their aims were not simply to entertain but to interest the viewer, capture his attention. The German filmmaker Hans Richter, for many years the head of the film institute at the City College of New York, spoke of the role of documentary film as "an instrument of great social importance . . . it must be used for better living and better understanding of problems . . . it is a fighting weapon."

In this high spirit, these filmmakers approached their tasks. Along the way, they learned their trade—including living with the fact that they sometimes lost their films to "accidents" and to circumstances beyond their control.

Robert Flaherty, the father of the documentary, lost his first two (untitled) films because of carelessness. Freak accidents resulted in his first film falling from his sled into the ice, and the second a year later going up in smoke. Thirteen years later, already an established director because of *Nanook of the North* (1922), he was making *Acoma, the Sky City* (1928). This incomplete film, too, was nearly destroyed in an accident. In fact, a number of sources list it as destroyed in a fire, but cameraman Floyd Crosby, who worked with Flaherty on the film, stressed years later that *Acoma* survived undamaged, if unfinished.

Another documentary filmmaker who lost a work to an accident was Hans Richter. He and Sergei Eisenstein had made the improvised and lighthearted 2-reeler *Storm Over La Sarraz* in 1929 in Switzerland. Richter assigned the film to Eisenstein for safekeeping, and the world-famous director promptly lost it.

Other stories can be told about French filmmaker Jean Epstein, who destroyed his film *Photogénies* (1924) after showing it one time to a circle of followers. Or Pare Lorentz, whose 1939 work *Ecce Homo!*—two-thirds complete—failed to be funded any further by the progressive government Lorentz had worked so hard to support. Or Joris Ivens, whose film *Woman of the Sea* (1944) would have brought Garbo out of retirement. But she was frightened by some Hollywood red-baiters from participating in Ivens's anti–Nazi film as World War II was coming to an end.

In the 1960s, a new crop of directors was gaining exposure in television. The young filmmakers Robert M. Young and Michael Roemer, for instance, began by making documentaries in the medium. They too were trying to come up with creative treatments of reality. Their only television collaboration was the full-length documentary *The Inferno* (*Cortile Cascino*, 1962) for NBC's White Paper series, yet their experience in making this film would turn them to fictional filmmaking.

In shooting *The Inferno*, the two discovered that their whole—their collaboration—was greater than the sum of their parts. They divided functions—Young handled the camera while Roemer wrote the script and worked with the cast or subjects—yet worked closely together. Filmed in cinema verité, their documentary is a series of sequences, almost like scenes from a play, about people struggling to survive in Sicily, in the poorest region of Europe. The filmmakers were trying to capture human experience and feelings in an original way yet remain within a logical framework.

Though the two were satisfied with the outcome, their television backer wasn't. NBC never aired the film because it was said to have lacked drama and confrontation. Shocked at having lost a chance to become established, Roemer realized it was time to turn to fiction and go independent.

Three years later, he and Young made the highly praised fictional film about black life in America called *Nothing But a Man*. In 1971 the two collaborated on the comedy-satire about urban travails called *The Plot Against Harry*. The film remained unfinished while the collaborators sought postproduction funds. Continuing to work in television, Roemer eventually completed and released the film in 1989. Robert M. Young left the medium of television and went on to establish his reputation directing *Short Eyes* (1978) and *The Ballad of Gregorio Cortez* (1983).

26. Jean Epstein (1897–1953)

Photogénies. 1924, 1,000 ft. Produced by Films Jean Epstein. Unreleased.

Marius et Olive à Paris. 1935, 70 min. (1100 meters). Produced by Cinemonde. Script by Jean-Michel Pages. Music by Jean Wiener. Photographed by Joseph R. Barth and Philippe Agostini. With Barencey (Marius), René Sarvis (Olive), Ila Meery, Laurette Clody (fiancee of Barbapoule), Micheline Cheirel (Alberte), Pitouto (Auguste Barbapoule), and Lilian Constantini. Unfinished.

The French director Jean Epstein has been called a "magician of the cinema" because of his use of stylized acting, gray slow-motion photography, and emphasis on detail in such films as *La Chute de la Maison/ House of Usher* (1928), *Finis Terrae* (1929), and *Le Tempestaire* (1947). Yet this influential director, who cared little for plot, made one experimental film that was never released and another that was not completed.

In April 1924, Jean Epstein made a film that would help establish his reputation as a leading avant-garde filmmaker. *Photogénies*, shot in Paris, was a short nonnarrative film that has been defined by the film historian Jean Mitry as an "essay of pure cinema." The experimental film, made at the request of the Théâtre de Vieux Colombier, was one of the first to endow ordinary newsreel with meaning and art. Using only snippets of edited newsreels, Epstein was able to convey the sense that buried treasure could be found in ordinary file footage.

Epstein dedicated the film to his mentor Louis Delluc, who had died earlier that year, and showed it to a group of enthusiasts. *Photogénies*, said one reviewer, represented "an indefinable something ... which differentiated cinema from all other arts." But after this showing, *Photogénies* was, it is said, "dismantled" by its creator and never released. Until Walter Ruttman made *Mélodie du Monde* in 1930, no filmmaker followed up on Epstein's idea.

By the mid–1930s, Epstein was out of favor: While sound films were all the rage, he continued to experiment with largely silent-screen images. Said Epstein, "I would have liked to limit speech to the role played by the titles [in silent films]." But he also felt it necessary "to ascertain what contribution slow motion ... could make to the sound track." In investigating the "language of things" Epstein hoped to create a kind of sonic close-up in which "slow-motion may enable all beings, and all objects, to speak. We can already see, but soon may hear, the grass grow."

In his films based on the works of George Sand, Alphonse Daudet, and other literary greats, Epstein's characters never went through life more quickly than his images; instead their daily routines made up the plot. His 1935 sound film *Marius et Olive à Paris* is a case in point.

Marius et Olive à Paris has been described by the producer, Cinémonde (also a film publication), as a "cinematographic fantasy ... a comedy in the manner of the Marx Brothers" about time and responsibility: Rejected by the Academy Phocéenes, Marius and his friend Olive leave Marseille and head for Paris. They marry and share a number of adventures. About halfway there, they meet the president of the academy, Auguste Barbapoule, who has the job of restoring life to the dead.

Scripted by Jean-Michel Pages, director of the publication *Cinémonde*, *Marius* was shot in January 1935 at the film studios of Photosonor de Courbevoie and the next month around Marseille and Aix. Epstein never completed the film, possibly because he didn't know how to. Nevertheless, the producer released a 70-minute version, whose editing and sound quality were not very good. Epstein disassociated himself from the release and his name did not appear as director. Still, *Marius et Olive à Paris*, like all of Epstein's work, was made with a pace which has been called the "rhythm of breathing."

27. Robert Flaherty (1884–1951)

Untitled film. 1914. Photographed by Flaherty. Unreleased.

Untitled film. 1915, 30,000 ft. Produced, scripted, and photographed by Flaherty. Unreleased.

Acoma, the Sky City. 1928. Silent. Produced by Fox Film Corp. Script by Flaherty and Randall H. Faye. Photographed by Flaherty, Leon Shamroy, and Floyd Crosby. Unfinished.

Guernica. 1949, 12 min. Produced by the Museum of Modern Art. Photographed by Flaherty. Titles by Richard Griffith. Script by William S. Lieberman. Assembled by David Flaherty. With Frances Flaherty and Iris Barry. Unfinished.

The American Robert Flaherty was the first filmmaker to have his work described as "documentary" in nature. The film theoretician and producer John Grierson described his work this way in 1926. The maker of the sweeping *Nanook of the North* (1922), Flaherty lost his first two films to accidents. Thirty-five years later his death would leave another work unfinished. This was "a tentative study" called *Guernica* to which Flaherty was never able to add voice, music, and a sound track.

Robert Flaherty began his film career almost inadvertently. An explorer, he was preparing to head out for northern Canada in 1913 when fellow explorer Sir William Mackenzie made a suggestion: "You're going into interesting country—strange people—animals and all that—why don't you include . . . a camera for making films?"

Flaherty liked the idea. He bought a Bell & Howell and spent the early part of 1914 shooting scenes of Eskimo culture: sledding, dancing, the building of igloos, the hunting for game. It was while he was shooting a deer hunt that his sled—containing his film—broke through ice. Most of the footage was lost.

Back in the warmth of lower Canada, Flaherty tried to edit and organize undamaged portions of the film but found it uninteresting. But he took consolation in the fact that he was planning another trip north. He would try to make another, better film.

Flaherty spent mid–1915 on the Belcher Islands of northern Canada, again filming Eskimo life and exploring the territory. He shot 30,000 feet of film that summer and sent a rough cut (work print) to Harvard University. It was lucky for him that he did. Soon thereafter the original nitrate negatives caught fire when Flaherty dropped a cigarette on them. The flames burned every foot of film and scarred Flaherty's hands.

Flaherty analyzed the surviving work print: "It was a bad film, it was dull—it was little more than a travelogue. I had learned to explore, I had not learned to reveal. It was utterly inept, simply a scene of this and that, no relation, no thread of a story or continuity."

Flaherty next determined to make a film following "a typical Eskimo and his family" in their daily lives for a year. Seven years later, he achieved this goal with *Nanook of the North*, a revolutionary film for its freshness, curiosity, humanity, and art.

In the period 1928–29 studios in Hollywood were adjusting their casting, their technique, and their production schedules to the making of sound films. Flaherty, meanwhile, in June of 1928 sought out the Fox Film Corporation. He wanted to make a silent documentary, building on the critical (though not financial) success of his last film, *Moana* (1926). Tentatively titled *Nanook of the Desert*, Flaherty's new project would "depict the life, customs, and habits of the Pueblo Indians" of the Southwest, as stipulated in a $2,000 contract the director negotiated with the Indians. The village of Acoma, located high atop the rocks in the New Mexico desert, was the setting for this latest project. Flaherty described the village as a "Gibraltar in a sea of sand."

As he had done with the film *Moana*, Flaherty collaborated with his wife, Frances, and brother, David. They picked the locations for shooting while Flaherty and a colleague developed the script.

Flaherty's treatment stressed the precarious nature of life in the Southwest for the agricultural Indians: the threatening wolves, lack of water, hostile Navajo and Apache neighbors. His main characters were the Pueblo Indians Lone Wolf and a young boy, and the Navajo woman Wild Deer. The story centered on the Indians' attempts to appease the gods so that it might rain. In this regard Flaherty investigated the importance of the rain dance for the Acoma.

On top of this, Flaherty uncharacteristically imposed a structured storyline that his colleague Randall H. Faye favored and which the producers insisted on. They wanted a love story between Lone Wolf and Wild Deer. This required inventing material—a way to rescue Wild Deer, who are to be sacrificed—that did not come from the culture under study.

While Flaherty was known to have at times fit his facts to his theories—for instance, while making *Nanook of the North*, he had Nanook build the biggest igloo of his life so he could film the interior scenes—he had, as John Grierson wrote in an obituary, "a genuine passion for the genuine."

Acoma, the Sky City, *1928. A reputed scene from Robert Flaherty's unfinished film. Actors not identified.*

Flaherty began filming in the fall of 1928. He shot the initial footage himself at Acoma. But when Fox's production chief, Winfield Sheehan, saw the rushes, he immediately sent a film crew to shoot at another location outside of Tucson. Assistant cameraman Floyd Crosby, who was dispatched to rescue the project, recalled Flaherty's work as the cinematographer: "He had no idea how to film the story. He photographed Indians coming over the horizon for five months, and Fox got a little tired of it. Finally [photographer] Shamroy took one sequence and broke it down into a story and they shot it."

Then in March 1929, Winfield Sheehan announced that Fox would no longer invest any more money in silent films. Directors who failed to become "acclimatized" to sound, he stated, would be let go. So, despite the fact that a good deal of footage had been shot, Flaherty saw *Acoma, the Sky City*, abandoned by the film studio.

Over the years, Flaherty was able to make use of this experience. For the films *White Shadows of the South Seas* (1929) and *Tabu* (1931), he again used young male leads as the vehicles through which he could document his stories. This presaged similar approaches in his later films *Elephant Boy* (1937) and *Louisiana Story* (1948).

After the success late in his life of *Louisiana Story*, Flaherty decided to use the medium of film to "reveal" a work of art. He was interested in shooting footage of Picasso's "Guernica," then located at the Museum of Modern Art. His work, silent and unfinished at the time of his death, was backed by Hemisphere Films at the urging of officials from MOMA. Flaherty's last work has been called by one writer a "microcosm of what is already a microcosm of the . . . Spanish Civil War."

The film critic Arthur Knight was there when Flaherty made his last film. He said that "what came out of his camera . . . was as much the raw material of a work of art as the Picasso sketches that preceded Guernica." Flaherty's *Guernica* is comprised of repeated camera movements. It starts with these titles, added after his death:

> Robert Flaherty was deeply moved by . . . Picasso's famous mural. . . .
> In the spring of 1949 he planned to film it. . . . Before attempting a
> detailed analysis, Flaherty wanted to try the mural from various
> angles. . . . You are about to see a photographer's first experiments in
> looking at a painting.

Flaherty's one reel of film opens with a full shot of the mural and shows two women seated in front of the painting (to give it perspective). His camera then slowly explores the canvas, sliding over Picasso's intricate details. It stops to concentrate first on the famous bull. It then moves on to the figures of the horse, the warrior, and the females. These shots include the woman with a lamp and the mother holding her limp child. Flaherty ends this reel as he began it, with a complete shot of Guernica and the two spectators.

28. Joris Ivens (1898–1989)

New Frontiers. 1940. Produced by the Sloan Foundation (New York) and Educational Film Institute (New York University). Script by Ivens. Photographed by Floyd Crosby. Unfinished.

Woman of the Sea. 1944. Produced by Lester Cowen. Script by Ivens, Vladimir Pozner, and Salka Viertel. Unfinished.

Song of the Rivers (Das Lied der Ströme). 1954, 90 min. Produced by DEFA. Script by Ivens and Vladimir Pozner. Photographed by Sacha Vierny and others. Music by Dmitri Shostakovich. Lyrics by Bertolt Brecht, sung by Paul Robeson and Ernst Busch. Unreleased in U.S.

Les Aventures de Till L'Espiegle. 1956, 90 min. Produced by Ivens for DEFA-Ariane studios. Directed by Ivens and Gerard Philipe. Script by Philipe and René Wheeler. Photographed by Christian Matras. Music by Georges Auric. With Gerard Philipe, Françoise Fabian, Nicole Berger, Jean Carmet, Fernand Ledoux, and Jean Vilar. Unreleased in U.S.

Joris Ivens was a highly prolific, controversial, and legendary documentary filmmaker who was born in Holland but resided in many parts of the world. In the period 1938–45, when he lived in the United States, he failed to finish two films because of opposition to the films' viewpoints. In East Germany ten years later, he directed *Song of the Rivers*, a compilation film shot in 32 countries; and his one commercial, fictionalized film (out of his more than 50 films in 50 years), codirected by Gerard Philipe, contained little propaganda. Called *Les Aventures de Till L'Espiegle*, this film has never been released in the United States.

In 1940, Joris Ivens completed *The Power and the Land* for the United States Film Service. It was about the importance of electrification to rural America. He then embarked on the film *New Frontiers* through official American institutions. This project would be an extension of *The Power and the Land*: a look at the social and economic problems in America, particularly the opening of the Far West, in the light of the New Deal. Initiated by the Sloan Foundation and New York University's Educational Film Institute, headed by Spencer Pollard, *New Frontiers* would, according to the producer, provide the answer to how "prosperity can come about or on what it would be based." It was to stress "the problem of unemployment as the location of the country's frontier." Pollard had written Ivens that he viewed "the Frontier picture as filling this gap for all our films completed before it appears."

Ivens was invited to develop the script, collaborating with Floyd Crosby, former director of photography for the United States Film Service. As the project took shape, Ivens decided that the economic development of the United States represented a "social" frontier which could be crossed only after the geographic frontiers of the Rocky Mountains and then the Pacific Ocean had been reached. On this notion he determined he would base his script.

Ivens chose the actors, selected the locations, and started shooting. The first scenes take place in Colorado. "In that fantastic countryside," wrote Ivens, "two men cross [the paths] of one another, each on a rocky peak separated by a precipice. One heads towards the West, the other East. When they get within shouting distance, they stop and talk."

In his script, Ivens stressed that the United States had to cross this new stage, that is, resolve the "contradictions of capitalism and knock down the social barriers." But Pollard didn't agree to Ivens's speaking about a better life for Americans and how new social services could bring it about. While he accepted the long-term, higher goals stressed by Ivens, Pollard found New Frontiers "somewhat vaguer and less urgent than a film about the frontier of unemployment would be." Then, when General Motors and the J. Walter Thompson advertising agency objected to the film's politics, Pollard halted work. So, having shot a considerable amount of footage, Ivens lost the chance to finish the film. The film was never edited, and is now lost.

After Ivens directed Our Russian Front with Lewis Milestone in 1941, and before he completed Indonesia Calling in 1947 in Australia, he tried, as it turned out, to make one last film in America. Woman of the Sea was to be the fact-based story of the escape of the Norwegian coastal steamer Galtsund, commended by a woman, from Nazi control. Greta Garbo, "retired" from films for the last three years, was invited to play the leading role.

Garbo was interested in the part but would not sign a contract until she'd read a finished script. Salka Viertel, the screenwriter (wife of Bertolt Brecht), was asked by Lester Cowen, the producer, to write the treatment, which was to include an invented love story. Ivens was brought in as director, and Vladimir Pozner, a Frenchman of Russian descent, was hired. During the writing, Garbo often visited the trio to inspire them. Ivens remembers this period as one "marked by the temptation of staging" films. "This evolution was the logical extension of what Pudovkin told me [in 1929].... Take a hero and let him develop in your story."

Song of the Rivers, *1954, Joris Ivens's homage to the workers of the world.*

When two-thirds of the treatment was completed, Cowen showed it to Garbo. While other readers reacted favorably to the treatment, Garbo didn't. She turned it down, even after Cowen offered to have it rewritten by others.

Garbo probably turned the part down because of political opposition from Sweden, which was neutral in World War II, and from the Norwegian Embassy in the United States. The year 1944 was also the year red-baiting began in Hollywood. In this regard, Garbo had been warned by her agent, Leland Howard, that Norway was about to become a Communist country. He also convinced her that the scriptwriter Viertel was "under the influence of Reds." He went so far as to say that war films were "outdated and nobody cared to see them."

Still, Cowen asked the trio to complete the script, which they did, in the hopes that another studio would buy it. MGM did find it commendable but rejected it for fear that, with the United States winning the war, no one cared about resistance to the Nazis any longer. Ivens then left the United States to become High Commissioner for Cinema in the Dutch West Indies.

In 1954, A. J. Liebling related the story of the woman commander of the *Galtsund* in the *New Yorker*.

In the 1950s, Ivens worked in Eastern Europe. An advisor to the DEFA (formerly UFA) studios in East Germany, he directed a film that contained footage shot along the great rivers of the world (the Amazon, Ganges, Nile, Mississippi, Volga, and Yangtze), 32 countries in all, and had excerpts from his own films *Borinage* (1933) and *New Earth* (1934).

Song of the Rivers, reported Georges Sadoul in *Cahiers du Cinéma* in November 1954, was a "hymn to men's grandeur, to the struggle which transforms poverty into splendor" and a work which "brings a great director to the high point of his art." The film is considered by supporters an homage to the "seventh" river—the "working-class movement." Versions of the film were produced in 18 languages; the English-language commentary is by Alex McCrindle.

Containing music by Shostakovich, lyrics by Bertolt Brecht, and songs by Paul Robeson, the film was banned in France and other Western countries, and unreleased in the United States.

Two years later Ivens produced and codirected the French–East German production *Les Aventures de Till L'Espiegle*, a film whose theme he'd long preached and desired to tackle. It's the story of the sixteenth-century Flemish folk hero who rids Flanders of the colonialist Spanish à la Fanfan La Tulipe. Till (Gerard Philipe) is a naive but creative leader who puts together a liberating force for his country after his father (Fernand Ledoux) is murdered in the Inquisition. Till and his loyal friend Lamme (Jean Carmet) join up with a Flemish nobleman to preach revolt, unite the many provinces, and save their Flemish prince. Till then marries his fiancée, Nell (Nicole Berger), when the country is free of the oppressors.

Ivens's direction of the film was compared to that of Christian-Jaque's *Fanfan la Tulipe* (1952). Ivens emphasized the historical and actual conditions of the period: He dealt with the Inquisition, the church and its tithes, the presence of mercenaries, the sufferings of the people of Flanders. He brought to life the character of Nell, who had been a nonentity in the initial treatment; he played up the peasants' role in the Resistance; and the director made sure that the viewer was aware that Till, who survives at the end, "is tied to the struggle for independence . . . that his strategems [were] to have great significance." In addition, Ivens was greatly impressed with de Coster's book, so he incorporated that author's dialogue and dramatic situations.

The critics in 1956 stressed that while the film "has East German money in it for the Eastern rights to the picture . . . there is no propaganda embedded in it except for the church heavies." However, United States distributors in the mid-1950s stayed away.

In 1957, Ivens moved to Paris. He resided there until his death. Though he and his wife (and longtime collaborator), Marceline Loridan, had no children, Loridan once said that the couple's films were their children. Ivens's last "child," a meditation on a lifetime of trying to "tame the wind and harness the sea" by filming them, called *A Tale of the Wind*, premiered in the United States in 1989. In it Ivens expresses the essence of his work: "Filming the impossible is what's best in life."

29. Pare Lorentz (1905–   )

Ecce Homo! 1938–39, 80 min. Produced by U.S. Film Service. Script by Lorentz. Photographed by Lorentz and Floyd Crosby. Music by Bernard Hermann. With Will Geer. Unfinished.

Pare Lorentz is the well-known New Deal documentary filmmaker of *The Plow That Broke the Plains* (1936) and *The River* (1940). In May 1938, Lorentz had broadcast an experimental program called "Ecce Homo!" over CBS and the BBC. He had simulated the sounds of a factory at work and employed a cast of actors, including Van Heflin, to narrate stories of men out of work because of automation. In August, as head of the United States Film Service, he expanded this experiment to the medium of film. In it, the central figure is a man known as #7790 (Will Geer). Lorentz's film follows this unemployed man in his search for work across the United States. He travels from the manufacturing plants of the Midwest, in the segment Lorentz called "the industrial symphony," to the West Coast, and then up the coast to the Grand Coulee Dam along the Columbia River in Washington. Lorentz and his cameraman, Floyd Crosby, director of photography for the Film Service, did not have an easy time gaining admittance to facilities such as White Motors in Cleveland, the auto plants in and around Detroit, including the Ford River Rouge facility, or other plants such as Dodge Forge and Foundry and U.S. Rubber.

After these sequences #7790 traveled to the Columbia River Valley and the construction site of the Grand Coulee Dam. The director encountered heavy rains and ran short of money. Lorentz then switched locations again, this time going to the Tennessee Valley Authority to shoot scenes of the Fort Loudon and Fontana (North Carolina) dams then being built.

In spring 1939, President Roosevelt was seeking funding for the Columbia Valley Authority. He asked Lorentz for a rough cut of the film to impress congressional leaders. The footage of the manufacturing processes and the work along the Columbia River "looked like Rembrandt," according to one viewer. Yet Lorentz, who showed the unfinished film to a host of people over the next year, could secure no more funding because in the election of 1940 the Republicans gained control of Congress. With war in

Europe raging, Lorentz halted work. His disappointment over Congress's failure to support what he saw as an important project was one of the reasons Lorentz, who had gotten Robert Flaherty and Joris Ivens to make films for the Film Service—it produced 5 films in all—resigned as head by 1941. Congress then abolished the agency.

Since the early 1970s, Lorentz, living in Armonk, New York, has reportedly been working on a historical project and writing his autobiography. His papers and films are housed in the Pare Lorentz Collection Room, University of Wisconsin–Oshkosh.

30. Hans Richter (1888–1976)

Metall. 1931–33, 100,000 ft. Produced by Prometheus (Berlin) and Mezhrab-pomfilm (Moscow). Script by Richter and Pearl Attachewa. Photographed by Katelnikov. Unfinished.

The German director Hans Richter was an avant-garde filmmaker, surrealist, and theoretician. He'd become famous early in his career for his animated films *Rhythmus 21* (*Film Is Rhythm*, 1921), *Rhythmus 23* (1923), *Rhythmus 25* (1925), and the surrealist work *Ghosts Before Breakfast* (music by Paul Hindemith and Darius Milhaud, 1928). But Richter was not above taking on commercial projects. In a career that spanned the '20s to the '60s, he was involved in a number of projects which failed to come to fruition. Perhaps the most interesting, and one which got him into an entangling alliance with his producer, is the film he began in 1931.

That year, Hans Richter began a documentary in Berlin for the left-wing film company Prometheus Film, in conjunction with a semiprivate Russian studio (backed by International Workers' Aid). They had asked him to undertake a project on the strength of his anti–Nazi feelings. It seems that in 1929 Richter had publicly called the Nazis "those bastards" after he'd been assaulted by them.

Richter accepted the job because he wanted to see Russia for himself, after having heard so much about it as "the land of the future." After much discussion, he and his backers settled on the idea of making a nonfiction film, called *Metall*, about a strike going on at an iron factory in Henningsdorf, near Berlin. The leader of the strike, named Sievers, went to Moscow to meet Richter and to help in preparation of the script. Also working with Richter was Pearl Attachewa, who'd been recommended by Eisenstein (and who would later become Richter's wife).

For two years Richter traveled between Berlin, Moscow, and Odessa, gathering details and filming scenes of the strike and the tactics used by the strike-breakers and their allies such as Nazis attacking convoys of food for the workers, or factory managers trying to trick the workers into thinking that the factory was operational by starting up the furnaces. But in 1932, when Germany and the Soviet Union signed a commercial agreement, Richter's ability to make the kind of film he wanted suddenly became

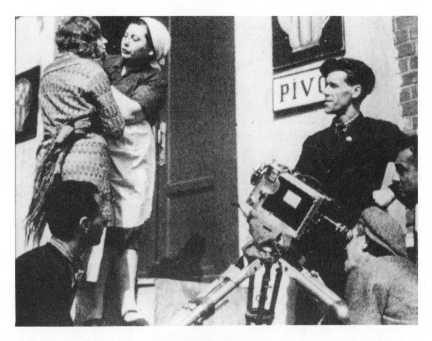

Metall, *1931–33.* Top: *Hans Richter (top right) directing his ill-fated anti–Nazi film with Katelnikov, photographer (bottom right). Others not identified.* Bottom: *One of the strikers (perhaps the leader Sievers).*

severely limited. What had started out as a documentary turned, instead, into a piece of fiction and propaganda for one of his backers or the other. Said the director, "They forbade me this, they forbade me that. . . . I was continually rewriting the script. I rewrote [it] seven times."

After two years, Richter had 100,000 feet of film, yet in practical terms this represented only some 5 percent of the film he had in mind. So, unhappily, Richter abandoned the project. Then Hitler came to power, and suddenly Richter was stranded in the Soviet Union because "during the Reichstag fire, the last week of January, 1933 . . . the Nazis cleaned out my apartment."

Richter got out by accepting an offer from the Philips company of Holland to direct the documentary *Hallo, Everybody!* Soon he was able, he rejoiced, to "rent an apartment in Paris . . . buy a car and a suit."

Other Lost Films

Storm Over La Sarraz (Sturm über La Sarraz). 1929, 2 reels. Directed by Richter, Sergei Eisenstein, and Ivor Montagu. Script by Richter. Photographed by Edward Tissé. With Richter, Eisenstein, Walter Ruttmann, Bela Balasz, and Leon Moussinac. Unreleased.

Baron de Crac. 1937. Script by Jacques Prévert, Jacques Brunius, and Maurice Henry. Design by Georges Méliès. With Michael Simon, Pierre Brasseur, and Jules Berry. Unfinished.

The Movies Take a Holiday. 1944, 65 min. Directed by Richter and Herman G. Weinberg. Unfinished.

At the close of the *Metall* fiasco, Richter had been an avant-garde filmmaker for 12 years. A few years earlier, he'd made a film more or less on the spur of the moment, and that one, too, had come to an unhappy end. In September 1929, he was a delegate to the Congress of Independent Films, held at the initiative of the French avant-garde at the old La Sarraz castle, near Lausanne, Switzerland. The meeting's aim was to cover the "Art of Cinema, Its Social and Aesthetic Purposes." All delegates, reported a trade paper, agreed to "oppose the international, stultifying, kitschy, dictatorial, capitalist movie industry that violates the artist's aims." The production of *Storm Over La Sarraz*, denied for a time, appears to be without doubt now.

So Richter, in collaboraton with Sergei Eisenstein, who was making his first appearance at a conference outside the Soviet Union, and Ivor Montagu, the filmmaker and writer, responded to the call for "good, artistic movies" by fashioning a parodic, "historical document of nonsense" at the end of the conference, according to Marie Seaton, Eisenstein's biographer. Photographed by Edward Tissé, it tells how the independent filmmakers come to lay siege to the castle in order to free Cinematic Art, a maiden (Jeannine Bhoussanousse) clad in white and suspended by rope from the castle, from Commerce (Bela Belasz, a scriptwriter) and Industry. Victorious Independent-General (Eisenstein) appears in helmet and a white sheet. Wallenstein (Moussinac, a film critic), General Tilly (Richter), and St. George (Ruttman, a filmmaker) also enter the fray.

After two reels were shot, the hostess of the congress, Baroness Hélène de Mandrot, asked Richter and company to halt their "eccentricities." Leaving La Sarraz, Richter handed the film over to Eisenstein for safekeeping. That was the last anyone saw of the film, for Eisenstein lost the negatives on the train somewhere in Europe. Only stills of the work remained in Richter's estate at the time of his death.

Richter's third unfinished project got its start in Paris in mid–1937 when he met the legendary filmmaker Georges Méliès. Although Méliès hadn't made a film in 25 years, Richter called himself one of the "lineal descendants of Georges Méliès. He was the first to know what the cinema was for."

The two had been introduced by Henri Langois, who had shown Méliès Richter's *Ghosts Before Breakfast* (1928). Having gone bankrupt in 1923, when he sold the nearly 500 films he'd made (most have since become lost or destroyed), and then having been "rediscovered" by the public in 1929, Méliès had managed to keep busy these many years classifying cinematic documents, writing his memoirs, and drawing designs. Impressed by Richter's work, Méliès was ready to reenter the world of filmmaking.

Méliès would create the designs for Richter's film *Baron de Crac*, the French equivalent of Baron Münchausen (1720–97), the German cavalry officer whose tales of his incredible adventures in Russia became classics. First published in English in 1785, Münchausen's stories were later put into German. Méliès was familiar with Baron Münchausen: He had made a silent film of his tales in 1911.

Richter's film was slated to be a satire about a so-called outrageous liar who understates the truth of "what is happening in the world today." The scriptwriters Jacques Prévert, Jacques Brunius, and Maurice Henry envisioned creating a "screen" behind which the veracity about events could be told: "This story," went the script, "takes place in a country that nobody knows, in a town nobody will ever know anything about."

The filmmakers were fortunate in one regard already. They had found a distributor for this project: Jean Renoir. He agreed to have his film company distribute the film, and in Paris had signed an agreement to this effect for 3 million francs.

However, in late 1937 the project came to a halt when Richter suddenly left Paris for Zurich to make the commercial films *A Small World in the Dark* (1938) and *Hans in Glück* (1938). Then before Richter could return, Méliès died in January 1938.

Richter remained interested in the film he'd left behind. He resumed work in Paris later that year. In sessions between Richter and the script-writers, Prévert came up with new scenes for the script, which Jacques Brunius and Maurice Henry rewrote. It appears that Richter and his collaborators worked on *Baron de Crac* for more than a year. But the idea of bringing the film to life ended when most able-bodied Frenchmen—including the cast and crew for this film—were mobilized when war began in September 1939. Richter found shelter in Switzerland.

The following excerpt from the script of *Baron de Crac* was published in the November 1960 issue (number 14) of *Premier Man*, which was devoted to the works of Jacques Prévert.

Baron de Crac

The Baron de Crac and his valet discovered a population with curious customs, in a town with absurd inscriptions, full of identical statues of the same personage, dressed in a raincoat and a derby on the head: the 'President'. Pretending to be foreigners, they met a charming man, a great admirer of the President, M. Dupays, who offered to guide them through the incredible town in a car fueled by coffee instead of gasoline.

The extraordinary state of affairs is suddenly interrupted: soldiers invade the castle and arrest Felicien on the accusation of being a negro. At the same time, they confiscate the paintings whose personages have, naturally, regained their immobility.

We discover the five paintings hanging in President Lagrandeur's private apartment.

The President is alone and, through a small window, he observes the animation reigning in the game room of the palace: the great festivities given on the occasion of the betrothal of the President's aide-de-camp to Aube Niquelle, Felicien's ex-fiancée, bring together the notables of the whole country.

The President has the aide-de-camp called, to dictate to him some new legal decisions that just passed through his head: 'Forbidden to laugh', for example. He also informs him of the banker Niquelle's nomination to the order 'of the hat'. He learns, in this connection, that Aube obstinately refused to consider herself betrothed to Hubert and that she rejects all his overtures.

—Never mind! The President will talk to the young girl.

Summoned, the girl, who always tells the truth with perfect simplicity, holds her position energetically: she detests Hubert, she intends to remain free, it is Felicien she loves, Felicien who has been disgracefully imprisoned.

Remaining alone, the President is visited by M. Mouche, high director of the President's protection services. The policeman Fregoli, specialist of secret passages, comes out of a filing cabinet to make his report.

The people lack distractions? The President will decide to organize a popular concert.

The people need speeches? The President will make a speech.

The people are wondering about the President's celibacy? On that point, M. Lagrandeur cannot give the people cause for satisfaction. He likes women, but they scare him. Only the women of past times could have suited him.... Women such as this Beate de Crac-Maille, so charming on her swing in that painting....

M. Mouche leaves the President to his contemplation, which animates itself so very slightly: Beate winks.

M. Lagrandeur rubs his eyes and suddenly, very much perturbed, hurries to his office, where he wants to put some business in order.

In the absence of witnesses, the ancestors come to life, as is their habit.

The Baron de Crac is very displeased with Beate's behavior and admonishes her sharply, which the pretty woman accepts ironically. Crac is jealous, it is a fact. Beate's motives can be guessed: if she leads the President on, it is only to arouse the Baron's jealousy and to test the sincerity of this great bluffer's feelings. Her game almost succeeds, since Crac, annoyed, soon descends from his painting and leaves the drawing room, declaring:

...Well, if that is the way it is, I too will find something to occupy myself with.

Here he is in the corridors, in a Louis XV costume. Fortunately, a dozen Louis XV valets are walking by, carrying refreshments. It is unhoped for luck: Crac, mingling with them, will not attract attention.

Meanwhile, the President Lagrandeur, in his office before a microphone, begins a speech, rather incoherent, grandiose, and burlesque, that the population listens to respectfully everywhere, in town as in the palace.

As the tone rises, the orator tires, he yawns:

...Enough weakness! On your feet! The dream weakens the people! The people must be awakened.

On these words, he falls asleep in his armchair.

In the painting, Baron de Crac's parrot has been showing some agitation for some moments now. And suddenly, he flies off, crosses the drawing room, enters the office, places himself in front of the microphone, and, imitating Lagrandeur's voice, he begins to speak:

...I think therefore I am! Gone with the wind! Shoot first! Tit for tat! ... etc.

After making the documentary *Die Borse* (*The Stockmarket*, 1939) in Switzerland and commercials in Holland until 1941, Richter left Europe for the United States. In 1942 he became director of the Institute of Film Techniques at the City College of New York, a post he would hold for more than a decade. Richter did not abandon filmmaking. In 1944, he tried his hand at putting together a compilation film entitled *The Movies Take a Holiday* (1944), codirected by film critic (and CCNY colleague) Herman G. Weinberg. The film is an anthology of avant-garde film clips from the works of René Clair, Jean Renoir, Marcel Duchamp, Fernand Léger, and Man Ray—all directors who found refuge in the United States during

World War II. But *The Movies Take a Holiday* was left unfinished when Richter turned to completing a film he'd been working on since he arrived in the United States—the well-known avant-garde film *Dreams That Money Can Buy* (1945). The color film's script was written by Man Ray, Marcel Duchamps, Max Ernst, Alexander Calder, and Fernand Léger.

Nearly all the films Hans Richter made before 1941 are lost or survive only in bits and pieces. The Museum of Modern Art in New York houses a Richter archive, and the British Film Institute holds some of Richter's films. Films available for viewing include *Rhythmus 21, Rhythmus 23, Ghosts Before Breakfast, Dreams That Money Can Buy,* and *Forty Years of Experiments* (1951–61).

VI. THE FRENCH PREDICAMENT: WAR AND AFTERMATH

Art lives on constraints and dies from freedom.

—André Gide

The start of World War II abruptly ended France's golden age of filmmaking. Hostilities and then the Occupation (June 1940–August 1944) turned the industry into a shell of its former self. The industry faced a predicament: to remain French yet serve others.

In September 1939 two dozen French productions were immediately suspended and then abandoned. Directors, actors, technicians were called up. By October, film production was allowed to resume when the government saw that entertainment was second only to food. But half-completed films by Marc Allégret, Christian-Jaque, and René Clair could not be saved.

A few films were completed under difficult constraints. One such work was Jean Renoir's *La Tosca*. The director had been invited to Rome by Mussolini in July 1939 to make a film and to lecture. It seems that the dictator was a fan of Renoir's *Rules of the Game* (1939). In Rome, Renoir was preparing the script for *La Tosca* when war broke out. He immediately returned to France and was mobilized as a captain in France's cinematographic service.

Yet by the spring of 1940, Italy was still at peace with France. The French Ministry of Information hoped to keep it that way. It asked Renoir to become a sort of goodwill ambassador by returning to Italy to resume filming *La Tosca*. Renoir shot a few scenes before the inevitable happened. On June 10, Italy declared war on France. Renoir again hastened home. This time, he asked his assistant, Karl Koch, to complete the film. Koch did just that, employing a non–French cast.

When Renoir eventually saw the film nearly 40 years later in the United States, he was said to have found it moving.

A second example of art triumphing over constraint also involved

143

Koch. He was the writer of Jacques Becker's first film, *L'Or du Cristobal*, and its assistant director as well. Becker worked on the film for about three weeks in the summer of 1939 before he was called for service. Finding himself without a director, the producer hired Jean Stelli to finish the job. Despite the fact that Becker disassociated himself from the finished product, *L'Or du Cristobal* was released in May 1940.

The timing was fortunate, because two months later France fell and was occupied. The film industry once again was thrown into turmoil. This time such major directors as Renoir, Clair, Feyder, Duvivier, Ophuls, and Benoit-Levy left France. Actors and technicians departed as well. Others such as Raimu retired until "le jour de gloire" returned to France.

The Vichy government then stepped in to fill the void. It reorganized the film industry while itself taking orders from the Nazis. The government created the Committee for the Cinematographic Industry (COIC), whose job it was to review and suppress film scripts, apportion film stock, and ration electricity. The Germans themselves organized the French branch of UFA called Continental Film Corporation. Light, popular, and "moral" films became the norm. The viewing of almost any film became extremely popular when filmgoers realized that the theatres were among the few heated buildings in most cities.

Individual filmmakers were impelled to respond to the crisis. Three thousand of them banded together to form the underground Cinema Committee for Liberation. Headed by producer Pierre Blancher, the committee's job was to "guard as best it could" the interests of French cinema. Blancher expressed the group's attitude in 1944: to make "very certain that no one who . . . collaborated with or assisted the Germans [would] ever be permitted to be associated with the [French] film industry."

Blancher indicated as "unmistakable" collaborators notable film personalities as Pierre Fresnay, Sacha Guitry, Henri Decoin, and Henri-Georges Clouzot. Clouzot and Fresnay were said to have made the "biggest anti–French" film—*Le Corbeau* (1943)—of the war years. Called by Blancher "a man who never amounted to much before the war," Clouzot wound up being barred from directing until 1947.

During the Occupation, French filmmakers made 221 films. Most have never been seen in the United States. Blancher has said that only thirty to forty were free of propaganda at the war's end.

The consequences of the Occupation extended into the postwar years. The progressive director Jean Grémillon, active in the committee and said to be "close to communists," found himself unable to realize a number of projects in the period 1946–48.

Director Edmond T. Gréville, who had directed in Germany before the war, was the first French director to attempt a Franco-German production after the war. By 1949, the German film industry was revived. German

Filmgoers had had enough of pictures that dealt with war guilt, persecution, and pacifism. They were calling for entertainment—romance, musicals, thrillers.

Gréville was invited to Munich to make the romantic, erotic film *Im Banne der Madonna*. He completed the film—and then the past came roaring back. It seems that German technicians had been Nazis. Mortified, the French never released the film.

31. Marc Allégret (1900–1973) and Yves Edouard Allégret (1907–1987)

Le Corsaire. 1939. Directed by Marc Allégret. Produced by André Daven and Marc Allégret. From the play *Le Corsaire* by Marcel Achard. Design by Serge Pimenoff. With Charles Boyer (as Kid Jackson and Frank O'Hara), Michele Alfa (as Evangeline and Georgia Swanee), Louis Jourdan, and Marcel Dalio. Unfinished.

Les Deux Timides (The Two Shy Guys). Directed by Yves Allégret. With Claude Dauphin and Pierre Brasseur. Unreleased.

Un Tour au Ciel/La Roue Tourne (A Round in the Sky). 1941. Directed by Yves Allégret. Script by Yves Allégret and Pierre Brasseur. With Pierre Brasseur. Unfinished.

Tobie Est un Ange (Tobias Is an Angel). 1941. Supervised by Marc Allégret. Directed by Yves Allégret. Produced by SPDF. Script by Yves Allégret and Pierre Brasseur. Photographed by Henri Alekan. Commentary by Yves Allégret. Unreleased.

Félicie Nanteuil. 1942, 99 min. Directed by Marc Allégret. Produced by Imperia. Script by Marcel Achard. From the novel *L'Histoire Comique* by Anatole France. Photographed by Louis Page, music by Jacques Ibert. With Micheline Presle (Félicie Nanteuil), Pierre Prévert, Mady Bery, Marcelle Prainse, Claude Dauphin (Aime Cavalier), Louis Jordan (Robert de Ligny), and Jean d'Yd. Unreleased in U.S.

Marc Allégret and his younger brother, Yves, the nephews of French writer André Gide, might have received more of the international fame their talent deserved had World War II not intruded on their directing careers. Marc Allégret began his film career in 1927, when he filmed his famous uncle's trip to Africa (*Voyage au Congo*). Directing until 1970, he applied a competent and conscientious approach to the direction of comedies and romances, many of which featured film talents he discovered such as Raimu, Simone Signoret, Michele Morgan, Gerard Philipe, Jeanne Moreau, Brigitte Bardot, Alain Delon, and Jean-Paul Belmondo.

Yves Allégret began his career by assisting his brother and other directors—among them, Alberto Cavalcanti and Jean Renoir—in the making of shorts in the 1930s. When he finally began to make full-length films, his specialty was the film noir. A prime example was his grave and chilling *Une Si Jolie Petite Plage* (*Riptide*, 1949) starring Gerard Philipe, scripted by Jacques Sigurd, and photographed by Henri Alekan. From 1944 to 1949, he was married to Simone Signoret.

In the summer of 1939, producer André Daven hoped to produce a screen version of Marcel Achard's popular play *Le Corsaire* with Marc Allégret as director. Despite the insistence of Achard, Daven refused to consider the stage play's star, Louis Jouvet, for the film; he felt that the film role required a younger man with a fine physique. He contracted Charles Boyer at $125,000 for the role. Jouvet, angered, blamed the author for the casting decision and never forgave Achard for what he saw as an act of betrayal.

Charles Boyer sailed for Europe in August to begin filming the costumed spectacle. Most of *Le Corsaire* was shot in the studio in Paris. The balance was to have been shot in Nice, where Allégret had a great ship constructed for the remaining few days of work expected. The rights to *Le Corsaire* had already been sold in the United States—the film was scheduled for release in the Christmas season of 1939—when World War II broke out on September 1.

Le Corsaire became a casualty of the war, one of a score of films that were sandbagged during this period. Allégret's production crew soon left to join the French army. Boyer first fled to the home of his recently widowed mother in Figeac, from which, it was reported, "no power in the world could make him return." Then, relenting, in the light of the fact that he had not served in World War I, Boyer, too, clandestinely joined the French forces. That ended, for the time being, any hopes Daven had of resuming film production. There had been too much publicity and money spent on the film to consider replacing Boyer. Boyer's stay in the army was short, though. After 11 weeks, his status as a lowly private finally discovered, he was quickly demobilized by the government.

The French film industry had fallen into shambles when war was declared. But by October, the government decided it was important to entertain the population and the troops, so film production was encouraged to resume. This effort was directed by offices of the Commissariat de l'Information. Producers were exhorted to develop "healthy and optimistic films," and some of the greatest stars, such as Jean Gabin and Pierre Fresnay, were even released from service to return to filmmaking. Daven, however, sought a way to complete *Le Corsaire* in Hollywood. He appealed to the playwright Jean Giraudoux, who headed the offices of the Commissariat, to be allowed to take the film abroad. Assembling cast and crew, he might have succeeded, for in June 1940 RKO announced it would distribute the film when completed. But that month, France fell. *Le Corsaire* was

Michelle Presle and Claude Dauphin in Marc Allégret's Félicie Nanteuil, *1942.*

abandoned, and Daven lost a fortune. Achard was tremendously disappointed, convinced that his play, properly mounted, would have made a wonderful film.

Up until France fell in June 1940, Marc Allégret's brother Yves served in the military's aerial photographic service. Then in early 1941, with half of France under German occupation, Yves Allégret began making full-length films. He worked under the name Yves Champlain so as not to be confused with his more illustrious brother. But no matter what the name, he ran into trouble making his first three films.

His first was called *Les Deux Timides* (*The Two Shy Guys*) and starred Claude Dauphin and Pierre Brasseur. The fact that it starred Dauphin put the film in jeopardy because Dauphin was an outspoken opponent of the Nazis. After the film's completion in February, Dauphin rejoined the Free French Forces. Consequently, when the Nazis found out about Dauphin's actions, they retaliated by prohibiting the film's release.

Yves Allégret then immediately turned to making a film entitled *Un Tour au Ciel* (*A Round in the Sky*), cowritten by and starring his colleague Pierre Brasseur. This time, it was Vichy law that affected the outcome of the movie. It seems that the government of Marshall Pétain prohibited the making of new or first-run romantic films. Yves Allégret had to abandon the work.

Yves Allégret's third film suffered an even worse fate. Called *Tobie Est un Ange (Tobias Is an Angel)*, the film was the cinematographic debut for Henri Alekan, who would later earn fame for *Beauty and the Beast* (1946). Filmed in Toulon in the unoccupied zone of the country. *Tobie Est un Ange* was one of the first films made by the Société de Production et de Doublage de Films (SPDF). Founded by Jean M. Thery in Marseilles in 1941, SPDF represented an attempt by one producer to meet the French government's call to resume filmmaking after the disasters of the war effort. But Allégret's *Tobie Est un Ange* was never released because it was destroyed in a laboratory fire.

In 1943, Yves Allégret codirected *La Boîte aux Rêves (The Box of Dreams)*, starring Simone Signoret. The film was not shown in Paris until 1945. So the younger Allégret, who is credited in most sources with directing only two films during the occupation (*Les Deux Timides* and *La Boîte aux Rêves*), actually expended a lot of energy and time trying to make four.

In 1942, also while under German occupation, Marc Allégret, meanwhile, made *Félicie Nanteuil*. The finely crafted tale concerns a great actress, who is the mistress of an aristocrat, and the superficial nature of her life in the theatre. As Félicie Nanteuil rises to the top in her profession, she is helped by a young actor (played by Claude Dauphin) who falls in love with her. When she spurns his affections, he becomes insanely jealous and commits suicide in her presence. For the first time in her life, the actress senses her disconnectedness from the lives of those around her. She becomes obsessed by the act of her spurned lover, who in death obtains over her a power he never achieved in life.

Based on Anatole France's 1903 novel *L'Histoire Comique*, *Félicie Nanteuil* was one of more than 200 films made in France during the Occupation, June 1940–August 1944. One reason many of these productions have never been shown in the United States is that they reflected Vichy ideology and spirit of collaboration. This stigma held to Marc Allégret's melancholy love story despite the fact that it was apparently intended to turn the public's mind away from its preoccupation with the war—and to consider the more personal issues of honesty and commitment—just as Anatole France's novel was an apparent attempt to deflect the public's obsession with the Dreyfus Affair of 1898.

As it turned out, the film was not released even in France until after the war because Claude Dauphin, one of its stars, had fled to England upon the film's completion. The Nazis were after him. There he made anti–Nazi broadcasts for the BBC. But the Germans had already banned his films.

32. Christian-Jaque (1904–   )

Tourelle III (Gun Turret 3). 1939. Photographed by Marcel Fratedal. With Bernard Blier. Unfinished.

Never acclaimed a great director, Christian-Jaque (born Christian Maudet) was nonetheless prolific. He made nearly 70 films in a career that spanned the years 1931–1977. The director enjoyed his greatest commercial and critical success in the 15-year period that began in 1937. It was then that he was one of France's most important filmmakers. He made his mark with the film *Boys School* (1938), scripted by Jaques Prévert and starring von Stroheim. He displayed a talent for directing action, comedy, or drama that did not disturb audiences, exhibiting a skilled hand at presenting a pleasing piece of entertainment.

In the fateful year 1939, Christian-Jaque had already directed two films (*Le Grand Élan* and *L'Enfer des Anges*). In late summer, he began *Tourelle III*, an adventure story that centered on the French Navy. This was the kind of drama he preferred to make. Christian-Jaque's *Les Pirates du Rail* (1937) had been a similar kind of story about Indochina (shot in France).

The director had registered with the local authorities in Toulon in order to be allowed to shoot footage along the Atlantic and Mediterannean coasts. The French navy had loaned out its fleets for the shooting. Years later, the director still recalled the "extraordinary" battle scenes filmed. But when the war began, Christian-Jaque's production, along with everything else in France, was thrown into disarray. Christian-Jaque halted filming because the vessel necessary to complete some scenes—the cruiser *Émile-Bertin*—was now needed for more important duties. Still, the director managed to do some "premontage" of the film, but when the Germans arrived in Paris, they promptly relieved Christian-Jaque of his film, on which editing had already begun.

During the four-year Occupation, Christian-Jaque continued to work in Paris. In fact, no French director made more films than his six. His notable productions, which he proudly refers to as having avoided propaganda, were *Who Killed Santa Claus?* (1941), *La Symphonie Fantastique* (1941), *Carmen* (1943), and *The Bellman* (1944).

Other Lost Films

God's Chessboard (L'Échiquier de Dieu). 1962. Produced by Raoul Levy. Dialogue by Jean Anouilh. Photographed by Armand Thirard. With Alain Delon, Dorothy Dandridge, Anthony Quinn, Akim Tamiroff, Omar Sharif, Elsa Martinelli, and Orson Welles. Unfinished.

Don Camillo et les Contestataires. 1970. Produced by Cité Films, Francoriz, and Rizzoli Films. Script by Bernard Revon, Leo Benvenuti, and Piro de Bernardi. With Fernandel, Gino Cervi (Peppone), Paolo Carlini, and Graziella Granata. Unfinished.

In 1962, Christian-Jaque suffered a second unfinished project. He was filming *God's Chessboard (L'Échiquier de Dieu)*, an epic superproduction about Marco Polo. Alain Delon was in the lead, backed up by Dorothy Dandridge and an international cast. Christian-Jaque shot only a few scenes, but one was the key to his film: a giant chessboard made up of real people. After a few weeks, the project was halted because of huge costs and trouble casting secondary roles. It nearly ruined the producer, Raoul Levy.

Two years later, the film was revived, but without director Christian-Jaque. Denys de la Patelliere and Noel Howard completed the film in Africa, Asia, and Yugoslavia. Because they deleted Christian-Jaque's few scenes, the film's title was changed to *The Fabulous Adventures of Marco Polo*. Horst Buchholz also replaced Delon in the lead. According to Christian-Jaque, none of his footage was retained in the 115-minute release.

In 1970, Christian-Jaque failed to finish a third film in his long career. This film was supposed to represent the final chapter in Fernandel's Don Camillo series. Shooting was halted when the star became too ill to proceed. He died soon thereafter.

Fernandel first appeared as the idiosyncratic Catholic priest forever at odds with his town's Communist leadership in the 1951 production *The Little World of Don Camillo* (directed by Julien Duvivier). Over the next 20 years he made *The Return of Don Camillo* (1952, Duvivier), *Don Camillo's Last Round* (1955, Carmine Gallone), *Don Camillo Monseigneur* (1961, Carmine Gallone), and *Don Camillo in Moscow* (1965, Luigi Comenici). In July 1970, Fernandel began the sixth film in the series, *Don Camillo et les Contestataires*.

In this episode, Don Camillo tries to come to the aid of his old adversary-friend, Mayor Peppone. The mayor is facing a political barrage from the whip in his own party. Don Camillo arranges for his old combatant to be defended by a young lawyer. Meanwhile, the mayor is facing troubles of a more personal nature as well. His adolescent daughter is estranged from her father because of his political beliefs, which have brought the heads of the village together to discuss the dissension within the party. With political and personal turmoil all around, Don Camillo leaves for the country, uncertain about what path he will eventually take with regard to the crises back home.

By August, 1970, Fernandel became too ill to work. Christian-Jaque then abandoned the film.

After Fernandel's death the following year, Italian director Mario Camerini began *Don Camillo et les Contestataires* from scratch. Gastone Mochin (as Don Camillo) and Lioner Stander (as Mayor Peppone) starred in this French-Italian production. The 95-minute film was released in 1972.

33. René Clair (1898–1981)

Air Pur (Fresh Air). 1939, 30 min. Produced by Edouard Corniglion-Molinier. Robert Bresson, R. Broc Dubard, assistant directors. Script by René Clair, Albert Valentin, Pierre Bost, and George Neveux. Photographed by Michael Kelber. Design by Max Douy and Eugene Lourie. Music by Maurice Jaubert. With Jean Mercanton, Raymond Cordy, Michel François, Bernard Gorse, Elina Labourdette, Yvonne Leduc, Jeanne Marken, Paul Olivier, Jane Pierson. Unfinished.

René Clair, the film stylist and innovator of the comedic and the ironic, has claimed that *Air Pur*, the one unfinshed film in his career, "would have been the first neo-realist film." For others, the surviving footage evokes the authentic feelings of Marcel Pagnol's films and Clair's own *Under the Roofs of Paris* (1930).

In November 1938, René Clair returned to France from Britain after an absence of five years. In that time he'd had only one successful picture—*The Ghost Goes West* (1935)—and four unrealized projects. Determined to make a successful film again in his native country, he began work on a film that used the services of several writers and assistant directors, including a young Robert Bresson. Uncharacteristically for him, however, he was not going to rely on studio-built exteriors to make this film. Instead, he would be shooting on location for only the second time, sixteen years after he'd made his first film, *Crazy Ray* (1923), the same way. Also, he was going to explore favorite themes of friendship and love.

Filming began on July 17, 1939, with a cast of nonactors and 13 children, aged 6–13. The story was a simple one—a trademark for Clair—of the introduction of urban youngsters to the joys of country life. Said Clair: "They do not know what a tree is. . . . The film is their reaction to the things of nature." In Paris Clair began filming the attempts of a city boy (Michel François) to join up with friends who have departed for a camp in the country. The friends are led by Yvonne (Elina Labourdette), a social worker. She is struggling against Fred (Jean Mercanton, son of the director Louis Mercanton), the boy's gangster brother, to have the children live a more normal life. On the streets of the city he and his friends behave like rats on the prowl. In the fresh air of the country, they will first experience beauty, love, and friendship. Clair records the character changes in the children with the change in environment.

153

Air Pur, 1939, René Clair's only unfinished production.

Clair completed one-third of *Air Pur* when World War II broke out.
Along with everything else, the French film industry collapsed. Producer
Edouard Corniglion-Molinier (who also halted production of Malraux's
L'Espoir), its great composer, Maurice Jaubert, and the actors disappeared
into the army. Clair managed to get the children back to their Paris homes.
He then left for the south. In May 1940, Clair shot new interiors of *Air
Pur* using new technicians and artists. When France fell, he left for Holly-
wood.

After the war, Corniglion-Molinier, who'd been an aviation commander (and would become minister of justice in 1957), tried to revive the
film. But the children were older; assistant director Dubard and composer
Jaubert were dead, although Jaubert's 11 minutes of music, called "Village
dans Paris," survived; and Mercanton, gravely ill, died soon after. Like *Le
Corsaire* and *Tourelle III*, *Air Pur* became a cinematic victim of the war.
Photographer Michael Kelber stressed that *Air Pur* "would have been one
of Clair's best" films, "tender and humorous." Thirty minutes of film remained unedited and unfinished.

Other Lost Films

All the Gold in the World (Tout l'Or du Monde). 1961, 90 min. SECA Films release. Script by René Clair. Edited by Louisette Hautecoeur. Music by Georges Van Parys. With Bourvil, Phillipe Noiret, Claude Rich, Annie Fratellini, Colette Castel, and Alfred Adam. Unreleased in U.S.

The Lace Wars (Les Fêtes Galantes). 1965, 90 min. Gaumont release. Script by René Clair. Photographed by Christian Matras. Music by Georges Van Parys. Designed by Georges Wakhevitch. Edited by Louisette Hautecoeur. With Jean-Pierre Cassel, Philippe Avron, Jean Richard, Genevieve Casile, and Marie Dubois. Unreleased in U.S.

Clair went on to make such hits as *And Then There Were None* (1945), *Beauty and the Devil* (1950), and *Beauties of the Night* (1952). Then in 1961 he made *All the Gold in the World*, a French-Italian production that was the first René Clair sound film not to be released in the United States. The director bitterly commented that it lacked enough flesh to satisfy the distributors.

A fable of urban progress versus rustic simplicity, the film is set in the sleepy village of Cabosse, where the citizens enjoy long life. Victor (Phillipe Noiret), a real estate man from the city, smells money. He buys up the town, except for two holdouts, Mathieu and his son, Toine (both played by Bourvil). Fred (Claude Rich), an advertising specialist, tries to market the town's assets: The place, he claims, is a modern fountain of youth. Mathieu dies protesting progress, but his son continues to resist change. At the finale, Toine gets the girl he's been courting; the real estate operator, about to realize his dream, dies of a heart attack as the land is about to be developed.

Shot on location, the film represents for some a "Clairien" triptych of liberty versus progress with *À Nous la Liberté* (1931) and *Le Dernier Milliardaire* (1934). Georges Sadoul compared it to the "admirable and faultless *Le Million*" (1931). Other critics found it only intermittently funny and lamented the fact that its subplot about the private lives of stars did not add substance to the film. Yet they admitted the movie contained several moments of comedy and humanity that reminded filmgoers of Clair's best work. In the poignant opening sequence, for instance, during which the old man meets his death tearing down a billboard, Clair cuts to a shot of the belfry, tolling for the man. In a more comic scene, Toine confesses his love to his girl who, he thinks, is just out of sight around the corner on a hilltop. The audience meanwhile sees her at the foot of the hill, running away.

René Clair's *The Lace Wars*, his twenty-eighth and last full-length film, was a French-Rumanian production three years in the making. It, too, was never released in the United States. It dealt with a subject new to him—

war—and was set in the eighteenth century. But despite its daring, European critics found it "lacked the delicate wit, balance, and comedic dryness to bring it off" (*Variety*, 4/20/66).

Shot outside the studios in natural settings, Clair's film portrayed the absurdity of war. In *The Lace Wars*, the rich periodically stopped the bloodshed for lunch. Joli Coeur (Jean-Pierre Cassel) is an adventurer who serves as a go-between for two rival dukedoms, one ruled by a princess (Genevieve Casile), the other by a prince (Jean Richard). Before he can bring about a reconciliation, fighting breaks out. This last Clair film was praised for "its many gags and malicious observations," its lush photography that attempted to give viewers a picture of how events might be remembered, its introductory explanation to the audience, and its ironic ending, with the camera showing a soldier's hat atop a grave.

After making films for 42 years, René Clair said in 1972: "I don't need to make another picture . . . because I would not like to repeat myself. . . . I have other things to do." He turned to the theatre in the early 1970s.

34. Jean Grémillon (1901–1959)

Le Printemps de la Liberté. 1948. André Paulve–UGC, production. Script by Grémillon. Photography by Louis Page. Music by Grémillon. With Fernand Ledoux (Nivose), Paul Bernard (Edouard Espivent), Arlette Thomas (Françoise), Jean Debucourt (Baron Etienne), Michel Bouquet (Jean), and Pierre Larquey (La Croque). Unfinished.

The artistic, musically inclined director Jean Grémillon, who began making films in 1923, ranks as one of France's finest filmmakers. His two dozen documentaries evoked eras when artists flourished while his twenty-two feature films explored the relationship between class and desire. Movement, particularly dance, was often present in his films. At the heart of Grémillon's cinema was a mixture of realism and fiction that threw a spotlight on "the unhappiness of daily happiness." Grémillon filmed his material in carefully composed shots in his native Brittany, a bleak environment which allowed him to emphasize the commonplace.

Grémillon is a director who, argues colleague Louis Daquin, "should be judged by the films he was not able to make." Ever since *La Ciel Est à Vous* (*The Sky Is Yours*), completed in January 1944, Grémillon had been unable to shoot any feature films. In 1945, he prepared a script called *The Paris Commune* (to be produced by Pierre Gerin), about the uprising after the Franco-Prussian War of 1871, which was brutally repressed. Then in 1946, Grémillon intended to film *Le Massacre des Innocents* (written by Charles Spaak, to be produced by Ciné-France), taking place in 1936–1946, with the Spanish Civil War, Munich, the collapse, the concentration camps, and the return in the ruins, for stages.

Grémillon was not able to mount these projects because "after the war, little by little," said Louis Daquin, "he was put aside." According to Henri Langois, head of the French Cinémathèque, his projects were the "victims of the cinematographic order that is ours." It seems that for the film establishment Grémillon's actions up to and during the Occupation were too controversial. He had worked in Germany in 1938, where he filmed *Gueule d'Amour*. After June 1940, he was a member of the Front National and, while not in the French Communist Party, he was associated with it.

In 1947, Grémillon was working with Charles Spaak on a scenario about a group of performers caught up in the Saint Bartholemew Massacre

157

of August 23–24, 1572, called *La Commedia dell'Arte* (to be produced by André Paulve). Ironically, the project was halted by the subsequent preparation of *Le Printemps de la Liberté*.

In February 1947, a delegation from the department of national education, part of the French Ministry of National Education, approached the producer André Paulve. It seems that the government wanted to organize commemorative events about the Revolution of 1848. It would provide a reimbursable advance of 40 million francs to the film company that would undertake production of an important movie devoted to the historical event. Despite protests from right-wing organizations, producer Paulve and the film company UGC agreed to assume the production of a film costing 100 million francs. They selected Grémillon.

Observers stress that Grémillon's unfinished film *Le Printemps de la Liberté* would have been a true "film d'auteur." For Grémillon, *Le Printemps de la Liberté* would prove more difficult to make than *La Ciel Est à Vous* (*The Shy Is Yours*, 1944), his greatest success, under the Occupation. Pierre Kast, who met Grémillon in 1945, details that the cineaste was "seduced by the historic and ideological scope of the proposed subject, very close to his preoccupations at the time when he was preparing *La Commune*." Grémillon himself had stressed at the National Congress France-USSR, in January 1945, that "it is not through dead history that people draw nearer, but through living history, of which the masses are the principal agents and that men make themselves.... The common hopes, the defeats, the tragedies, and the victories are the surest and most solid bonds."

Between June 15 and November 11, Grémillon wrote three versions of the story, reducing the scope of the action to satisfy financial contingencies. Grémillon planned his tribute to the individual with a "feeling of the commonplace, of the intimate, of the personal." He would integrate the terrible events of 1848 around the lives of Jean and Françoise on the scale of Gance's *Napoleon* (1927) and Griffith's *Intolerance* (1917).

On January 1, 1948, still without any guarantee about actual filming, Grémillon began writing the dialogue and laying out the technical cutting of the film, had designer Barsacq prepare small-scale models of the spectacular effects, and had a stage manager and three assistants prepare the work schedule. On March 13, Grémillon gave a first reading of the work at the French Cinémathèque.

The photography was being directed by Louis Page, from whom Grémillon was getting ready to exact a performance as difficult as that for *La Ciel Est à Vous* and, noted Kast, "where, going against recipes for perfection, Grémillon and Page had been able to find the greatest originality on the photographic medium in the 'banal' and 'commonplace.'"

Slated to cost 100 million francs and call for thousands of extras in 1947, the film would cost 300 million a year later. Despite inflation, UGC continued to back the project on condition that the government advance its share. In addition, observers stressed the prestige—and foreign currency—the film would garner overseas. Then just as suddenly, the project was cancelled. According to Kast, Grémillon learned from his morning newspaper that he was to lose his funding. The minister of national education—the very man who had been encouraging Grémillon two weeks before—was proposing that the credits from the movie be transferred to finance ceremonies commemorating Chateaubriand.

Le Printemps de la Liberté was shelved because of a financial crisis within the funding agency. Pierre Kast railed against this abandonment of the great filmmaker, who, he pointed out, had passed up the chance to make his first movie in five years in order to take on this project.

The script and music of the unfinished film—of which no footage was shot—survive. On July 11, 1948, a radio adaptation of *Le Printemps de la Liberté* was broadcast by the Parisian channel of Radiodiffusion Française. The published script contains illustrations by the film's designer, Leon Barsacq, and an introduction and notes to the film by Pierre Kast.

The following excerpt from the script of *Le Printemps* was published in *Le Printemps de la Liberté* de Jean Grémillon.*

Le Printemps de la Liberté

Sequence LIV

IN THE BOTTOM OF THE QUARRY

...several platoons of twelve Mobile Guards are shooting the rebels......
....
...who are brought in five at a time.
....
   Smoke and terrible noise fill
the whole inside of the quarry.   ORDERS: Fire!
                                               repeated every five seconds.

....
   Françoise and Jean out of breath,
panting...
....
   Mobile Guards without weapons
pile up the corpses.
....
...even more numerous, the prisoners continue coming.
....
   Françoise and Jean closer, their
eyes on the horrible spectacle ...

*Published 1948 by Bibliothèque Française.

when Françoise starts

FRANÇOISE: Look... Look...

. . . .

They see father Nivose arriving, among four companions of the neighborhood.

. . . .

BELOW

Nivose, impassive, waits his turn.

. . . .

A non-commissioned officer to the officer in charge of the platoon.

NCO: Faubourg Saint-Antoine... barricade leader ... arms in hand
OFFICER: To be shot.

. . . .

Two Mobile Guards take Nivose away.

NIVOSE: You can kill all of us... You will not kill the Repub...
VOICE: Fire...

Nivose collapses in a pool of blood.

. . . .

A little further, Mobile Guards drag the corpses to pile them up.

A GUARD: What a job!...
ANOTHER ONE: Oh, don't exaggerate, there wasn't more than a fourth of innocents in the whole bunch.

. . . .

An officer of the Mobile Guard gives an order to some men.

THE OFFICER: It's cleaned up everywhere? Make another round in there... I want you to leave the whole place nice and neat.

The men go into the galleries.

. . . .

ROTUNDA

Jean and Françoise huddle against the wall.

FRANÇOISE: It's the end... Jeantou... it's the end... They're going to take us...
JEAN: Put your cheek on mine, Choisie.
FRANÇOISE: No... look at me.
X...: There are two who're hiding.

Shouts are heard coming from below.

. . . .

Is Françoise going to shout? Jean places his hand over her mouth.

BELOW

It's the ragpicker and la Puce
they got out of their hole.

AN OFFICER: No weapons...
good... they go with the
prisoners...
...and now the fireworks.

The troop goes out.
. . . .

ROTUNDA

Jean and Françoise lean out and
see the last Mobile Guards leaving
the quarry.
. . . .
They look at one another... will
they escape the massacre? No...
they start when they hear:
Françoise takes the two wedding
rings out of a pocket of her blouse.

VOICE: Ready.

. . . .
They put them on one another's
fingers.
. . . .
Their hands join.
. . . .
JEAN:

JEAN: For the best, Choisie.

. . . .
FRANÇOISE:

FRANÇOISE: For the best, Jeantou.

. . . .

EXTERIOR OF THE QUARRY

The cannon is aimed at the top of
the quarry

AN OFFICER: Fire...

. . . .
The Tree of Liberty is mowed
down by the shell.
. . . .

ROTUNDA

A fall of sand and stones buries
Jean and Françoise, while, through
the rumble, the echo of the quarry
returns the two mingled voices.

ECHO: CHOI—SIE.
JEAN-TOU
FOR-THE-BEST.

. . . .

EXTERIOR QUARRY

The troop has set off and moves
away toward the town.

. . . .

ROTUNDA

Jean has freed himself from the
fallen sand and stones and hurries to
Françoise.

JEAN: Françoise... Françoise...
FRANÇOISE: I'm all right...
Jeantou... and you?

. . . .
They raise their heads.
. . . .
There is a large hole over them.
You can see the sky and the fallen
tree.
. . . .
By holding on to the roots...
. . . .
...they are able to get out.
. . . .
From above: you can see the two
of them drawing closer...
. . . .
...then detach themselves against
the sky:
They are free.

While serious music rises quickly and
brings up the word.

END

Other Lost Films

L'Étrange Madame X. 1951, 91 min. Produced by André Collignon. Script
by Marcelle Maurette. Photographed by Louis Page. With Michele Morgan, Henri
Vidal, Maurice Escande, Arlette Thomas, Robert Vattier, Paul Barge, and Louis
Comte. Unreleased in U.S.

Caf'Conc'. 1951–52. From an idea by Pierre Kast. Music by Grémillon.
Unfinished.

L'Amour d'une Femme. 1953, 100 min. Produced by Pierre Gerin. Script
by Grémillon. Photographed by Louis Page. With Micheline Presle, Massimo
Girotti, Gaby Morlay, Marc Cassot, and Roland Lesaffre. Unreleased in U.S.

In the last ten years of his life, Grémillon tried to make fiction films,
but continued to find commercial projects—and success—elusive. Thus he

only occasionally turned to feature films when not involved with documentaries. Two films explored the theme of impossible love in the present social climate.

In 1951 Grémillon directed *L'Étrange Madame X*. It is the sad story of Irene (Michele Morgan) and Étienne (Henri Vidal). Irene is a rich woman pretending to be a maid. She is in love with Étienne, a carpenter. When they secretly have a child, she seeks a divorce from her husband. But faced with the fact that he is totally against the idea, she is forced to give the child to a wet-nurse. The child dies, and it is then that Étienne discovers the truth about her. He breaks with her. In the end she overcomes her despair and returns to her world.

In 1953, Grémillon returned to this theme in *L'Amour d'une Femme*. In this story, Dr. Marie Prieur (Micheline Presle) falls in love with a young engineer, Lorenzi (Massimo Girotti). He wants to marry her, but requires that she abandon her profession. She is tempted, but he realizes that her vocation is her "priesthood." He leaves her, and she is overcome with a "profound sadness. Henceforth, she is alone," as the French reviews described it. She soon finds work; her life continues.

Between the realization of these two films, Grémillon in 1951 began the film *Caf'Conc'*, a full-length film about the café-concert scene at the beginning of the century. From an idea by assistant Pierre Kast, Grémillon hoped to explore further an era he'd looked at briefly in his 1950 documentary *Les Charmes de l'Existence*. The latter film evoked the period through its artwork. In *Caf'Conc'* Grémillon intended to link actual footage of music halls with some original material.

From the war of 1870 to the war of 1914, the cafe-concert was the main form of popular entertainment for the French for the simple reason that it was cheap entertainment. Each town had a cafe equipped with a piano and a stage where someone put on a show. Except for the large towns such as Marseille, Lyon, or Bordeaux, the provinces had no caf'conc'. The industry was centralized: It was out of the 150 halls in the capital at the end of the century that a succession of stars emerged and spread throughout the country.

Grémillon hoped to briefly recapture the years which starred such talents as Maurice Chevalier, the comedians Dranem and Polin, the singers Mayol and Polaire, the English piano player Harry Fragson, and the singer of military songs Paulus.

In all quarters of Paris there had been cafe-concerts. In the center of the city on the boulevards could be found the Eldorado (opened during the Second Empire), the Scala (which boasted amazing programs), the Petit Casino, the Parisiana, and the Alcazar d'Hiver; towards the Bastille were the Concert Parisien, the Concert de l'Époque, and the 2,000-seat Ba-Ta-Clan. In the summer, the establishments of the Jardins des Champs-Élysées, the Alcazar d'Été, the Ambassadeurs, and the Horlage would open. On the exterior boulevards could be found the Gaite Rouchechouart, the Trianon, and the Cigale.

Patrons, performers, agents, and composers would mingle, dine and listen to local singers of romantic songs (called *chanteurs de charme*), soldier songs, tramp songs, etc. In this atmosphere one could buy new songs, seek out talent, or try to land a job.

In mid–1952, the film *Caf'Conc'* was still being listed by the French trade publications as in production. It would seem that the movie could have been a kind of *Children of Paradise* 30 years later. Carne's 1945 film centers about a popular theatrical form around the middle of the nineteenth century (the Funambules), while caf'conc' was a similarly popular form of theatrical entertainment in the 1880s and onwards; and the Funambules were as much reviled in their time as the caf'conc' were in theirs.

But soon thereafter Grémillon dropped the film. It's not entirely clear why, but he or the producer may have abandoned the film because two competing films were about to come out: Jacques Becker's *Casque d'Or* (1952) and John Huston's *Moulin Rouge* (1953). (In 1954, a short film on the cafe-concert, starring Maurice Chevalier and directed by Barthomieu, came out.)

With the exception of a few titles, Grémillon's work has not been released in the United States. The few feature titles available include *Maldone* (1928), *Gardienes de Phare* (1929), *La Petite Lise* (1930), *Gueule d'Amour* (1937), *Remorques* (1941), *Lumière d'Été* (1943), *La Ciel Est à Vous* (1944), *Le 6 Juin à l'Aube* (documentary, 1945), and *Pattes Blanches* (1949).

Grémillon's work unreleased in the United States includes his score or so of short documentaries filmed between 1923 and 1958, and the following features: *La Vie des Travailleurs Italiens en France* (doc., 1926), *Un Tour au Large* (doc., 1926), *Dinah la Métisse* (1931), *Pour un Sou d'Amour* (1932), *Gonzague/L'Accordeur* (1933), *La Dolorosa* (Spain, 1934), *Centinella Alerta* (Spain, 1935), *La Valse Royale* (1935), *Pattes des Mouches* (French-German, 1936), and *L'Étrange Monsieur Victor* (French-German, 1938).

35. Edmond Thunder Gréville (1906–1966)

Une Femme dans la Nuit. 1941, 105 min. Directed by Gréville and Abel Gance. Produced by Jean Mugell. Script by Jacques Companeez. Adaptation by Jacques Prévert, Pierre Laroche, and Pierre Rocher. Photographed by Henry Burel. With Claude Dauphin, Viviane Romance, Marion Malville, Lysiane Rey, and Jane Marken. Unreleased in U.S.

Im Banne der Madonna (Under the Madonna's Spell)/Der Bildschnitzer vom Walsertal (The Sculptor of Walser Valley), 1951, 79 min. Produced by Atlas. With Maria Holst, Siegfried Breuer, Viktor Staal. Unreleased.

Edmond T. Gréville made films that emphasized a nostalgia for terrestrial paradises, with characters on an incessant search for freedom. Gréville's images were baroque and confounding, yet displayed an affection for those who exhibited a spirit of originality and independence. The psychological and the erotic were his primary motifs, and the stories were movingly and lyrically told. This is true especially of *Remous* (1932), *Princesse Tam-Tam* (1935, released in the United States in 1989), *Mademoiselle Docteur* (1937), *Menaces* (1939), and *Passionnelle* (1947).

Of English-French parentage, Gréville made most of his films in France, but worked in England and other European countries. In a career that spanned 35 years, he made two films that were banned. One was found objectionable by the Nazis; the other was made—unknown to Gréville— with the assistance of former Nazis.

In 1941 Gréville was in occupied France, completing the film *Une Femme dans la Nuit*, begun by Abel Gance. Vivian Romance portrays a woman who leaves her husband for a freer life. Injured in an accident, she is helped by a young doctor. She is attracted to him and stays to become his assistant. Years later, when she learns her husband is ill, she returns home. Then when her husband is found dead, suspicion falls on the doctor.

Une Femme dans la Nuit was shot in Avignon in early 1941. Jacques Prévert and Pierre Laroche adapted the novel *Manon Lescout* in an "inverse sense," making the woman the one who seeks a change in life. But since only two of their scenes were retained, Prévert and Laroche had their names removed from the release.

165

Im Banne der Madonna, 1951 (actor unidentified). This film is characteristic of director Edmond T. Gréville's work: baroque and confounding.

Completed in 1941, the film was not released until 1943 because the Nazis objected to the lifestyle of the heroine. In addition, the ubiquitous Claude Dauphin was in the film. An outspoken opponent of the Germans, his presence in any French film of the Occupation almost surely guaranteed its suppression by the Nazis.

Gréville immersed himself with enthusiasm in each of his subsequent undertakings, even the most obscure, whether it was discovering the *Haut-de-Cagnes* in 1942, when he assumed the "technical supervision" of a documentary by Jacques Canolle on traveling comedians (released in 1947 as *Le Chariot de Thespis*), or in the making of the first postwar Franco-German film, *Im Banne der Madonna (Under the Madonna's Spell)*.

Gréville was not unused to working in Germany. He'd made two films in Berlin before Hitler's rise to power.

Called to Munich in 1951 to film a very Grévillian story of a sculptor in love with his model, Gréville had hardly finished shooting when he fled, having discovered that most of the backers and technicians were former Nazis.

Gréville's French backers decided not to release the film. Gréville made his next film back in France.

36. Marcel Pagnol (1895–1974)

La Prière aux Étoiles. 1942. Films Marcel Pagnol, producer. Script by Marcel Pagnol. Photographed by André Thomas. Design by Robert Giordani. Music by Raoul Moretti. With Pierre Blancher (Pierre), Josette Day (Florence), Julien Carette, Pauline Carton, Fernand Charpin, and Jean Chavrier. Unfinished.

The playwright-director Marcel Pagnol was the first filmmaker elected to the French Academy. He reached his height during the period 1933–39, when his plays became films (*Topaze, Marius, Fanny*), and he himself established a reputation behind the camera for evoking life in southern France through such movies as *Angèle* (1934), *César* (1936), *Regain* (1937), *Le Schpountz* (1938), and *The Baker's Wife* (1938).

Under the Occupation Pagnol directed the regime's first French film — *The Well-Digger's Daughter* (1941), which, in turn, was the fifteenth film of his career. Yet in the next thirteen years Pagnol completed only four films, and little of his later work, particularly such extensive films as *Manon des Sources* (1952) and *Letters from My Windmill* (1954), is remembered. Perhaps it is because during the war years Pagnol began an intimate project, said to be partly autobiographical and containing allusions to Pagnol's brother Paul, who had died in 1940. Pagnol worked on *La Prière aux Étoiles* (*Prayer to the Stars*) from August 1941 until June 1942, then halted. He didn't resume directing films again until 1948 (*La Belle Meunière*).

In Marseille, under the watchful eyes of the Nazis, Pagnol, then in his mid–40s, filmed *La Prière aux Étoiles*, a melodrama in the form of a fairy tale about Florence (20) and Pierre (40), "two creatures whom," according to the script, "life has disappointed." To Pagnol, the fairy tale was said to be "maybe the simplest and most noble form, the most poetically realistic in all of literature."

The man and woman have met at a cacophonous amusement park (Luna Park) and sworn eternal love for each other. It is at this moment that Florence's prayer to the stars — "The desire to love is smothering me and the nights of my twenty years are so black by its absence" — appears to have been answered after years of living an ignominious life (she's been a kept woman). Now her protector is more than willing to disappear, and a life of promise looms ahead. But her new love, Pierre, is uncomfortable with the knowledge of her past. He risks spoiling everything.

Pierre Blancher and Josette Day in La Prière aux Étoiles, *1942, directed by Marcel Pagnol.*

At the amusement park, in the climactic scene that lays bare Pagnol's attitude towards life, the couple visits a fortune teller. She pointedly tells Pierre that Florence "can only live from your love . . . and will die from your death. . . . For a love to give you real life, it must have the force to give you death." Sensing a great hesitancy on the part of Pierre, the fortune teller pleads with him to recognize the happiness that awaits him. As she's about to be paid for her services, she turns to Pierre one last time:

You love the stars, the stars love you, it's forty francs. Don't let go madam's hand. You have money in your right hand pocket. I do not give change for fifty francs. Besides, you would not take it. People like you don't have the right to be preoccupied with petty things: The stars have given you love—never take any change.

In attempting to film this bare, lyrical love story (dedicated to his wife and star Josette Day), Pagnol sketched out a "little world" full of humor but absent any picturesqueness. This he did by contrasting the cheap settings within the amusement park with the more luxurious surroundings outside. Yet Pagnol had to know that the chances were good he'd never finish *La Prière aux Étoiles* during the war years. His fierce sense of independence— he brooked no censorship—coupled with the inevitable pressures of outside interference, numerous mishaps and poor technical support on the set, and equipment shortages as a result of the war were bound to threaten the success of the project. Finally, abandoning the film, the director himself noted, "We had only bad film, whose manufacture had been improvised, which gave us reels that could not be projected."

Pagnol's unfinished *La Prière aux Étoiles*, along with the script, apparently survived in his papers.

VII. ON THE WRONG SIDE
OF THE WAR

G. W. complained often and was worried what people, especially his friends, would think about him since they did not know about the unhappy circumstances in which he found himself.

—Gertrude Pabst, wife of G. W. Pabst

Returning to the United States, the land of his father's birth, in 1926, German actor Emil Jannings bolstered his reputation in the closing years of the silent era. Signed to a $400,000 contract by Paramount, Jannings said he "learned American ways. I have learned filming schedules must be lived up to ... that authors, directors, and American actors are artists." He went on to stress that "In Europe ... the men who make pictures ... are either artistic and unbusinesslike or they are too businesslike and forsake the artistic side."

A few years later another great German filmmaker, director G. W. Pabst, also came to Hollywood seeking to further film art. But both he and Jannings eventually returned to Europe. Then during World War II, these two film giants remained and worked in Nazi Germany.

Pabst's allegiance during these years in particular cast a pall over his career. An acknowledged "cineaste," Pabst moved from France to his native Austria in April 1939. After the war began he wavered. Finally, he is said to have decided to flee to the West. But en route to Rome from his home in south Austria in October 1939, he suffered a hernia aboard a train. He and his family (including a 15-year-old son) were trying to reach a ship bound for New York.

According to his wife, they had to act by the end of 1939; their United States citizenship, gained in 1934, would be lost because of nonresidence if they did not return in time.

Pabst was operated on in Vienna. While he was recuperating, his doctors discovered he had diabetes. He and his family returned to the family estate when they determined overseas travel was out of the question. But Pabst's actions came under a cloud only when he actually began directing in Germany. His first full-length film in the Third Reich garnered him the

171

Best Director Award at the Fascist-controlled Venice Film Festival in 1941. There is no evidence he ever tried to leave Germany while Hitler was in power.

Both G. W. Pabst and Emil Jannings left a film unfinished as Germany was coming to a standstill in the waning days of the war. The Allies wound up impounding Nazi productions in circulation or about to be released. They substituted their own subtitled productions or they released dubbed American, British, and Russian productions, which for the most part were films of light entertainment. By January 1946, nearly 200 theatres in Germany were showing Allied films.

Notable German filmmakers were not forgotten. Those deemed to have been in service of the state—Jannings, actors Werner Kraus and Heinrich George, directors Veidt Harlan, Leni Riefenstahl, and Karl Ritter—were put on trial. Riefenstahl was sent to prison by the French government. Others disappeared from films for a while. Jannings was barred for life.

G. W. Pabst was allowed to retire to his estate in Austria. He resumed directing in 1947.

When the war ended in Germany and Japan, the victors moved to re-establish local filmmaking facilities. The Americans sent veteran German producer Erich Pommer to supervise production in the American sector of Germany; the British licensed German companies in Berlin and Hamburg; while the Russians fashioned Deutsche Film Aktiengesellschaft (DEFA) out of the old UFA studios now in East Germany. Wolfgang Staudte, having begun directing in 1945, became a prized director at DEFA.

In Japan, film production was at a standstill until 1946. The United States authorities then implemented a policy of reviewing existing Japanese films to weed out any that dealt with the subjects of militarism, racism, nationalism, and feudalism. Further, any films judged violent, exploitive, sexist, or antisocial were suppressed.

Japanese producers had to submit scripts for review, and the subsequent productions were previewed by United States authorities. This meant films had to portray the democratizing process underway in a positive light, including the rehabilitation of soldiers, the emancipation of women, the unionizing of organizations, and the development of the country.

Under the United States Occupation, young director Kon Ichikawa saw his first effort banned.

37. Kon Ichikawa (1915–)

A Girl at Dojo Temple (Musume Dojoji). 1946. Produced by J. O./Toho Co. Script by Ichikawa and Keiji Hasebe. Music by Takashi Hattori. With Kubuki dolls by Puppe Kawasaki. Unreleased.

The Japanese director Kon Ichikawa is best known for the antiwar films *Harp of Burma* (1956) and *Fires on the Plain* (1959). At the same time, his filmmaking has displayed a penchant for humor and black comedy. In the mid–1960s, he stated, "I'm still a cartoonist and I think that the greatest influence on my films (besides Chaplin, particularly *The Gold Rush*) is probably Disney." A glimpse of this emphasis was shown in his first film, which was censored by United States authorities in 1945. His second film remains unfinished by him.

The young Kon Ichikawa had intended to film *Rashomon* in 1945, but was dissuaded by his colleagues from attempting such a great subject. Since he was then only an illustrator—about to direct his first film— with the Toho film company, he was advised to begin work on a much simpler subject. He chose the Kubuki story "A Girl at Toho Temple." As it turned out, the young director was forced to use puppets instead of animation; there were not enough illustrators because of the labor shortage in Japan.

Ichikawa's first film was based on a tale of a monk in love. Anchin, a bell-maker, is completing work on a new bell for Dojo Temple. Kiyohime, the woman he loves, is sacrificed to the gods so that he may finish the job. Yet because of his work, ironically, his loved one is not entirely lost to him. Only Anchin is able to ring the bell, and when he does, Kiyohime's spirit emerges to dance.

When the film was ready for release in 1946, Japan was under United States military occupation. All Japanese films had to be cleared with United States authorities before distribution. Because the script for *A Girl at Dojo Temple* had not been reviewed by the authorities and contained "feudal remnants," according to Ichikawa, the film was seized by the Americans and never released. The film is now lost; only some planning sketches survive.

173

Other Lost Films

1001 Nights with Toho (Toho Senichi-ya). 1947. Produced by Shin Toho Co. Photographed by Akira Mimura. With Hisako Yamane, Susume Fujita, Tataro Kurokawa, and Hideko Takamine. Not finished by Ichikawa.

Ichikawa's second film, *1001 Nights with Toho*, was the debut production of the newly formed film company Shin Toho. The director shot a bit of footage, then stopped. The film was completed when footage from other films was tacked on. The "finished" product was then used as promotional material for satirical comedies the new studio intended to make. No prints of the film exist, although the negative is at the film company in Tokyo.

In 1956, Ichikawa displayed the other side of his "two kinds of films." His antiwar *Harp of Burma* won the San Giorgio Prize in Venice, and he gained an international reputation.

38. Emil Jannings (1884–1950)

The Merry Monarch (Die Abenteuer des König Pausole). 1932–33. Produced by Algra Films/Société des Films Tobis. Directed by Alexis Granowsky. Script by Fernand Crommelinck and Henry Jeanson. Photographed by Rudolph Maté. Music by Karol Rathaus. With Emil Jannings (Pausole), Josette Day (Aline), Sidney Fox (Diane), Jose Naguero (Giglio), and Armand Bernard (Taxis). Unfinished.

Where Is Mr. Belling? (Wo Ist Herr Belling?). 1945. Directed by Erich Engel. Produced by Bavaria-Ateliers, Munich. Script by Curt J. Braun. Photographed by Franz Koch. With Emil Jannings, Dagny Servaes, Heli Finkenzeller, Kurt Muller-Graf, and Alice Treff. Unfinished.

The talented German actor Emil Jannings, who gave the first Oscar-winning performance for *The Way of All Flesh* (1927) and *The Last Command* (1928), failed to finish two important films in his career. (A third, called *Der Letzte Appell*, a Nazi production set in the German navy, was started at the outbreak of World War II. Before filming was halted, Jannings himself directed a few scenes.)

Born to an American father and German mother in Switzerland, Emil Jannings (T. F. Emil Janez) began his film career in Germany in 1914 and worked in Hollywood from 1927 to 1929. Because of a heavy German accent, Jannings returned to Germany with the introduction of sound. Beginning in 1930, he made all of his sound films in Europe, including the famous *The Blue Angel* (1930) under Josef von Sternberg.

In 1932, Jannings agreed to star in the Austrian production *The Merry Monarch*, a satire about a bawdy ruler of a Mediterranean island who takes 365 women as wives. Russian theatre director Alexis Granowsky set out to shoot three versions of the film in three languages: French, German, and English. Jannings was to star in the German version and, despite his accent, in the English adaptation, alongside Josette Day and the American actress Sidney Fox. The French-language version featured André Berley as the king, and Edwige Feuillere as Diane. The photographer for all three versions was the famous Rudolph Maté.

Financing the film was tricky. Its chief patron was a French woman who, it is said, had a yen to make a mark in films. But stops and starts in the funding halted filming a number of times.

175

Expenses, meanwhile, were high. Granowsky filmed *The Merry Monarch* on the Côte d'Azur, where, according to film historian Herman G. Weinberg, "the prettiest girls were ferried out . . . (and) for weeks the company disported themselves, continually wiring their . . . backer to send more money."

Then suddenly the money stopped altogether. When word came that the backer had apparently committed suicide, the production fell apart.

In 1934, the French version, called *Les Aventures du Roi Pausole*, was released at about 75 minutes. It was described by the publication *Miroir de Monde* as a humorous political, artistic, and social satire containing quite a bit of nudity. Surviving stills of the film show a movie, according to Herman G. Weinberg, "with a kind of Lubitsch aura and a striking visual handsomeness" about it.

The unfinished version of *The Merry Monarch* is in the Cinémathèque Française and the Cinémathèque Royale de Belgique. There are apparently no German or English versions extant. Jannings himself made only one reference to the film in his memoirs, published after his death: "As I was shooting *Roi Pausole* in the Epinay Studios, near Paris, the news reached me that a new government had been formed overnight in Germany, under Adolf Hitler."

When the Nazis came to power in January 1933, Jannings, though never a party member, lent his support to Goebbels's cultural vision of a new Germany. He completed nine films in Nazi Germany. For his efforts, he received the Goethe medal in 1939. He was made a director of the German film studio UFA in 1940, and the following year was named by the Nazis "Artist of the State."

On December 12, 1944, in Munich, Jannings began his last film, *Wo Ist Herr Belling?* This drama was to be the story of a responsible family man who leads a double life. On the one hand Herr Belling is an ordinary train engineer, and on the other he is a man climbing the career ladder trying to become an industrialist.

Wo Ist Herr Belling? was being directed by Erich Engel (1891–1966), the prominent stage producer who, in the span of two decades, literally worked in two German worlds: in the late 1920s with Brecht and the stage director Reinhardt, and in the 1930s and 1940s in Nazi Germany, making a number of above-average films along the way.

In January 1945, Engels was forced to halt work on Jannings's film because of the star's failing health and evident despair over Germany's losing the war. Then after the collapse of the Third Reich, Jannings was banned from all further work in films by the Allies.

At the time of Jannings's death in 1950, *Wo Ist Herr Belling?* was remade by Erich Engel as *Mr. Bruggs' Strange Life* (*Das seltsame Leben des Herrn Brugg*, 89 min.).

39. G. W. Pabst (1885–1967)

The Molander Affair (Der Fall Molander). 1944. Terra Films/Prague.
Script by Ernst Hasselbach and Per Schwenzen, from the book *Die Sternegeige*
(*Violin of the Stars*) by Alfred Karrasch. Photographed by Willy Kuhle. Music by
Werner Eisbrenner. With Paul Wegener, Harold Paulsen, Walter Frank, Irene von
Meyendorff, Robert Tessen, Werner Hinz, Will Dohm, Theodor Loos, Fritz Ode-
mar, Hermine Ziegler, and Nikolai Kolin. Unreleased.

The Austrian director G. W. Pabst was at the height of his powers
when the Nazis took control in Germany. Pabst had established his reputation as a penetrating investigator of psychology in a half-dozen realist films:
Pandora's Box (1929), *Diary of a Lost Girl* (1929), *Westfront 1918* (1930), *The
Beggar's Opera* (1931), *Kameradschaft* (1931), and *Mademoiselle Docteur*
(1937). Yet his only unfinished film, *The Molander Affair*, is representative
of the director's most controversial period — the six years he spent directing
films in wartime Nazi Germany — and casts a long shadow over the meaning of his career.

When Hitler came to power in 1933, Pabst went to France to make two
films and then to Hollywood to direct *A Modern Hero* (1934). Unable, however, over the next two years to get other assignments in the United States,
he returned to France. From 1937 to 1939 he directed three features, the
last being *Jeunes Filles en Détresse* (*Girls in Distress*, 1939), a film inspired by
Leontine Sagan's *Mädchen in Uniform* (1931) and shown at the 1939 Venice
Film Festival (and unreleased in the United States). Then when World
War II broke out, Pabst publicly announced his desire to leave France and
become an American citizen. Instead, he slipped into Austria and went on
to Nazi Germany. Seemingly a director of left-wing political views, Pabst
by this action immediately put his allegiance into question.

To make matters worse, Pabst remained in Germany throughout the
war. In 1940, according to one account, he offered his services to Goebbels
and edited a "documentary" about the role of the Luftwaffe in the Polish
campaign of September 1939, called *Baptism of Fire* (*Feuertaufe*, directed
by Hans Bertram). In the months that followed, the film was shown in Norway and Denmark before the Nazis overran these nations. After the war,
the Allies banned the showing of the hardcore Nazi film.

In the next three years Pabst completed two films which were released

177

by the Nazis: *Comedians* (*Komödianten*), 1941, which depicts the creation of a German National Theatre; and *Paraclesus*, 1943, the story of the metaphysicist von Hohenheim. For these films, Pabst was allowed to select his talent from among the best Germany had to offer. *Comedians* won the gold medal at the fascist-controlled Venice Film Festival of 1941.

In 1943, Pabst traveled to Prague to begin work on *The Molander Affair*. The film, an adaptation of Alfred Karrach's novel *Violin of the Stars*, was to be a psychological study about the need to confront the truth about oneself. In the film, young violinist Fritz Molander is forced to secretly part with his precious Stradivarius in order to pay for his first concert. But when he finds that the violin he trades in is a fake—someone has stolen the priceless instrument—Molander questions whether he can remain a musician without the real violin.

Actual filming began in 1944 at the Barrandow-Ateliers Studios and was reportedly completed later that year. But the editing was still underway when the Russians entered the city. The director, cast, and crew fled back to Germany. The fate of their project is still disputed. French researchers Charles Ford and René Jeanne claim the Russians confiscated the film and distributed it in East Germany and the satellite countries. Another investigator, David S. Hull, contends the film was destroyed when the postproduction laboratory, where the film was being processed, was bombed. The unfinished film is now reported to be in the Czec State Archives in Prague.

At the end of the war, Pabst moved to Austria, where he was well received but did not make a film for three years. His first postwar effort turned out to be *The Trial* (*Der Prozess*, 1948), a story, ironically, about a Jew unjustly accused of a crime. In a further irony considering the director's recent past, the film won Pabst another round of honors as best director at the Venice Film Festival of 1948.

Pabst made films until 1956. Four postwar films and one from 1924 called *Countess Donelli* have not been released in the United States.

Other Lost Films

Countess Donelli (Grafin Donelli). 1924, 81 min. Produced by Maxim Films. Script by Hans Kyser. Photographed by Guido Seeber. Design by Hermann Warm. With Paul Hansen, Henny Porten, Friedrich Kayssler, Ferdinand von Alten, and Eberhard Leithoff. Unreleased in U.S. Now lost.

Before Georg Wilhelm Pabst became internationally known with the 1925 film *Joyless Street*, he had already directed two films in Germany. One, *The Treasure*, made in 1923, was hailed by critics but faired poorly. It was released in the United States in 1931. The other, called *Countess Donelli* was made in 1924, and never shown in the United States. It is now lost.

Countess Donelli was a vehicle for Henny Porten, Germany's first superstar, whose career was sagging in the mid–1920s. In the film Donelli (played by Porten) faces financial ruin after the death of her husband. She falls in love with a man who—unbeknownst to her—breaks the law to help her. Years later the consequences of his act nearly ruin their lives.

Pabst was praised for his direction of the star. This was the first of several films Pabst would make with the photographer Guido Seeber and the set designer Hermann Warm. Warm had established his reputation with the expressionist film *The Cabinet of Dr. Caligari* (1919). He would go on to work on such classics as Carl Dreyer's *The Passion of Joan of Arc* (1928) and *Vampyr* (1931).

Two Italian films Pabst made in the early 1950s were poorly received by the critics in Italy, and then ignored in the international market. *The Voice of Silence* (*La Voce del Silenzio*, 1952) boasted a dozen writers and an international cast (Jean Marais, Aldo Fabrizi, Eduardo Cianelli) in a story about men seeking emotional renewal at a Jesuit retreat. Pabst's strip scenes, regarded as risqué in France, were edited out of the film in Italy. *Crazy Affairs* (*Cosí da Pazzi*, 1953) was a story about a woman mistakenly institutionalized as psychotic. Pabst employed his long-time scriptwriter, Leo Lania, in taking up a subject that had interested him before the war: psychology.

In 1955, Pabst was back in West Germany. There he directed *It Happened on July 20* (*Es Geschah am 20 Juli*), a psychological investigation of the attempt by German officers to assassinate Hitler in mid–1944. *Variety* (7/13/55) announced, "Pabst's touch is evident in the dramatic photography, where certain scenes achieve real artistry." Bernhard Wicki stars as Count von Stauffenberg, the leader of the opposition to Hitler. What's also interesting is that this film was literally competing against a rival film (*Der 20 Juli*, directed by Falk Harnack), released one day earlier, on the same subject. The critics thought Pabst's "effort figures to come off somewhat better.... Wise promotion could turn this one into a sleeper."

Pabst's final career film was called *Through the Forests, Through the Fields* (*Durch die Wälder, Durch die Auen*, 1956), the story of the romantic nineteenth-century composer Carl Maria von Weber. It was Pabst's only film in color and starred Karl Schonbock and Eva Bartók.

Pabst lived for another 11 years, but because of ill health he never mounted another film project.

40. Leni Riefenstahl (1902–   )

Black Cargo (Die schwartze Fracht). 1956. Produced by Sternfilm GmbH. Script by Kurt Heuser and Helge Pawlinin, from the novel *Hassans schwartze Fracht* by Hans Otto Meissner. Photographed by Heinz Holscher and R. von Theumer. With Riefenstahl and O. E. Hasse. Unfinished.

Leni Riefenstahl was dubbed Hitler's favorite director. An actress since 1926, she directed her first film, *The Blue Light,* the year before Hitler came to power. Then, two years after his reign began, she produced the powerful propaganda vehicle *Triumph of the Will.* Detained and imprisoned after the war, she was ostracized from the film world at her release in 1949. Nevertheless, she attempted to realize a number of film projects in the 1950s. She failed to finish *Black Cargo* when the Suez Canal War of 1956 (ironically, in the light of her past) put her in position of having to wait for events to unfold—she who 20 years earlier had been in all-powerful position of having to wait for no one.

In April 1956, Riefenstahl was in Kenya recovering from a very serious car accident. Heading towards the Tana River near Nairobi, Riefenstahl's driver had swerved to avoid hitting an animal and gone off a bridge. Incapacitated, Riefenstahl remained in Africa "possessed by a project . . . that I did not want to give up." She had conceived of filming a story, as she had written, about which "men have kept silent . . . [the] problem of the slave trade. The treatment is original, but is based upon facts and authentic records."

A few months earlier, in Munich, Riefenstahl had read Hemingway's *Green Hills of Africa* and an account in Stuttgard's *Suddeutsche Zeitung* called "Missionary Exposes Slave Trade in Africa." The director, absorbed by the idea of Africa, immediately wrote a treatment which she called "Black Drums." She then met Andreas von Nagy, a zoologist who worked in Africa, and who became a consultant to her, and the big-game hunter and writer Hans Otto Meissner, whose book *Hassans schwartze Fracht* Riefenstahl found full of excitement. That excitement inspired Riefenstahl and Meissner to collaborate on *Die schwartze Fracht.*

Now the director had to raise money. She sent a proposal to every studio she could think of. Without waiting for replies, she put together a list of expedition members and booked passage to Africa, which von Nagy had described as possessed of limitless film subjects, a photographer's dream.

On the flight to Africa, Riefenstahl had a premonition and, for the first time in her life, wrote a will. She then suffered the accident that put her in a Nairobi hospital. When back on her feet in the fall of 1956, Riefenstahl gathered a cast and crew to begin filming the semidocumentary *Black Cargo*. Some of it would be staged with a cast of professional and nonprofessional actors. It appears that from her point of view, it was a documentary since it had ethnological veracity and geographic accuracy.

Riefenstahl put herself in the lead as an anthropologist who is following up on the work of her recently deceased husband. He died under mysterious circumstances while studying the history of a tribe in central Africa. Digging further into the life of the people, the anthropologist is horrified to discover that tribal members are still being sold into slavery by neighboring Muslims. With the help of a British agent, she manages to have the awful practice halted. At the same time, she discovers reasons for her husband's death.

Riefenstahl managed to complete test shooting of some scenes a few days before the Suez Canal War broke out in October. Then she was faced with a dilemma. The equipment she needed to continue filming (cameras, Cinemascope optics, reflectors, and color film) had not yet passed through the canal — and wouldn't be allowed through until hostilities between Israel and Egypt were settled. At the same time, the rainy season was almost upon her. It threatened to bring everything to a halt.

Two months later, the war over, her equipment proceeded safely through the waterway — but now the rainy season had started in East Africa. This made it nearly impossible to transport anything over land.

Riefenstahl decided to return to West Germany, wait out the weather, and seek additional funding for her film. Then a final incident brought her project to a halt. Two of her associates were injured in a car accident. At that point Riefenstahl abandoned *Black Cargo*.

In discussing the work of Leni Riefenstahl, one cannot but be struck dumb by Riefenstahl's reaction to slavery: "A shocking report. But is it even conceivable that such horrors can still exist today?" While slavery remained a serious human rights problem in central Africa until the mid–1960s, Riefenstahl's role in, and continued silence about, the Holocaust in her own backyard raised eyebrows about her postwar activities. It is likely that Riefenstahl was seeking a vehicle — a number of which she had found since entering films — to once again tell the story of a "strong-willed woman in an adventurous situation."

41. Wolfgang Staudte (1906–1984)

The Man Whose Name Was Stolen (Der Mann, dem man den Namen stahl). 1945, 86 min. Produced by Bernard F. Schmidt, Tobis Co. Script by Staudte and Josef Maria Frank. Photographed by Edward Hoesch. With Axel von Ambesser, Ruth Lommel, Gretl Schorg, Paul Henkels, and Leopold von Ledebur. Unreleased.

Women Overboard (Frau über Bord; also called Kabine 27). 1945, 7500 ft. Produced by Tobis Co. Script by Curt J. Braun. Photographed by Friedl Behn-Grund. With Axel von Ambesser, Heinrich George, Anneliese Uhlig, Charlotte Schellhorn, Karl Schonbock, and Carl-Heinz Schroth. Unfinished.

Mother Courage and Her Children (Mutter Courage und ihre Kinder). 1956, 2000 ft. Produced by DEFA. Script by Staudte and Bertolt Brecht. Design by Max Douy. With Hélèn Weigel (Mutter Courage), Simone Signoret (Lagerhure), Bernard Blier (Feldkoch), Françoise Spira (Kathrin), and Erwin Geschonneck (Feldprediger). Unfinished.

Wolfgang Staudte, the influential postwar German director, became an actor in 1931. In 1940 he had a part in the notorious anti–Semitic film *Jud Suss*. Its director, Veidt Harlan, said that "virtually every actor ... performed under duress." Three years later Staudte got his first directorial assignment for the government-controlled Tobis production company. Then in 1945, he started filming his first serious effort, *The Man Whose Name Was Stolen*, a satire about bureaucracy. Staudte's caricature of bourgeois mentality brought the director unwanted attention: The Nazi's propaganda minister, Joseph Goebbels, banned the production and threatened to have Staudte sent to the Eastern front.

Staudte was allowed to direct another film only because his actor-friend Heinrich George intervened on his behalf with the Tobis production company. With the war drawing to a close, Staudte completed shooting the "family comedy" *Woman Overboard* but did not cut the nearly 7500 feet of film.

In 1946, while living in West Germany, Staudte made the first postwar German film, *Murderers Among Us,* for the state-owned studio DEFA in East Germany. The film, which starred Hildegard Knef, was a look at war guilt. It was hailed as "remarkable" and "full of imaginatively visualized

Scenes from Mother Courage and Her Children, *1956.* Top: *Director Wolfgang Staudte, Simone Signoret and Hélène Weigel on the set.* Bottom: *Simone Signoret.*

From Mother Courage and Her Children. Top: *Bernard Blier (as Feldkoch).* Bottom: *Director Wolfgang Staudte rehearses a scene with Simone Signoret.*

moments." In 1948, working for DEFA in East Germany, he made a revised version of *The Man Whose Name Was Stolen* under the title *The Strange Adventures of Mr. Fridolin B. (Die seltsamen Abenteuer des Herrn Fridolin B.).* This time the film was released. Playing the lead was Axel von Ambesser, the actor who starred in the unreleased 1945 film.

In 1956 Staudte started one last film for DEFA. *Mutter Courage* was one of the most eagerly awaited productions from the East German DEFA company, which had taken control of the former UFA studios at Babelsburg, near Potsdam. Based on the play by Bertolt Brecht—who coauthored the movie script with Staudte—the film would tell the tragic story of a canteen-woman and her children during the Thirty Years' War.

Staudte envisioned *Mutter Courage* as a Cinemascope production on a grand scale. Art director Max Douy described the film this way: "The film was lovely to do.... There were 80 sets erected on the great lots at DEFA ... prepared down to the last detail; we'd made the sketches ... drawn all the images." According to Simone Signoret, Staudte was giving "the work the same kind of attraction that a Western has with audiences all over the world."

For the starring role Staudte cast Hélène Weigel, Brecht's wife, who had starred in the role on stage. Production began "enthusiastically," according to a critic, but trouble soon developed between director and star. Weigel, it appears, "could not adapt her style of acting to that demanded for the film," said this same critic. She was comfortable working in a stage setting; Staudte was directing a screen adaptation. Brecht's constant presence further irritated Staudte. Resentful of the famed playwright's attempts to interfere with his method of directing Weigel, Staudte even tried to have the set closed to him.

As Brecht's spokesman, Hélène Weigel interfered in the making of the film. She was described by Douy as "a sort of unofficial Minister of Culture for the government; when she said anything, everyone said 'Yes, Mrs. Weigel!'" It seems that at one point the government allowed her to stop the filming and direct it herself in the stage sets accepted by her husband. Simone Signoret, who was playing Weigel's deaf and dumb daughter, remembers, "There were all the East Berlin politics in which I was not involved: Staudte was trying to give the film an international cast, with big sets ... and not at all how Brecht had perhaps imagined it himself." Signoret herself finished her role then returned to Paris.

During the shooting, Staudte sought to reassert control by replacing Weigel. He tried to get Bertha Drews and Thérèse Ghiese, the latter a close friend of the Brechts. But both refused for personal or contractual reasons. Staudte finally stopped shooting the film after 2000 feet, citing "irreconcilable differences ... with the dramatist."

The producers soon after announced that production of *Mutter*

Courage would be resuming under the direction of Erich Engel. Weigel would remain in the starring role. Engel and Brecht then made it known that they had "come to an agreement . . . about the form the film was to take." But when Brecht died in August 1956, shooting was again halted.

In 1961, DEFA finally released a filmed version of Brecht's play, written and directed by Peter Palitzach and Manfred Wekworth. Hélène Weigel was in the lead. The footage Staudte shot was not incorporated into the final version. He was said by Douy to have been "shattered by this affair."

After this failed effort, Staudte began directing in West Germany. Up until the mid–1960s and the beginnings of the New German Cinema, he was perhaps the only West German director of any note. He won the German Film Prize in 1975 and the Federal Cross of Merit in 1979.

VIII. FACING THE
REALITY OF WAR

*The penalty of realism is that it is about reality and has to bother for ever
not about being "beautiful" but about being right.*
                                            —John Grierson, 1942

The filmmakers Michael Curtiz, Luciano Emmer, John Ford, and
Alfred Hitchcock were forced to leave films unfinished or unreleased
because of the interruptions of, or their treatments of subjects dealing with,
war.

Curtiz was working in his native Hungary following the close of World
War I when the country became communist. Curtiz fled because the nation's film industry was nationalized.

Luciano Emmer began making films in Mussolini's Italy during World
War II. His reaction to the call for realist films was to try to undermine the
regime. It got him into trouble.

Also during World War II, Alfred Hitchcock decided to make what
he called a "contribution" to the war effort. He made two shorts about
the "resistance" the French were showing. Containing his usual brand
of humor, the two French-language shorts were not appreciated by
France—and were never released in France, or for that matter, in the
United States.

Finally, at the height of the Vietnam War, John Ford made two documentaries on military subjects. An experienced documentarian, Ford's
prowar films were found out of favor during the antiwar years and not
shown.

42. Michael Curtiz
(Mihaly Kertész, 1888–1962)

Liliom. 1919. Produced by Phoenix Films, Hungary. Script by Mihaly Kertész. Adapted from the play *Liliom* by Ferenc Molnar. With Ika Lenkeffy, Gyula Czortos, Nusi Somogyi, Jeno Balossa, Lajos Rethey, Jeno Viragh, and Aidar Sarkadi. Unfinished.

Of the nearly 180 films Michael Curtiz (born Mihaly Kertész in Hungary) directed between 1912 and 1961 in Europe and America (including *Yankee Doodle Dandy,* 1942, and *Casablanca,* 1943), he failed to finish only one film: *Liliom* (1919).

In 1912, Curtiz acted in *Today and Tomorrow,* one of the first films produced in Hungary. Its success gave him a chance to direct four pictures within the next two years. Already in competition with Alexander Korda, Curtiz went to Scandinavia to study film production. Working with Victor Sjöström and Mauritz Stiller, he developed a preference for filming in the outdoors quickly but efficiently.

During the Great War, Curtiz served in the Austro-Hungarian Army along the Russian front, and was twice wounded. He finished the war as a newsreel cameraman making propaganda films—one of the first of a breed—in Constantinople.

Then from 1917 until he left Hungary in the middle of 1919, Curtiz directed exclusively for the film studio Phoenix Films. This production company was keenly interested in emulating the star system so popular in the United States. Through Curtiz's influence as director of production, Phoenix Films also became known for the quality of its stories. By the time he was 30, Curtiz had directed 50 films. Along with Alexander Korda and Paul Fejos, he had become one of Hungary's most important film directors.

In March 1919, Béla Kun established the first communist regime in Hungary. A month later, Kun nationalized the film industry on the advice of producer Alexander Korda, who, though not a party member, had been appointed to the Communist Directory for the Arts, charged with maintaining control of the industry. Korda and other producers saw this move as a way to rid the state film industry of the distributors—the middle men—

who were said to have made most of the money, to have "perpetuated the inequalities of the capitalist system" and stymied the chances for a true national cinema. Until Béla Kun was overthrown in August 1919, filmmakers in Hungary were, for the first time, to make films the state decreed permissible. During Kun's 120-day rule, the Hungarian Councils Republic produced three dozen films, which contained party-line propaganda.

Michael Curtiz began filming *Liliom* during this tumultuous period. His was the first attempt to film Molnar's comedy-fantasy of 1909. Hollywood and France would later make four other versions, beginning with *A Trip to Paradise* (1921). *Liliom* would also become the source for the 1945 Broadway show *Carousel*.

Liliom, a good-looking, trigger-temper carnival barker, marries innocent Julie. When he loses his job, insecurity overwhelms him and he takes his anger out on his wife. He learns he is to be a father just as he becomes involved in a botched hold-up attempt. Then, unable to face the prospect of prison, he kills himself. He goes to purgatory, and serves 16 years, after which the Heavenly Magistrate allows him one chance to redeem himself. Wanting to give something to his now grown-up daughter, Louise, Liliom steals a car and offers it to her. When she rejects is, he slaps her, and is returned to hell. Louise asks her mother why the slap didn't hurt. "There are times," Julie replies, "when a slap becomes a caress."

Nationalization of the film industry disrupted the shooting of *Liliom* after it had hardly begun. Unwilling to put up with the regime, Curtiz fled Hungary with his wife. According to the French film publication *Cahiers du Cinéma*, he went to Sweden, where he completed his fifty-first film, *Odette and the History of Illustrious Women*, featuring a 14-year-old Greta Garbo in the role of Marie Antoinette. (Other film sources make no mention of this film.) From late 1919 until 1926, he made about 25 films in Austria and Germany, before coming to the United States.

As in the case of his compatriot Paul Fejos, Curtiz's Hungarian films are now lost.

43. Luciano Emmer (1918–)

Destino d'Amore. 1943. Produced by Dolimiti Film Producing Co. Directed and scripted by Luciano Emmer, Enrico Gras, and Tatiana Grauding. Unreleased.

Land of Mussolini's Birth (Il Paese del Nascita Mussolini). 1943. Produced by Dolimiti Film Producing Company. Unreleased.

Luciano Emmer is a highly regarded director of documentaries on art and artists. He has shown great skill in editing. In the 1940s and 1950s, when he made a number of shorts, he often produced films noted for their mood and pace, particularly *Giotto* (*Racconto da un Fresco*, 1940), *Il Paradiso Terrestre* (on Bosch, 1946), *Leonardo da Vinci* (1952), and *Picasso* (1954). In 1950, when he began making feature-length films, he made *Sunday in August* (*Domenica d'Agosto*), a humorous, neorealist film about the bourgeoisie.

Luciano Emmer got his start in films in Italy during World War II. He, Tatiana Grauding (his wife), and Enrico Gras formed the Dolimiti Film Producing Company to explore the world of film and to express their opposition to fascism. Working at home studios, the three first tested their ability through editing to bring to life static objects. Unaware as to what they would come up with, they created the short *Destino d'Amore* in 1943. The outcome was a satire of the romance between a maid and an Italian soldier at the front. The three filmmakers told their story through their editing of the postcards the lovers sent to each other.

But the official reaction was not what they expected. The Ministry of Culture banned the work for being "a ridiculous insult to the love life of the heroic fascist soldier."

Their next film was called *Land of Mussolini's Birth*, a work Emmer was forced to produce on orders of the Italian ministry. Emmer demonstrated his skill by making another film that caused trouble. A surrealistic work, it tells the tale of a woman wearing black shrouding and carrying a scythe who roams Il Duce's birthplace. Feeling threatened by this piece of cinema, Mussolini destroyed all copies of the film, and outlawed similar kinds of efforts on the part of the three collaborators.

Emmer and his wife immediately fled to Switzerland, but Gras remained behind, having been forced to join the Italian Army. After the war, the three reunited. Up until 1949, Emmer, Grauding, and Gras went on to create their score of notable short documentaries about artists and painting, which a critic hailed for rekindling "the spirit of inquiry and exploration in the field of cinema. Their freshness and sincerity, and the complete disregard for the commercial that is reflected in their personalities and wit, are happy signs of perhaps greater things to come."

44. John Ford (1895–1973)

Vietnam! Vietnam! 1972, 58 min. John Ford, executive producer. Produced by Bruce Herschensohn. Directed by Sherman Beck. Script by John Ford and Thomas Duggan. Narrated by Charlton Heston. Unreleased in U.S.

Chesty. 1976, 28 min. Made-for-TV movie. Directed by John Ford. Produced by James Ellsworth. Written by Jay Simms. Photographed by Brick Marquard. Music by Jack Marshall. Commentary by John Wayne. Unreleased.

The American film master John Ford recapitulated the lives of American heroes in 40 years of sound films. Yet his last two film projects, vigorously defending United States military conduct in the Vietnam War, were never distributed in the United States. *Vietnam! Vietnam!* was regarded as an embarrassment by release time in early 1972 when antiwar sentiment was high. *Chesty*, the portrait of a career military officer, excited little interest.

John Ford was not unused to making documentaries about war. As a navy lieutenant commander in World War II, he served as chief of the Field Photographic Branch of the Office of Strategic Services. His team, including Gregg Toland, Budd Schulberg, Garson Kanin, and Robert Parish, shot documentary footage for propaganda. War's end found the director, now a rear admiral, preparing a film for intended use as evidence at the Nuremberg Trials (The film was not shown.)

The documentary *Vietnam! Vietnam!* (originally titled *Inside Vietnam*) was a production of the United States Information Agency (USIA), shot in Vietnam and the United States in the last three months of 1968, when America was electing a new president. John Ford, although in Saigon, did not participate directly in the filming nor did he direct. Instead he lent his name to the project, and served as executive producer, rewriting the script and overseeing the editing of the film. By agency standards, the film was costly ($250,000) and long. More than 60,000 feet of film was shot and then pared down by Ford to express his point of view.

Charlton Heston narrates the one hour, two-part film, full of techniques Ford usually avoided: zooms, soft-focus photography, and shades of gray. The first part of the film, entitled "Vietnam: The People and the War," opens with stills of headlines from the era and emphasizes some of

Unidentified actors in Vietnam! Vietnam!*, 1971, directed by John Ford and sponsored by the United States Information Agency.*

Ford's well-known themes: the war's toll on families and homes and the misery of old men, women, and children. The film then goes on to cover the search for POWs, the role of the Soviet Union, and the peace demonstrations back home. Director Ford, who in 1964 said, "I love America, I am apolitical," also presents the theme that the United States had to take the war to North Vietnam to end it.

The second half of the film, entitled "Vietnam: The Debate," comprises discussions of the war featuring such personalities as William Fulbright, President Lyndon Johnson, Dean Rusk, and Eugene McCarthy. Its theme is most clearly enunciated by Dwight Eisenhower:

> If you're going to fight a war, I believe in winning—because you're losing lives. And this one thing ought to be the number one priority. And whenever you get into a war ... get everything you can, as fast as you can, use everything you can, and get it over with.

The question, concludes the segment's narrator, is whether the "flame of freedom" in Vietnam "would be a permanent light ... or would be extinguished."

Since Ford's documentary was a USIA film, it was prohibited by law from any public screenings in the United States so as not to influence public policy. Characterized as a "dead duck" that would "stay in the can" by an information agency official after Ford completed editing the film in June 1971, *Vietnam! Vietnam!* became available for private showings in 1972 after newspapers reported its existence. *Vietnam! Vietnam!* opens with the phrase "A John Ford Film" and concludes without any end title.

John Ford's last military documentary, *Chesty*, was made for television. It looked at the career of Lt. Gen. Lewis (Chesty) Puller, who served in the Marine Corps during the Vietnam War. Ford worked on the film between August 1968 and April 1970, shooting scenes of the general at his home in Virginia, visiting the tombs of Robert E. Lee and Stonewall Jackson, and paying calls to VMI and the Marine barracks in the nation's capital.

Chesty includes footage from Ford's 50-minute documentary *This Is Korea* (1951), a compilation that contains footage he never shot but which, nonetheless, expresses his point of view. But soon after, when the 60-minute film was ready for release, television stations weren't interested. Ford shortened *Chesty* by half to make it more attractive, but there were still virtually no takers. The one public showing of the film was at Filmex in Los Angeles in April 1976, three years after Ford died. The host of the evening, who provided the commentary in the film, was John Wayne.

45. Alfred Hitchcock (1899–1980)

Aventure Malgache (Madagascar Landing). 1944, 31 min., in French. Produced by Crown Film Unit of the British Ministry of Information. Photographed by Günther Krampf. Sets by Charles Gilbert. With the Molière Players. Unreleased.

Bon Voyage. 1944, 26 min., in French. Produced by Crown Film Unit of the British Ministry of Information. Script by J. O. Orton and Angus McPhail. Photographed by Günther Krampf. Sets by Charles Gilbert. With John Blythe (Sgt. John Dougall) and the Molière Players. Unreleased in U.S.

In his long career, Alfred Hitchcock left unfinished his first directorial effort, called *Number Thirteen* (1922); two medium-length films, made in French for the Allied war effort, were never released in the United States. One, titled *Aventure Malgache* (1944), which was banned in 1944, is unique in Hitchcock's career. The director stirred controversy by modeling the characters on coarse-speaking Gaullist supporters and commenting on France's recent history of Vichy collaboration and colonialism.

In April 1944, Hitchcock returned to Britain after an absence of four years. Jean Mercure, today a theatre director, was in London then as an adviser to the director and noted that "the English have entrusted Hitchcock with two middle-length films on the Resistance." Hitchcock, who saw himself as "overweight and overage for military service," told François Truffaut years later, "I knew that if I did nothing [for the war effort] I'd regret it for the rest of my life." At the request of Sidney Bernstein, who headed the film section of the British Ministry of Information, Hitchcock shot *Aventure Malgache*, which turned out to be one of the few films of the era that showed how the French reacted to the armistice of June 1940. He made this and his other French short with the assistance of French advisors—they helped, for instance, reconstruct De Gaulle's headquarters on the set and assured that his portrait was in evidence—and employed the Molière Players, exiled French actors.

Aventure Malgache, filmed entirely in French, has dialogue supplied by the French actor and Resistance fighter Claude Dauphin. Concentrating on the obstacles that plagued the efforts of a lawyer named Clarousse to organize opposition to the Vichy-controlled government of Madagascar, the film begins with these titles:

195

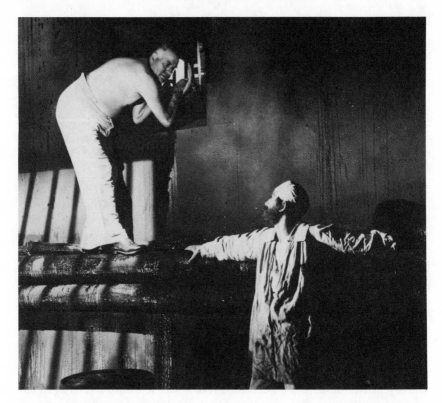

Aventure Malgache, *1944. Gaullists (played by the Molière Players) in prison in Madagascar.*

> The whole world has resounded with the dramatic episodes of the Resistance in France. You know this heroic period ... better than we do. The story we are about to tell you will not teach you anything.... If we tell it, it is because it is true. And because it shows that in the most distant possessions of the French Empire ... the same spirit animates the people....

> London 1944. A handful of actors ... were charged by the French military authorities with forming a troupe to stage shows for the soldiers, civilians, and the many Englishmen who know and love France. One of the actors ... had been a lawyer in Madagascar before the war. On June 28, 1940 ... but let us listen to his story.

Hitchcock begins the film by showing the actors working out their roles and then flashes back to show Clarousse's Resistance efforts on Madagascar. The lawyer attempts to set up clandestine departures to London. Later on he tries to install a secret radio transmitter "to speak to the French, but also to the Madagascans, to the Indians and to the Chinese, in a language they could understand." Betrayed by a supposed supporter, Clarousse is tried and condemned to death by the island government. Only the fact that he is a veteran of Verdun saves his life.

Sentenced to hard labor, he is shipped off to prison, but is rescued by the British. He convinces the British to help him set up his transmitter. He then radios: "Friends, let us proclaim the political and economic autonomy of Madagascar, and side with the Allies." He fails to convince the hard-core Pétainists, who see the British as their enemy.

When in May 1942 the British finally secure the island, the Vichy-supporting government changes course. Hitchcock shows them welcoming the liberators with parades and flags. But the Gaullists are upset that their allies now occupy the island. They fear the implications of appearing to be followers of the English.

To further underline the ambiguity of the reactions among the French to the Resistance, Hitchcock focuses on exchanges between the theatre actors. One actor exclaims to Clarousse, "I begin to see my character: greasy, slimy, a prick like Laval." Later on, dressed as a gendarme, he says to Clarousse, who is attired as an English general: "You claim nature has endowed me to play the role of the vile Michel [a Vichy supporter]. It's an insult coming from a 10th-rate lawyer. Pig! Asshole!" Clarousse responds with "Shut the fuck up." Called to account for why they're verbally "killing one another," Clarousse responds, "We are rehearsing." They then go on stage, at which point *Aventure Malgache* ends.

In this film, Hitchcock used Günther Krampf as photographer. The man who had photographed Slatan Dudow's anti–Nazi film *Kühle Wampe* (1932) evocatively employed expressionistic shadows to fill in the interior and prison scenes of *Aventure Malgache*. He would do the same for the dark streets of *Bon Voyage*.

Bon Voyage—strange title for a story about Allied resistance—is Hitchcock's lesson in the art of interpreting appearances in time of war. It is told two ways: In a straightforward fashion, it starts off with the interrogation in London of an RAF pilot (John Blythe) by a French agent. The pilot describes how he escaped German-occupied France with the help of his underground guide, a Polish officer named Stephane, and a young woman named Jeanne. At the conclusion of the interview, the French officer reveals the startling fact that Stephane was a member of the Gestapo and, more surprisingly, the Nazis wanted the pilot to succeed in escaping.

Then, in flashback commentary, the same events—shown from the point of view of the bad guy Stephane—reveal the true costs of the escape: the capture and death of those who helped the RAF pilot along the way. This meant the lives of several Resistance fighters and, worst of all, that of Jeanne.

The murder of Jeanne—comparable to a murder scene in Hitchcock's

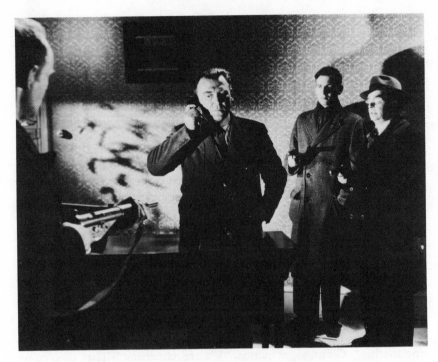

Bon Voyage, *1944. The German agent is caught at last.*

film *Topaz* (1969)—is the high point of the film. After she bids the pilot, "Goodbye RAF, have a good trip," and he flies to freedom, she takes out her notebook and phones her friends that all is well. At that point, Stephane grabs the phone and his gun appears in close-up. Seeing she is evidently shocked, he says, "I won't make you wait." There's a shot and the woman falls. The agent then claims the notebook and the dead woman's watch and ends the phone conversation with, "The carrier pigeon has flown away."

Hitchcock, however, doesn't leave it there. He uses a classic backward tracking shot to show three Resistance fighters capturing the Gestapo agent. The RAF pilot is consoled in the end by the interrogator: "You're thinking of the poor little Jeanne. . . . Yes, all that's terrible. But maybe someday . . . there will be another tomb under the Arc de Triomphe: that of the Unknown Civilian."

When the war ended, Hitchcock worked on a documentary about the concentration camps. Footage of the film shot in Germany was released in the mid–1980s. With no family left in England but a sister, Hitchcock returned to Hollywood. There he and the scriptwriter for *Bon Voyage* began work on *Spellbound* (1945).

Aventure Malgache and *Bon Voyage* can be found in the archives of the British Film Institute, London.

Other Lost Films

Number Thirteen. 1922, two reels. Script by Anita Ross. Production by W. and F. Film Service. Photographed by J. Rosenthal. With Clare Greet and Ernest Thesiger. Unfinished.

In 1920, Alfred Hitchcock got his start in films writing and designing titles for Famous Players–Lasky at their Islington studios in Britain. That year Hitchcock's first try at directing a one-reeler (*Always Tell Your Wife*) fell through when he became ill. By 1922, the Islington branch of the American company had turned out a dozen undistinguished films. Its survival was in doubt. Like a lot of other people during this year of films, Hitchcock was given another chance to direct.

The film's script was by Anita Ross, who was a publicity representative for the studio and who knew Hitchcock. In Hollywood she had worked with Chaplin, so her ideas for the film and suggestion that Hitchcock direct carried some weight.

Hitchcock referred to the film as *Number Thirteen*; the records of the Famous Players–Lasky studio refer to it as *Mrs. Peabody*. It seems to have been a comedy, starring American actress Clare Greet and a British stage actor. When it was in mid-production the American owners closed the studio. The film, which Hitchcock told Truffaut "wasn't very good, really," is now lost.

But Hitchcock did not forget his first star. Clare Greet performed in his 1929 film *The Manxman* and in three other films, including his English film *Jamaica Inn* (1939).

IX. MATTERS OF STATE

Every work of art which is known to the public influences public opinion. Remember Oscar Wilde's quip, that there was no fog before Turner painted it.

—Jean Renoir, 1959

The art of the cinema is the creation of illusion. The "art" of propaganda is to make people think that they are thinking for themselves when they are actually being manipulated. Beginning in the 1920s, filmmakers from the Soviet Union achieved worldwide praise while making use of propaganda and their "scientific" film techniques to serve social purposes. Until the 1950s, their techniques impressed other filmmakers outside the country eager to make "artistically progressive films."

The great filmmakers from authoritarian regimes have understood as20 well as any that illusion depends on the carefully calculated reactions of the audience. Working under restrictions themselves, they were rarely immune from official censors. Still, a number of directors from Russia, Eastern Europe, and other undemocratic regimes at times hesitated to serve the state in its call for more propaganda. Such highly respected directors as Mikhail Kalatazov, Lev Kuleshov, V. I. Pudovkin, and Sergei Yutkevich then found themselves under the glare of the state. Even lesser known colleagues, with less to say or less talent at their disposal, sometimes created films that came under scrutiny. For instance, the team of Alexander Alov and Valdimir Naumov, who collaborated in making competent works for the Soviet screen from 1951 on, found that their 1965 film *Nasty Incident*, based on a Dostoyevski story, could not be released. For reasons of state, with "reasons" sometimes never provided, these directors found their works suppressed.

In the late 1960s in Czechoslovakia, eminent filmmakers saw their films banned. Karel Kachyna's two late works from the "Prague Spring," *Funny Old Man* (1969) and *The Ear* (1970), touched on the effects of the political trials of the 1950s and the system the Communists created. Jiri Menzel's *Larks on a Thread* (1969) satirized the "reeducation of bourgeois elements" within the country, while Evald Schorm's *The Seventh Day, the*

201

Eighth Night (1969) was a moral tale that revealed the characteristics of people who submit to manipulation.

In India in 1971, the highly regarded director Satyajit Ray made the short documentary *Sikkim*. Apparently too controversial a look at the culture of an Indian minority, the government banned its showing. The only copy of the film has remained forgotten for the last 20 years in the archives of an American university.

Even by the 1980s, a director as skilled and highly regarded as Soviet filmmaker Gleb Panfilof (born 1937) could find that "no action taken by me or anyone else would have any effect" on getting his film *Tema* (*The Theme*, 1980) released.

A director whose films alternate between tragedy and Frank Capra-style comedy, Panfilof made three films beginning in the late 1960s. His third, called *I Wish to Speak* (1975), which depicted life in a closed society, was hailed by European critics as one of the best Soviet films of recent years. Then the director ran into trouble with *Tema*, about a playwright unable to find intimacy in a rigid Soviet system. Shown at the Moscow Film Festival in 1981 and then in Tallinn and Leningrad, *Tema* had the temerity to postulate that Soviet dramatists would waste their talents for the state.

Told by a party official that *Tema* was very good, even shocking, Panfilof also heard the official announce, "We cannot release it. You must wait." The director found himself unable to make films about "real life, modern life"; Panfilof's art remained unseen until the advent of *glasnost*.

In 1990, Panfilof's *Tema* made its premier in the United States. It was quietly shown on PBS. In addition, the changing political atmosphere in Europe has broken the logjam of some unreleased films that still exist. Schorm's *The Seventh Day, the Eighth Night* premiered in the United States at Joseph Papp's Film at the Public Theatre (New York City) in June 1990; Kachyna's *The Ear* was the official Czechoslovak entry at the 1990 Cannes Film Festival; and Menzel's *Larks on a Thread* was voted best film at the 1990 Berlin Film Festival.

46. Juan Antonio Bardem (1922–   )

La Muerte de Pío Baroja. 1957, one reel. Produced by Caro Baroja. Photographed by Carlos Saura. Unfinished. With Pío Baroja.

The Spanish director Juan Bardem became internationally well known for the films *Death of a Cyclist* (1955) and *Calle Mayor* (1956). These films dramatized the alienation many felt under Franco's rule. Bardem's main character was often named Juan. To escape his humdrum, vegetative existence in a repressive regime, Juan was often forced to find outlets that took the form of insignificant busy work and hobbies. Unable, finally, to take it any longer, Juan would somehow draw up the courage to reevaluate his surroundings and ask for change.

In the late 1950s Bardem took a keen look at those who thought only of themselves and refused to stand up for what was right: "Selfishness, I mean the fight against it, is the main subject to . . . Spanish realism that myself and others attempt to create. I believe that in everything that I have done till now, under cover of simple anecdote, this theme reappears, orchestrated in major or minor keys."

It was almost natural, then, that Bardem turned to an example of someone who had established a reputation for courage. Bardem, a communist, made a film about the last days of one of Spain's most acclaimed writers, the Basque Pío Baroja y Nessi (1872–1956).

Educated as a physician Pío Baroja early on became associated with change. Not yet 26, he was already identified with the so-called Generation of 1898. These were young men who sought through their words and opposition to end the torpor, corruption, and dogmatism of their nation in the wake of defeat in the Spanish-American War. Members of this informal group included the writers Unamuno, Antonio Machado, and Ganivet.

Baroja was a prolific chornicler of his times. Camilo José Cela, a contemporary, stressed that Baroja opened the doors to a novelistic Spain, revealing the possibilities of the novel: "The entire Spanish novel after Baroja stems from him." His popular works include *Memoirs of a Man of Action* (22 vol., 1913–34), about nineteenth century Spain, and *The Struggle for Existence* (3 vol., 1945), about the underworld in Madrid.

Juan Bardem's film *La Muerte de Pío Baroja* is the story of the famous

Pío Baroja in La Muerte de Pío Baroja, *1957. This unfinished film by Juan Bardem looked at one of the true Spanish heroes during the rule of Franco. The stills here are from the footage used for the 1965 short* La Ultima Vuelta del Camino, *assembled by Pío Baroja's nephew.*

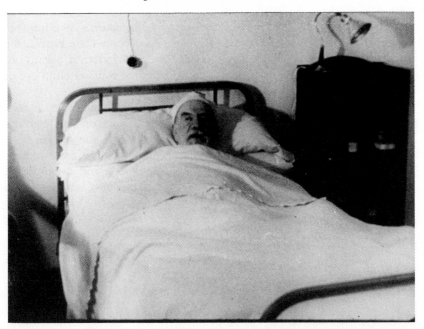

From La Muerte de Pío Baroja. Top: *Baroja near death.* Bottom: *Baroja's funeral, 1957.*

writer's last days. A short made, according to film sources at Filmoteca Española (Madrid), at the behest of Pío Baroja's nephew Caro Baroja, the unfinished *La Muerte de Pío Baroja* is nevertheless of interest because of the subject matter Bardem explored while under the ever watchful eye of Franco.

Using cameraman Carlos Saura, who would later establish his own reputation as a director, Bardem shot one reel of footage on the life of the respected writer. Then, apparently, when director and sponsor disagreed on what was to follow or how they were to proceed, shooting was halted.

Caro Baroja eventually took possession of all footage and incorporated it into his own 1965 short *La Ultima Vuelta del Camino* (*Last Turn in the Road*).

In his most recent production, Juan Bardem is said to be filming *Lorca, Muerte de un Poeta* (*Lorca, Death of a Poet*).

47. Slatan Dudow (1903–1963)

How Does the Berlin Worker Live? (Wie lebt der berliner Arbeiter).
1930, 2000 ft. Produced by Welt-Film Series. Photographed and scripted by
Dudow. Unfinished series.

**Kühle Wampe, oder Wem gehart die Welt (Cold Bellies, or Who Owns
the World?).** 1932, 6600 ft. Produced by Prometheus (Berlin). Scripted by
Dudow and Bertolt Brecht. Unreleased.

Bulgarian director Slatan Dudow made 10 films in his career. His first
full-length film and his last film went unfinished.

In Berlin in 1930, Slatan Dudow, an avowed communist, intended his
first feature-length film, *What Does the Berlin Worker Want?* (*Wie der berliner
Arbeiter wohnt*) as the first in a series of short "proletarian documentaries"
collectively entitled *How Does the Berlin Worker Live?*

In making *What Does the Berlin Worker Want?* Dudow used a hidden
camera to make a film that, a reviewer wrote in August 1930, "does not appease, but arouses, that shows the proletariat its wretched existence in an
unadorned manner." Shooting under difficult circumstances, the director
captured on film dark burrows used for living quarters—six, seven, eight
people in a narrow room—in the southeast and the north of Berlin. He
showed ragged and sick children, the dying old, Berliners out of work, the
hungry, people being forceably evicted from their homes, and an unemployment office on Gormann Street, where "applications for work were
heaped up to the size of a huge mountain." Then, to contrast this picture
of despair, Dudow filmed the "beneficiaries" of German order who enjoyed
life in castlelike villas in the Grunewald section of Berlin, surrounded by
their healthy children and well-treated dogs.

What Does the Berlin Worker Want? so alarmed the German authorities
that they banned it, putting to rest any ideas Dudow had for finishing his
series. Experienced in the theatre—his 1929 experimental short *Soap Bub-
bles* (*Seifenblasen*) looked at the Soviet stage—Dudow turned to writing and
directing plays with Bertolt Brecht, who, in turn, coscripted Dudow's next
film. Known as *Kühle Wampe* (*Cold Bellies*) or *Who Owns the World?* it
became Dudow's masterpiece. Nearly completed just before Hitler came

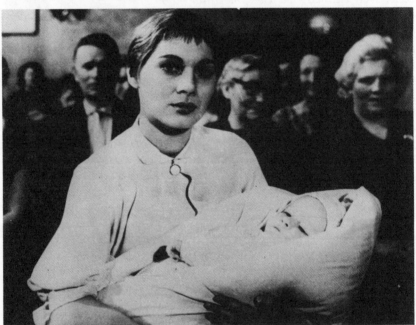

Christine, 1963. Annette Woska portrays Christine in Slatan Dudow's unfinished last film.

The director Slatan Dudow (wearing eye patch) on the set of Christine.

to power, when the production company went backrupt, *Kühle Wampe*—named for an unemployed workers' barracks near Berlin— was an explosive piece of propaganda about communists routing Nazis.

What distinguished this work about the lives of ordinary working-class people in Germany were the views and dialogue of Brecht and the filmmaking skill of Dudow. The playwright's discussion, for instance, aboard a crowded train about the place of coffee in society, whether it should be sold below market prices, given to the poor, or dumped into the sea, aroused passions to the hilt. Dudow's editing of footage that captured thousands of extras—exhibiting the influence of G. W. Pabst and Soviet filmmakers—resulted in an ultrarealistic document of a society at the end of its rope.

Kühle Wampe suffered the same fate as Dudow's first effort: It was banned, decreed the authorities, for "insulting Hindenburg and religion." No complete version of the film exists today.

When Hitler came to power. Dudow fled to Switzerland. There he again wrote and directed plays. In 1946 he moved to East Germany; three years later he joined the DEFA studios and resumed filmmaking. His films were political tracts, anticapitalist and anti–West, yet they displayed talent. The most highly regarded were *Women's Fate* (1952), a vitriolic story of a philanderer and the woman he seduces, and *Stronger Than the Night*

(1952), a tale of communist resistance to the Nazis. In 1956 Dudow made the *Captain from Cologne*, a virulent story about the reunion of former Nazis.

Other Lost Films

Christine. 1963. 105 min. Photographed by Helmut Bergmann. Design by Joachim Otto. With Annette Woska (Christine), Gunther Haack, Horst Schulze, Armin Mueller-Stahl, Friedo Solter, Gunther Schubert, Elsa Grube-Deiser. Unfinished.

In 1963, veteran director Dudow turned his attention to the problem of women's liberation. In filming *Christine*, Dudow tried to remain true to the principle of epic realism which he had discovered with Brecht 30 years earlier. Besides, he was a dramatist at heart and needed the structure of drama to present his proletarian-revolution world view. His story had a heroine: a girl with four illegitimate children who becomes a woman and mother assuming her place in society.

In July of that year, Dudow died of injuries sustained in an auto accident. His death prevented our getting to know his movie about Christine.

48. Mikhail Kalatozov (1903–1973)

Nail in the Boot (Gvozd v sapogye). 1932. Script by A. Bezimensky. With Akaki Khorava. Unreleased.

The Georgian filmmaker Kalatozov made his first film, *Blind*, in 1930. In a portent of things to come, his second film that year, *Salt for Svanetia*, was criticized for its "negativism," "naturalism," and "formalism." Much in the manner of Bunuel's *Land Without Bread*, it depicted the harsh realities of life in a primitive Soviet village. An American critic said (*Close Up*, 1931): "Kalatozov ... established his point of view at once in the bold image and stern grand angles." During World War II, the negative was destroyed; a print survives in the archives of Gosfilmofond.

Two years later, an even bolder effort by Kalatozov was suppressed altogether. *Nail in the Boot* took a critical and realistic look at Red Army maneuvers. In the climactic scene, a soldier loses one of the army's trains he was charged with protecting in training exercises. The reason? A missing nail in his shoddily made boot causes a foot injury at a key moment in the defense of the train. The mishap is still more ironic because in civilian life the soldier works in a shoe factory.

The film was banned by Soviet military commissars, who charged it was an affront to the glory of the Red Army. To no avail, Kalatozov denied the charges. In 1932, the Russian publication *Proletarskoye Kino* published his rebuttal. *Nail in the Boot*, Kalatozov claimed, was no attack on the army's inefficiency but a statement about the interdependence of industry, national defense, and civilian life. The film remained banned despite the unusual public nature of the dispute.

Kalatozov did not make another film until 1939, when he completed *Manhood*, a film about his country's aviation industry. He had withdrawn for seven years to his native Georgian city of Tiflis (Tbilisi) to be an administrator in a film studio. He was in familiar territory again. In the late 1920s he worked there as a cameraman for the director Lev Kuleshov.

In 1957, Kalatozov achieved international prominence with his twelfth film, *The Cranes Are Flying*, about wartime Russia, which won him the award as best director at Cannes. The film's focus on romance rather than propaganda—a Kalatozov trademark—marked a departure for the Soviet Union at this time. Among other things, the film made mention of draft dodgers. (Could this be viewed as an affront to the Red Army?)

49. Lev Kuleshov (1899–1970)

Steam Engine No. B-1000 (Paravoz No. B-1000). 1927. Produced by Goskinprom Gruzii. Script by Serge Tretiakov. Photographed by Mikhail Kalatozov. With a cast of nonprofessionals. Unfinished.

Theft of Sight. 1934. Artistic Supervisor: Lev Kuleshov. Produced by Mezhabpom. Script by Kuleshov, L. Obolensky, and L. Kassil. Directed by L. Obolensky. Unreleased.

Dohunda (The Beggar). 1936. Produced by Tajikistan Studio. Script by Osip Brik, from the novel by Nasreddin Aini. With Kamil Yarmatov, Tasia Rakhamanova, Komarov, and Svashenko. Unfinished.

Lev Kuleshov, the film theoretician and originator of the "Kuleshov effect," was once one of the "Big Five" in Soviet cinema, ranked alongside Eisenstein, Pudovkin, Vertov, and Room. In fact, Kuleshov taught more than half of the best-known Soviet directors since 1920 (including Pudovkin, Eisenstein, Kalatozov, and Parajanov). Yet in his 50 years in films, he, too, failed to finish a number of films. One major effort, *Steam Engine No. B-1000*, his film commemorating the tenth anniversary of the Revolution, was halted midway by the authorities. Of his score of films, only *The Extraordinary Adventures of Mr. West in the Land of the Bolsheviks* (1924) and *By the Law* (1926) are available for viewing in the United States.

In 1919, Kuleshov helped found the State Film School in Moscow. It was there that he propounded his theory of montage that called for the interweaving of shots of objects with shots of an actor's face to heighten viewers' awareness of an actor's mood. The viewer, he said, assigns meaning to facial expressions depending on the footage intercut. Kuleshov, eager to develop a "director's cinema" in which actors would be sensitive to what the director wanted, searched for "general laws governing the relationship of actor movement to cutting and composition." The net effect of this was that many of his pupils became directors.

The mid–1920s saw Kuleshov make his first full-length feature, *The Extraordinary Adventures of Mr. West in the Land of the Bolsheviks*, an American-style comedy starring Pudovkin (with a shot of Trotsky at the end of the film). *By the Law*, an adaptation of London's anti–capital

213

punishment story, "The Unexpected," also dated from this period. Together, the two films helped place Kuleshov, an acknowledged leader of "left cinema," in the pantheon of Soviet filmmaking.

In 1927 Kuleshov began working at Goskinprom Gruzzi (State Cinema Industry of Georgia) in Tiflis, which offered more room for experimentation. The suggestion to work there came from Serge Tretiakov, a scriptwriter for Eisenstein. Tretiakov also provided Kuleshov with the script for *Steam Engine No. B-1000*, the story of a locomotive's life from Czarist days through 1927, the tenth anniversary of the Revolution. Photographer Mikhail Kalatozov, then a cameraman at the film studio, threw himself into the project. But his effort would be wasted. According to the director, only the crowd scenes were shot before production was halted by the studio. Kuleshov was forced to stop the film because he was presenting a far too sympathetic portrayal of Trotsky.

The next year, Kuleshov and Kalatozov went on to make *The Sausage Factory*, a "very beautifully filmed" short, according to Kuleshov. The film is now lost. In 1930, Kalatozov himself became a director, and ran into his own filmmaking problems.

In 1933, Kuleshov directed his last great effort, *The Great Consolar*, the film that threatened to put a stop to his career at the age of 34. The film not only denounced the "counterfeit heroics" of American movies, but also attacked artists who sold out to the state, who created the "beautiful lies" their leaders wanted to hear. The fact that he was castigating himself did not mollify his angry critics. Kuleshov was denounced at the meeting of the Congress of Film Workers in 1935 for being an unrepentant representative of the "Formalist" school of the 1920s. Kuleshov had failed to make propaganda in a film that displayed a discernible style or form.

At the same meeting Kuleshov "confessed" that his recently completed film *Theft of Sight*, which he had supervised, was a "bad picture." Made while Soviet cinematography was celebrating its fifteenth anniversary, *Theft of Sight* dealt with the fight against illiteracy.

At first, Kuleshov had planned to shoot the movie alone, but when the film studio's administration turned down his choice of leading lady (A. S. Chochlowa), Kuleshov turned the reins over to another director. The new director had no better luck in finding a lead. Kuleshov reported that 16 actresses were tested for the role. When shooting was completed, 200,000 rubles had been spent. Claiming he "hadn't given himself up wholly to the work" and that it wasn't his "favorite child," Kuleshov requested permission to reshoot parts. The film studio turned him down and never released it.

Kuleshov's next project, *Dohunda*, suffered as well. An epic story, based on a well-known novel, about the Revolution and the establishment of Soviet power in Tadzhikistan, the film focuses on Jedgor, nicknamed Dohunda (the beggar), his hard life, and his great love for the beautiful Gulnor.

When Jedgor's beloved is made to marry a rich man, Jedgor enlists in the Army. After his region's liberation, he meets Gulnor again—she still loves him—and they find happiness together.

In making the film, Kuleshov and his screenwriter, Osip Brik, traveled through the young Soviet republic, familiarizing themselves with its historical sources, the Koran, and literature about central Asia. Everything went well until the film was sent to Stalinabad (now Duschanbe) for editing.

The raw material was screened without Kuleshov's knowledge and created a ruckus. As the director later pointed out, it was to be expected that the people at this meeting would understand nothing about the film; they knew nothing about movies, and many of them could not even understand Russian (the language spoken in the film). The local press saw the film as "a great distortion of reality and a false, schematic interpretation of Aini's [the author's] poetry."

B. Schumayatsky, the Soviet film censor, all too quickly then suppressed the film. Kuleshov still hoped to edit the material in later years, but found that the passions ignited by the film were still strong enough to endanger anyone attempting to ressurect the work. So the film Kuleshov called "cherished" was abandoned forever.

Dohunda suffered a fate similar to Eisenstein's *Bezhin Lug*, also shot in 1936. Suppressed by the state's chief censor, Kuleshov's unedited film disappeared, and its creator was forced to practice self-criticism. The one bright note came in 1956, after the death of Stalin, when Soviet director B. Kimjagarov made a version of *Dohunda* based on some surviving fragmentary footage of Kuleshov's lost film.

In 1941, Kuleshov wrote his massive work, *Fundamentals of Film Direction* (never translated into English). At the urging of director Sergei Yutkevich, he continued to make films, mostly for children, at the Detfilm Studio until 1944. Then, through the efforts of Eisenstein, he became head of the Moscow Film Institute. He remained unknown in the West and forgotten in his own country until Jay Leyda's book *Kino* brought his work to the attention of the film world in the early 1960s. He received the Order of Lenin in 1967.

In 1965, Kuleshov was asked whether production stopped in 1927 on *Steam Engine No. B-1000* for the same reason that Eisenstein that same year had to redo *Ten Days That Shook the World*. "Your hypothesis is correct," he said, referring to Eisenstein's glowing treatment of Trotsky in his film.

When Kuleshov died in March 1970, he was buried alongside the poet-playwright-screenwriter Vladimir Mayakovsky in the Novodevicha Cemetary in Moscow. In the same cemetery are buried Turgenev, Chekov, Gogol, and other distinguished artists, statesmen, and scientists. His death marked the passing of the old guard in Soviet filmmaking.

Unshown Films

The films by Kuleshov unavailable in the West are:

The Project of Engineer Prite, 1918 (2 reels survive).

The Unfinished Love Song, 1919.

On the Red Front, 1920 (2-reeler, and first Soviet film to combine documentary footage and actual acting scenes).

The Death Ray, 1925 (8 reels; 4th and 8th reels missing).

Your Acquaintance/Journalist, 1927 (6 reels; only reel two survives).

The Gay Canary, 1929 (6 reels; partially preserved).

Breakthrough, 1930 (1 reel).

Forty Hearts, 1931 (5 reels).

Horizon—The Wandering Jew, 1932 (7 reels; Kuleshov's first sound film, thought lost; at Film Institute, Moscow).

The Great Consoler, 1933 (8 reels).

The Siberians, 1940 (10 reels; children's film).

Incident in a Volcano, 1941 (7 reels).

Timur's Death, 1942 (6 reels).

We Are from the Urals, 1944 (9 reels).

50. Vsevolod I. Pudovkin (1893–1953)

The Murderer Takes to the Road (Ubiitsy vykhodyat na Dorogu). 1942, 7 reels (1715 meters). Produced by Studio-Central, Alma-Ata. Directed by Pudovkin and Yuri Taritch. Script by Pudovkin and E. Bolshintsov (from a Brecht play). Photographed by Boris Volchok and E. Zaveliev. Design by Alexis Berger. Music by Nicholai Krioukov. With Valere Kulakov (German soldier), Pyotr Sobolevsky (German soldier), Olga Zhizneva (Clara), Ada Voitsik (Marta), A. Antonov, Boris Blinov, Oleg Zhakov, and Sophie Magarill. Unreleased.

V. I. Pudovkin acted in and directed films from 1921 to 1953. During this period he made *Mother* (1926), *The End of St. Petersburg* (1928), *Storm Over Asia* (1929), *Deserter* (1933), and *General Suvorov* (1941). His work *The Murderer Takes to the Road* is the only completed film by this great Russian director never released.

The German invasion of the Soviet Union in 1941 forced Pudovkin to abandon plans for a sequel to his great sound film *General Suvorov*, and retreat to the countryside. At new film studios in Alma-Ata in central Asia, he began making propaganda newsreels, combat documentaries, and films for a compilation work called the *Military Film Albums.* One result was *The Murderer Takes to the Road* (subtitled The Face of Fascism/School for Villainy). The film is based on a series of short plays and sketches by Bertolt Brecht about the early years of Nazi control in Germany.

The theme of the film is fear: the simple numbing fear of betrayal many people felt in Hitler's Germany; a fear that destroyed normal life and made citizens self-conscious before the closest family members, even children.

The emotion-filled seven-reeler, like nearly all of Pudovkin's films, used the manipulation of space to enhance the story. By contrasting intense close-ups with huge openings-up of the screen, Pudovkin placed his characters solidly in their environments. Soviet officials, however, according to an observer named Karaganov, found the tale of Nazi horror too close a parallel to life in the Soviet Union. Wartime exigencies led communist officials—the party, the NKVD (now the KGB), and the Young Communist League—to encourage the act of informing as a patriotic duty.

In addition, the source for the film, Brecht, had been banned in the Soviet Union. The country was then in a life-and-death struggle with Hitler, and the times demanded something else. The film was put on hold. Over the years, all references to it were expunged from official histories of Soviet films.

This film signaled the start of restrictions on Pudovkin by communist officials. The director of the highly praised *Storm Over Asia* was assigned to commissar D. Vasiliev, the same man who had made sure that Eisenstein stuck to the "approved" script for *Alexander Nevsky* (1938). Under official scrutiny, Pudovkin in 1943 made *In the Name of the Fatherland* (codirected by D. Vasiliev, and based on K. Simonov's play *The Russian People*). As a story about Russians opposing the S.S., the film displayed little of Pudovkin's emotional range and fantastic shots. The party's chief censor, A. S. Scherbakov, said, "Pudovkin's film is a failure."

Three years later Pudovkin made *Admiral Nakhimov* (1946), a film about the defender of Sevastopol during the Russo-Turkish war of 1853. But his work was condemned by the communist party's central committee this way: "Pudovkin . . . undertook the production of a film on Nakhimov without studying the details of the matter, and distorted historical truth. The result was a film . . . about balls and dances." Pudovkin released a revised version in 1947. Containing more battle scenes, the remade *Admiral Nakhimov* won prizes at Locarno and Venice and garnered the director the Stalin Prize that year.

Except for *General Suvorov*, Pudovkin's later films are not readily available in the West.

51. Laszlo Ranody (1919–1983)

Stars (Csillagosok). 1950. Produced by Jeno Katona. Script by Erno Urban. Photographed by Gyorgy Illes and Istvan Paszior. With Maria Fonay, Maria Majlath, Vioja Orban, Josef Bihari, Jeno Bodnar, Jozsei Juhasz, Janos Maklary, Zoltan Maklary, and Gellert Raksanyi. Unreleased.

Veteran Hungarian director Laszlo Ranody attempted to make his first film in 1943. A stage drama, it was rejected by the censors. Ranody worked for seven years as an assistant director before he tried again to make his own film. In 1950, he filmed *Stars*, a contemporary story of a farmer's cooperative in his native Hungary. *Stars* was banned by the authorities for ideological reasons. It has never been released.

In the postwar era when Ranody made this film, the Russian director Pudovkin twice visited Hungary in his capacity as a film adviser. He said that many of the country's filmmakers filmed "as though one saw the world through a telescope at a distance of many kilometers."

Hungarian productions were vehicles for propaganda. As a means with which to demonstrate the problems covered in the press, the cinema in Hungary had one role only: to give a picture of what life should be like. The camera rarely took note of what life was actually like for the average human.

It is plausible to assume that Ranody crossed the line in making *Stars*. A director with a law degree whose doctorate was in film law, Ranody may have looked a bit too closely at working-class conditions. He may have failed to embellish the film with enough optimism; the lawyer-director might have commented on something sensitive and controversial.

Ranody did not complete—and have released—a film of his own until 1954. This was a comedy called *The Love Travelling Coach*.

Ranody supervised television productions and directed ten films over the next 25 years. Nearly all were adaptations from literature. Ranody more than once adapted the work of Zsigmond Moricz. His most successful films were *Be Good Till Death* (1960), *Skylark* (1964), which netted Antal Pager the Best Actor prize at Cannes, and *No Man's Daughter* (1976).

Hungarian film documentation indicates that the film *Stars* is in the archives of the Institute of Theatrical and Film Sciences, Budapest.

52. Sergei Yutkevich (1904–1985)

Light Over Russia (Tsvet nad Rossiei). 1947. Produced by Mosfilm. Script by Nicholai Pogodin. From the play *The Kremlin Chimes* by Pogodin. With Mikhail Gelovani (Stalin), Nicholai Kolesnikov (Lenin), Nicholai Okhlopkov (Zabeline), Boris Livanov (Vladimir Mayakovsky), Vemyamin Zuskin, and Nicholai Kryuchkov. Unreleased.

The Russian director Sergei Yutkevich began making films in 1926. He managed to make two dozen films in 50 years, collaborating with Eisenstein and Abraham Room. His work, which covered a broad range of contemporary and historic subjects in a realistic style, forms a transition between the first and second generation of great Russian filmmaker. In addition, Yutkevich was concerned with dramaturgy and sought out dramatists to develop material for him.

Sergei Yutkevich had a reputation as a director without problems. Yet in the Soviet Union he made few movies that did not cause him difficulties. He had to spend three years, for instance, tailoring his 1934 film *Miners* (*Shakhory*) to official requirements before it would be released in 1937. Then after the war, one of his films ran into real trouble, and his career was in jeopardy. While Yutkevich was never openly accused, he saw his 1947 film *Light Over Russia* banned by Stalin. It is probable Stalin reacted negatively for a number of reasons. One was that Yutkevich was born in Leningrad.

Throughout his life, Stalin demonstrated an implacable loathing towards the city which until 1924 was called St. Petersburg. This meant artists, survivors of the siege of World War II, political leaders, and others could be targets of his wrath. In the period 1947–48, Stalin even purged the party of Zhdanov, Leningrad's loathsome party secretary and "savior" of the city during the siege, his close associates, and 2,000 lesser officials. The more important ones were arrested and shot. Althouh no one has said it outright, it is thus very plausible that Yutkevich just might have been the wrong man making the wrong film at the wrong time. What may have saved his neck, ironically, was Stalin's curious respect for artists.

By 1947, when Yutkevich completed *Light Over Russia*, Stalin had instituted a longstanding requisite of reviewing everything produced by the

Soviet film industry: nothing was released without his approval. His favorites were civil war films in which he was depicted as the hero. Stalin would even speak about any outstanding portrayal of Stalin in the third person. Thus, any film—and those people associated with it—that ran short of outright glorification faced censure. In *Light Over Russia*, Stalin appeared in only two or three scenes at Lenin's side.

Further, the subject matter of *Light Over Russia*, too painful for Stalin to contemplate, might have been a contributing factor to its ban. *Light Over Russia* (also called *Dawn Over Russia*), some of it in color—color was important for Soviet films that year—recounted how in the cold and hunger of winter 1920, Lenin's idea to electrify one-sixth of the world took shape. It recounts how a great engineer, named Zabeline, opposed to the Revolution, let himself be convinced to work for his country. A parallel theme—the arduous restoration of the Kremlin Chimes, silent since 1917—symbolized the reconstruction of the Soviet Union's industrial machinery. To achieve his aim, director Yutkevich inserted documentary footage of the construction of the country's first dam on the Volkhov River and the first power stations. He also included allusions to the poets Alexander Blok and Vladimir Mayakovsky (also a playwright, screenwriter, and actor) and to Moscow's poets' cafes, where literary giants recited their verses and debated their adversaries.

The film's color sequences, meanwhile, foretold, as Yutkevich recounted, "a vision of the triumphant and victorious youth, our today, that, for the characters of the film, represented an unattainable dream." They centered on the hero named Rybakov, who also figured in the industrial construction.

At the end of the World War II, however, the Soviet "dream" was in shambles. Nothing worked, there was little food, people were on the move everywhere. At the same time, the Russian people were, according to observers, chauvinistic, a trait that showed itself in the belief that Russians were the inventors of most of the technical (and also nontechnical) wonders of the world. To have to admit that they once lacked electricity in the 1920s, and then again in the 1940s, was to go against an age-old myth encouraged in, and accepted at, all levels of society.

The upshot of all this was that Yutkevich's career was threatened by the ban. Yutkevich, labeled a "teenage artist of the Revolution" in the 1920s, once said "my country has give me everything. Trusting in me, it has given me the right for work for the 'most important of all the arts.'" He now found himself able to make only two films between 1948 and 1953, the year Stalin died.

In 1954, when the political climate eased in the Soviet Union, Yutkevich thrust himself on the international scene. His historical spectacle *Skanderberg* received a special jury prize at Cannes, and two years later he won the Best Director award there for *Othello*. Despite the change in Yutkevich's fortunes, the ban on his 1947 film remained in effect.

Light Over Russia no longer exists, but stills and fragments of the film survive because in 1960, shortly before Nicholai Pogodin's death, the dramatist-scriptwriter and the director tried to reconstruct the film. Much of it was missing, but Yutkevich found two scenes. He included them in a montage film called *The Most Human*, based on his Leninist films of the late 1950s and early 1960s. In addition, the scenario and the shooting script were rediscovered by A. Volgar, Pogodin's literary heir.

Of his vanished project, Yutkevich eventually exclaimed: "God, how I regret that the Soviet audience could not have seen this film! In my opinion, it was Okhlopov's best performance and he was inspired as Zabeline, I am not afraid to say. Better than any other, this character coalesced with the image of Don Quixote, graying and ungainly, in a long old-fashioned frock-coat."

The full script of *Light Over Russia* was published in Moscow in the 1970s. The following excerpt from the script was published in the book *Youtkevitch* by Jean and Luda Schnitzer.*

Light Over Russia

RED SQUARE

P.m. 19 Lenin:
—The clock of the Kremlin must not remain silent. Yet, it is silent.

Rybakov, moved, with emotion:

—Vladimir Illytch, I'm off to look for clockmakers. In all of Moscow... I'm going right now...

Lenin has put his hand on his shoulder:

—Yes, yes, clockmakers, it's very important. This carillon makes me lose my sleep... Yet, try to see farther, more broadly...

Lenin sighs deeply:

—You know, and only between us, Rybakov, I dream sometimes. I'm taking a walk by myself and I dream about the future...

I 1   Rybakov listens, holding his breath.

*Published 1976 by L'Âge d'Homme.

P.m. 20 After a short silence, Lenin catches the lapel of
Rybakov's peacoat and says gently, as if it were the
most banal thing in the world:

—I've been thinking a long time about the electrification of Russia.

Voiceless, Rybakov stares at him with admiration.

Lenin screws up his eyes:

—Well, Rybakov, what do you think of my idea?
We'll succeed, in this electrification of Russia?

Rybakov:

—Comrade Lenin, you're looking at thousands of
kilometers before you...

Lenin shaking his finger at him:

—Not a word about it in the meantime, huh? Don't
mention it to anyone. I'm the only one to know,
along with two, three comrades. If you talk about it,
they'll call me insane. Inspite of everything, it's only
a dream.

Gen. 2.5 He walks away. Rybakov at his side.

(Dissolve to black).

X. TOO HOT TO HANDLE

We strain with mighty straining
At a measly little gnat
And swallow a rhinoceros
And not an eyelid bat

—anonymous lines

It seems so quaint and long ago that battles were once waged over the use of the words "virgin," "pregnant," or "damn"; that men and women couldn't be shown in bed together; or that "lustful" kissing was prohibited. Yet the fact that films were considered mere entertainment made them suspect—and subject to censorship. Artistic or not, the treatment of sex was bound to be too hot to handle by some people. As Hollywood's chief censor for the producers and the distributors, Will Hays, said in 1924: "It is mighty essential that the more or less prevalent type of book and play not become a prevalent type of picture."

In the United States and elsewhere, the censor appeared when the un-draped body was shown on the screen. In Europe, the censor also banned violent subject matter, portrayal of cruelty, approval of suicide, and blasphemy.

Hollywood's own attempts to clean up its backyard began in the 1920s and 1930s, when drug use and open sex was rumored to be the norm in Hollywood. Will Hays, President Harding's campaign manager in 1920 and his first postmaster general, was called in to head the Association of Motion Pictures Producers and Distributors—to make sure films stayed in line with a new self-professed moral code on the part of filmmakers. By the time Hays left office, 10 states could be counted which already had censors; 100 cities had set up their own Hollywood watchdogs; and the other states were considering censorship bills of their own.

In 1927 Hollywood went a step further: It imposed self-censorship. A three-man committee, headed by Irving Thalberg, issued what became known as the "Don'ts and Be Carefuls" of filmmaking. In brief, they pro-hibited references to or scenes of much that was in anyway controversial—nudity, references to genital hygiene, scenes of childbirth, "perversion," prostitution, etc. The coming of sound only made things worse. By 1934, an official production code was put into effect. This meant scripts that might in any way be controversial had to meet with the approval of an overseeing body before they could be filmed.

The United States Supreme Court bolstered the acts to suppress films by ruling in 1941 that censorship was a proper exercise of police power— that it did not violate the First and Fourteenth amendments. This ruling allowed local officials to close down movie houses.

World War II brought an openness and new perspective to the country. In the postwar years, the Supreme Court overturned its 1941 decision—film content was to be protected by free speech and the freedom of the press guarantees of the Constitution. Hollywood, however, was slower to react. So filmmakers such as Thorold Dickinson, making the American/British production *Then and Now* in 1947, and Hiroshi Teshigahara and Ruy Guerra in the early 1960s remained at the mercy of restrained distributors. Their films remained unseen in the United States despite the fact that the production code was revised in 1966 and a rating system was introduced in 1968.

The Swedish director Victor Sjöström could claim a special credit. His 1912 film *The Gardener/Broken Spring Rose* was banned in Sweden for its daring content. Discovered in the Library of Congress in 1979, it finally "opened" in Sweden in 1980. But it remained unreleased in the United States these many years.

53. Thorold Dickinson (1903–)

Then and Now. 1947. Script by Thorold Dickinson and Simon Harcourt-Smith, based on Somerset Maugham's novel of the same name. Producers: Two Cities Films and Regency Productions Co. With Trevor Howard (Machiavelli) and George Sanders (Cesare Borgia). Unfinished.

Thorold Dickinson's unsuccessful attempt to make the film *Then and Now* illustrates the risks inherent in submitting one's ideas for approval to a guiding authority, particularly in a socially repressive era.

In early 1947, Dickinson, the British director of thrillers such as *Gaslight* (1940), was assigned the task of filming Somerset Maugham's *Then and Now*, whose rights had been acquired by the British film studio Two Cities. Two Cities teamed up with the American studio Regency Productions Company to coproduce the film. By November, Dickinson and a colleague developed an intricate story that centered on Machiavelli's private loves (based on his play *La Mandragola*) and his public struggle (as secretary of the Florentine Council) to prevent Cesare Borgia from ruling Florence in the late fifteenth and early sixteenth century. In Italy, Dickinson selected location shots and envisioned the story, which would be told in flashback from the following opening: A mule, with a body on its back, is descending a trail. A figure comes into view and lifts up the head, and yells, "Cesare Borgia."

In December 1947, with the cast selection already underway and set design and costume under consideration, the British producers received a letter from Hollywood. It seems that the Hollywood coproducer, headed by Arnold Pressburger, had on its own discretion submitted the film script for review to the Motion Picture Association of America. Stephen Jackson of the association responded:

> In its present form a picture based on this material would be in violation of the Production Code and could not be approved by us. This . . . arises from the fact that the secondary theme . . . is a story of seduction, adultery and illegitimacy, which are treated for romantic comedy. . . . At the outset, we direct your particular attention to the need for the greatest possible care in the selection and photography of the dresses and costumes for your women. . . . The intimate parts of the body—specifically the breasts of women—(must) be fully clothed. . . .

227

Two Cities was faced with a list of three dozen specific objections, particularly to material dealing with Machiavelli's private life. The studio considered altering the film's "secondary" theme dealing with Machiavelli's personal affairs—in this case his seducing the wife of a wealthy friend—by using material from Molière's *L'École des Femmes* (*School for Wives*). But Molière's play dealt with the love of an old man for a young woman, a story-line the producers also could not envision filming under the censorship of the period. Unable to come up with an adequate subtheme that would at least suggest the more intimate subject matter in Machiavelli's life—and that could be filmed—the British producers of *Then and Now* shelved the film.

The script for *Then and Now* can be found in Thorold Dickinson's papers.

54. Ruy Guerra (1931–)

Oros. 1960. 15 min., in color. Produced by Niemeyer. Script by Ruy Guerra. Photographed by Di Luca. Unreleased.

Oxumare's Horse (O Cavalo de Oxumare). 1961, 30 min. Produced by Niemeyer. Script by Ruy Guerra and Miquel Torres. Photographed by Di Luca. With Irma Alvarez, Haroldo Barbosa, and Miguel Paiva. Unfinished.

The Hustlers (Os Cafajestes). 1962, 92 min. Produced by Magnus Films. Script by Guerra and Miguel Torres. Photographed by Tony Rabattoni. With Jece Valadao (Jandir), Daniel Filho (Vava), Lucy Carvalho (Wilma) and Glauce Rocha (prostitute). Unreleased in U.S.

Ruy Guerra, who was born in Mozambique, is a Brazilian director who has made only a dozen films in thirty years. His most recent films are *Erendira* (1983) and *Kuarup* (1989). "In contrast to his generation," a Brazilian paper once wrote, "Ruy Guerra has not given up his critical and uncompromising vision of society." A result is that he has had difficulty finding backing to make—and complete—films. Ruy Guerra's films center on individuals in extreme situations, and focus on their relationships to societal structures.

Ruy Guerra entered filmmaking by making shorts. His first efforts, called *Oros* (1960) and *Oxumare's Horse* (1961), were made at the behest of a soccer-film producer eager to turn out something else. *Oros* was a documentary on the last stages of the building of a dam in Northeast Brazil. "The movie was not what I would have wished for," said Guerra in 1973, "that is, to film a dam being built over several years.... I had no direct sound and I could not have any interviews." *Oros* was completed as a working copy, but the standard copy was never made by the producer Niemeyer. "For business reasons," speculated Guerra, "the movie was paid for but never exploited."

Oxumare's Horse was written in a year by Guerra and colleague Miguel Torres. Produced by the wealthy Niemeyer, who was probably seeking a prestigious product, it was supposed to be a medium-length film about the Afro-Brazilian *candomble* ceremony of the Northeast: the forbidden fetishistic temples, the ritual slaughter of roosters and rams, black magic, and the women, possessed by the spirits, who become the "horses of the gods."

Guerra believed that in *Oxumare's Horse* he succeeded in "giving a sense of time that was at once objective and subjective." According to the director's description, the plot centers around a white woman and a black man. The woman loves the man, but refuses him for fear that any child they produce would suffer the consequences of being of mixed race. The woman imagines giving herself to God in penitence, and much of the film's action involves her initiation rite.

According to Ruy Guerra, the *candomble* ceremony, which has a public and a secret side to it, "is very much tied to psychoanalysis, to all the tribal context." Guerra presented images of much that had been done thanks to blackslaves—not the negative heritage, the tortures, but all that colonialism left that was beautiful, now found in museums. While recognizing the beauty inherent in a sequence of Christ figures, for instance, the director underlined the "cries, the suffering that permitted their creation" by concentrating on the secret initiation rite of the white woman, who is supposed to give herself to Saint Oxumare. Her anguish was "to feel what people can become in the name of beauty and what her own son could become."

By filming the secret ceremony, Guerra attracted enormous publicity. He was warned that no one had yet been able to complete any movie involving the *candomble*. For example, in 1950, Henri-Georges Clouzot was in South America to make *Voyage to Brazil*. He was concentrating on the secret ceremony—and failed to realize his project. Guerra scoffed at the warnings and went on to film the crucial scenes: the beautiful white woman (Irma Alvarez) finds she can't come to give herself wholly to Saint Oxumare, and shaves her head. She meets a black man, and they make love near a sewage dump.

It turned out that the film had unintended effects. The Argentinian actress playing the lead had a magnificent skull and became even more beautiful bald in a role that completely captivated her. Guerra described her as being "seduced by the Afro-Brazilian ritual." After the producer's associate objected to the film, the movie was halted. Guerra says he was never able to find out the precise reason for the interruption. *Oxumare's Horse* remains two-thirds complete.

The rushes of *Oxumare's Horse* are in Brazil, in the possession of the producer. Had the film been finished, stressed Guerra years later, distribution would have been easy enough for Niemeyer, who, Guerra believes, holds a great deal of power in distribution networks.

Guerra's next film was *The Hustlers*. This film put him on the international stage. It presents one day in the lives of four people in Rio de Janeiro. Concentrating on a playboy named Jandir, the film describes how he deals with the prospect of bankruptcy staring him in the face: He decides to blackmail his uncle. The scheme, at first, involves photographing the man's mistress in the nude and then, when that doesn't work, taking pictures of his daughter. Guerra employed documentary footage shot with a hand-held camera to give a feel for the "world of the street." At a time when other Brazilian filmmakers were looking at the misery of the Northeast and urban slums, Guerra was turning his camera, as one critic noted, towards the "country's moral underdevelopment" and pointing his finger directly at the "film-going" middle class.

The Hustlers was the first Brazilian film to show frontal nudity. *Variety* found some of the nude sequences "delicately handled and magnificently lensed. They have a sincere artistic quality and are without erotic overtones." Some other scenes, the publication pointed out, "may evoke censorship problems." This prediction turned out to be true; the film was banned in Brazil for its "immoral, nauseating, and repugnant" nature. The official responsible for its prohibition called the film "an apology for crimes of rape, kidnapping, licentiousness, drug usage and crimes against Christian morality and behavior." While others called the film "the most important [Brazilian film] since *Ganga Bruta* (1933), and it was awarded the Grand Prix at Cannes in 1962, it was denied entrance into the United States because of its "pornographic" nature.

In his later career, Ruy Guerra went on to win the Silver Bear at the Berlin Film Festival twice—for *The Guns* (1964), a film he had tried to make in 1958 in Greece but was barred from filming, and its sequel, *The Fall* (1978).

55. Victor Sjöström (1879–1960)

The Gardener/Broken Spring Rose (Tradgardsmastaren). 1912, 950m (3 reels). Directed by Sjöström. Scripted by Mauritz Stiller. Produced by Swedish Biograf Theatre (Svenska Bio). With Sjöström (Hans, the gardener), Gösta Ekman (son), Lili Beck (girlfriend), John Ekman (general), Gunnar Bohman, and Mauritz Stiller. Unreleased in the U.S.

Victor Sjöström was a Swedish director and actor. He is perhaps best remembered for his starring role as the old man in Ingmar Bergman's *Wild Strawberries* (1957). Yet he directed more than 50 films in only 20 years. Besides Sweden, he worked in Hollywood and Britain. His important works include *A Man Was There* (1917), *A Girl from Stormy Croft* (1918), *The Sons of Ingmar* (1919), *The Phantom Carriage* (1921), *Love's Crucible*, (1922), *He Who Gets Slapped* (with Lon Chaney, 1924), *The Divine Woman* (with Greta Garbo, 1928), *The Wind* (with Lilian Gish, 1928), and *The Red Robe* (produced by Alexander Korda, 1937). *Love's Crucible* was destroyed in a fire in 1941, and *The Divine Woman* is lost.

In the years 1912–16, the Swedish directors Sjöström (Seastrom) and Mauritz Stiller were mastering the medium of film. Each director averaged eight films per year during this learning period. Nearly all their work from these years was not shown in the United States and is now lost. Sjöström's early work *The Gardener* or *Broken Spring Rose* is of particular interest because it reflected the "elemental" themes central to his work: the human struggle against both the psychological nature of man and the forces of the natural world. This film was thought lost until recently.

In 1911 Sjöström, along with Stiller, was recruited into the Swedish Biograf Theatre (Svenska Biografteatern), located in Lidingö, outside Stockholm, by its owner, Charles Magnusson. He was seeking directors to handle the increased film production. Both having had experience in live theatre, Sjöström and Stiller became fast friends. They lead Sweden into its golden age of silent films from 1914 to 1921. Of those years, Sjöström said that neither he nor Stiller considered the possibility that their work would be remembered and discussed for years. Their timing, he said, was a matter of luck.

Victor Sjöström began directing films in mid–1912. His first effort ran into trouble. The film bore a title indicative of the role he felt nature played in the lives of people. (Many of his films would bear titles reflective of a physical reality.) Called *The Gardener* or *Broken Spring Rose*, it was scripted by Stiller and starred Sjöström himself; his wife, Lili Beck; and Sweden's Barrymore, Gösta Ekman. Stiller also had a part. Sjöström took seven days to make his film, an unusually long time for the era in which he was filming. He took care to tell his story.

Broken Spring Rose is the tragic story of a young woman, played by Lili Beck, who is in love with a gardener's son (Ekman). His father opposes the affair. When the young man is out of town, the gardener rapes the young woman. From this point on, her life goes downhill. She becomes the mistress of a general, and then turns to prostitution. In the last scene in the film, she is "among the roses of the summer where the rape took place" because of the "violence of the gardener's nature." She curses the "murderer of her happiness." Then her soul, as described by the film's title, "swings to the blue sky."

The film was promptly banned in Sweden, the ostensible reason given by the industry's overseer that "the film as such is opposed to good conduct and justice through its depiction of death as something beautiful." Svenska Bio sought to overturn the ban. The film studio arranged a special screening for Sweden's prime minister. But Prime Minister Staaf would not overrule the film's suppression.

Broken Spring Rose opened in October 1912 in Copenhagen, where the newspaper *Politiken* praised the movie for its "ravishing beauty" and emotional story. Like his other early films, Sjöström's film was a social drama filmed on location, highlighted by Sjöström's developing skill in characterization and economical use of sets and landscapes. Sjöström made clear what his interests were in filmmaking. He examined forces in conflict, whether natural or human, and integrated the physical world into his work. He viewed nature as both a mystical and a physical force humans had to contend with.

Sjöström went on to make *Ingeborg Holm* (1913), the story of a widow who lacks any kind of support to raise her children. This film is the only other work from this period still in existence.

The Gardener, never released in the United States, was lost for 67 years until a copy was found in the film collection of the Library of Congress in 1979. It premiered in Stockholm in 1980.

56. Mauritz Stiller (1883–1928)

The Dummy (Mannekangen). 1913, 300m. Directed by Stiller. Produced by Svenska Bio. Scripted by Harriet Block. Photographed by Julius Jaenzon and Hugo Edlund. With Lili Ziedner (Lili), Karl Gerhard, Stina Berg, Dagmar Ebbesen, Sven Pettersson, and Eric A. Petschler. Unfinished.

The Dagger (Dolken). 1915, 1,350m. Produced by Svenska Bio. Scripted by Stiller and Ester Julin ("Alex Vichetos"). Photographed by Julius Jaenzon. With Lili Beck (Julia), Lars Hanson (Herbert), Bertil Junggren, Rasmus Rasmussen, and William Larsson. Unreleased.

The Odalisque from Smyrna/Constantinople/The Girl from Sevastopol. 1924. The Trianon Film Company, producer. Script by Stiller and Ragnar Hylten-Cavallius, based on the story by Vladimir Semitjov. With Greta Garbo (Nina) and Einar Hanson (fiancé). Unfinished.

The film director Mauritz Stiller is perhaps best known as the man who discovered Garbo. He cast Greta Gustaffson in *Gosta Berling's Saga* (1924). He also gave her a new name. But before he established this new star, he and his colleague Victor Sjöström were instrumental in bringing Sweden to the attention of filmgoers around the world in the years 1914–21.

Between 1912 and 1916, when the director Mauritz Stiller (a Finnish Jew) was developing his narrative skills at Stockholm's Svenska Bio film studio, he made 32 films. His early work emphasized comedy, melodrama, thrillers, and sensational affairs. Nearly all of his work from this era, never released in the United States, is now lost.

Stiller's film style employed fast editing, emphasis on detail (especially the sets, props, and costumes), and a strong heroine, in contrast to the hero, who is usually anything but. In his comedies, the heroine also displays keen intelligence and great spirit.

In his second year of filmmaking, he started *The Dummy*, a coarsely humorous, burlesque-style film that he never finished. In 1915, he filmed a thriller called *The Dagger*. It was promptly banned and never shown in his native country and neighboring Norway because of its sensational nature and subject.

His other early films never released in the United States are *When*

Unidentified actor and actress in The Dagger, *1912. Banned by the censors 80 years ago, Mauritz Stiller's film dealt with a violent subject in a baroque manner.*

Mother-in-Law Rules, The Vampire, The Child, Mother and Daughter, The Black Masks, The Tyrannical Sweethearts (all 1912); *When Love Kills, When the Alarm Sounds, The Unknown Girl, The Modern Suffragette, Life's Conflicts* (begun by Sjöström), *For the Sake of Love* (all 1913); *The Playfellows, The Stormy Petrel, The Red Tower, The Shot, When Artists Love* (all 1914); *His Wife's Past, The Avenger, The Master Thief, The Wedding Night, The Mine Pilot, The Lucky Pin* (all 1915); *Love and Journalism, The Battle for His Heart, The Wings* (all 1916).

Only five of Stiller's early films were ever released in the United States. They were *The Brothers* (1913), *On the Fateful Roads of Life* (1913), *The Borderers* (1913), *Madame de Thebes* (1915), and *The Ballerina* (1916).

In 1920, Stiller made the international hit *Erotikon*. In 1924 he hit it even bigger with the now famous four-hour film *The Saga of Gösta Berling*. After its international success, when it was hailed as an "unparalleled epic of the screen," and Garbo, a costar, praised as "a Nordic princess" whose "bodily movements are like quicksilver," the film's Berlin exhibitors, Trianon, asked Stiller to direct a film for them.

Stiller had in mind just the film. Called *The Odalisque from Smyrna*, it would, he insisted to the producers, star Garbo. Stiller then promised Garbo even more acclaim from this picture than from their previous effort. The subject matter, he told her, was perfect for a major motion picture: a sweeping love story—the director had fashioned the lead character after Garbo—of a good Russian girl (Nina) who, during the Great War, leaves Sevastopol, in Russia, for Constantinople, where her lover is supposed to have disappeared. But on the dangerous journey by barge the woman is kidnapped and enslaved in a harem. Fortunately, after a number of harrowing episodes, she escapes and reunites with her fiancé.

Garbo quickly agreed to this project, for which she was to receive 500 marks a month. Stiller wanted to shoot the film in Turkey because beautiful locations would be provided free of charge. In addition, Stiller believed that because films were rarely made in Turkey, this project would receive a great deal of publicity. Further, he intended to make use of a number of mob scenes, and the extras, he felt, would be easy to find among the Turks.

Stiller, Garbo, Hanson, and Hylten-Cavallius—19 Swedes in all—reached Turkey for a two months' stay just before Christmas, 1924. The director spent a few days scouting out the main locations, but Kamel Ataturk's government would only let him shoot in a few select sites. About to start the main filming, Stiller realized he was short of cash. Immediately he cabled the producers at Trianon for one million marks, but received no reply. The director halted the shooting to head back to Berlin.

At Trianon, Stiller found that his chief backer within the company had resigned and, still worse, that the producers had gone bankrupt—the devastating inflation was in full swing in Germany. He was forced to recall Garbo and the rest of the cast from Turkey while he tried to find financing within the German film industry. But he could find no backing, not even from the studio of his colleague G. W. Pabst. Despite the severe economic conditions, Stiller had, paradoxically, acquired the reputation of a man "careless with a mark."

Garbo reacted to the turn of events with "Don't worry.... Everything will be all right.... Stiller will take care of everything." But *The Odalisque from Smyrna* was to remain unfinished. Diagnosed as having cancer in 1928, Stiller apparently committed suicide at the age of 45.

Much of Stiller's early work was in existence until September 1941, when fire destroyed most of the negatives of silent Swedish films housed in an archive in Stockholm. The loss included nearly all of Victor Sjöström's films directed before 1916. Of the 32 films Stiller made until 1916, all were lost but one: *Love and Journalism* (1916); only fragments of *The Dummy* (36m), *The Borderers*, and *His Wedding Night* (1915) are extant.

Photos of Stiller's *His Wife's Past*, *The Avenger*, *Madame de Thebes*, *The Master Thief*, *The Ballerina*, and *The Wings* are preserved in the Library of Congress's Prints and Photographs Division.

57. Hiroshi Teshigahara (1927–)

"Ako." 1964, 30 min. Produced by National Film Board of Canada. Script by Kobo Abe. With Miki Irle. Unreleased in U.S.

In 1964, the surrealist Japanese director Hiroshi Teshigahara participated in the making of a 4-part compilation film entitled *That Tender Age, or the Adolescents* (*La Fleur de l'Âge, ou Les Adolescents*). Produced by the National Film Board of Canada, which has made many films about young people in documentary and fiction form, the film was shown in its entirety in Europe.

In the United States, however, Teshigahara's episode, called "Ako," was deleted because of its depiction of aggression and sexual activity and its pessimistic vision.

Teshigahara participated in the making of the 110-minute film *The Adolescents* the year after he achieved international recognition with *Woman in the Dunes* (*Suna No Oona*). Each of the participating directors provided a segment about female adolescents (14 to 17 years old). Gian Vittorio Baldi directed a segment about a spoiled 14-year-old Italian girl who, with only time on her hands to hang around a magnificent villa and contemplate her dead father, drives her mother's lover away; the Canadian Michel Brault told the story of two girls who, attending a winter carnival in Montreal, are attracted to the same boy; and Jean Rouch has two rich and young Parisiennes exploring life in the big city.

Teshigahara's story stands out from the others. Written by Kobo Abe, who scripted some of Teshigahara's best films, the "Ako" episode, while lacking full character development, is grim yet forceful. It is an example of Teshigahara's belief that "history and cultural patterns may change over time, but fundamental human problems do not."

The adolescent Teshigahara depicts is the 16-year-old Ako. She works at a monotonous job; and when not at work the only boys she seems to know are the ones interested in her body. In one encounter she is nearly raped, yet she remains optimistic in outlook despite this and other distressing events.

Injured in an automobile accident in 1970, Teshigahara disappeared from view in the West, although he was quoted in 1989 as saying, "It never

237

occurred to me that I had stopped filmmaking. I continued to make small documentary films and experimental works on film." Seventeen years after his last commercial work, *Summer Soldiers* (1972), Teshigahara made *Rikyu*, a political tale set in seventeenth-century Japan.

XI. ABRUPT HALTS

Those who know how the production of films is organized find it . . . inexplicable that a good film can appear on the screen from time to time. Doubtless such an accident is due to a moment of distraction on the part of its producers, and a more efficient organization will probably one day reduce to nil the number of such unforseeable accidents.

—René Clair

It is no accident when a major director abandons a film—"one's child"—as Eisenstein referred to his experience having to forego the completion of *Que Viva Mexico!* in 1932.

The seven directors and actors discussed in this section abandoned works for many reasons. Clouzot and Wicki each abandoned a film in 1964 for reasons of health; Keaton walked away from a project because he wasn't paid; Dulac in 1922 and Deren in 1944 suspended work for art's sake; and Chaplin in 1916 and 1922 and Ozu in 1935 shelved works for personal reasons.

Some mysteries about unfinished or unreleased films have had happy endings. Widely reported to have been shelved, a few were actually completed and shown.

This was the case with two films starring Sarah Bernhardt. The great stage actress made only eight films in her career. After her first, *Hamlet's Duel* (1900), she said of the cinema: "It exorcised the old curse of the actor's art—its impermanence." From 1908 on, when she returned to film acting, she tried to establish herself as the first screen star, calling the arena of films "my last chance at immortality."

So at the improbable age of 64, she agreed to star in the film version of Victorien Sardou's 1887 play *La Tosca*, which had been written specifically for her. André Calmettes was directing her as the famed singer Floria Tosca. He filmed the two-reeler in a day. When the Divine Sarah saw her performance, she asked Calmettes not to release the film.

That same year Sardou died. According to a number of film sources, Calmettes granted her wish. The next year he shot *La Tosca* with Cecile Sorel in the lead. In late 1909 the publication *Moving Picture World* described this second version of *La Tosca* as "superbly mounted . . . unquestionably the finest picture we have seen."

239

Then in 1912, Bernhardt scored a triumph in *Queen Elizabeth*. It was time to capitalize on her film stardom. The 40-minute version of *La Tosca* was dusted off the shelf and released. The reaction was not what Bernhardt had expected years earlier. Critic G. F. Blaisdell, writing in *Moving Picture World*, called "Bernhardt in La Tosca" an "unusually" short film that nonetheless preserves the "essentials of the great play."

Bernhardt went on to complete three more films. In 1923 she was starring in *La Voyante*. She died with a few scenes left unfinished. While it's true she didn't complete the film, the actress Jean Brindeau filled in for her. The picture was then released in France by directors Louis Mercanton and Leon Abrams.

A final story concerns the works of three directors who died in mid-film in the 1960s. In 1961, the Polish director Andrzej Munk, making the film *Passenger*, lost his life in an automobile accident. But an edited version, by Witold Lesiewicz, of scenes shot by Munk and linked with stills was released in 1963. In 1965, the Hungarian director Ladislao Vajda died of a heart attack while making *La Signora de Beirut* in Spain. With two-thirds of the film completed, the producer called in another director to finish the job. Despite the claims of a number of film sources to the contrary, this film was completed and released.

Finally, veteran Soviet director Ivan Pyriev was making *The Brothers Karamazov* in 1968. Sixty-seven years old, he was celebrating his fortieth year of filmmaking when he died. The 220-minute film was completed by the lead actors Mikhail Ulyanov and Kirill Lavrov.

58. Charles Chaplin (1889–1972)

Life. 1916. Essanay Film Manufacturing Co., Jesse T. Robbins, producer. Script by Charles Chaplin. Photographed by Harry Ensign. With Chaplin. Unfinished.

The Professor. 1922, 2 reels (2,000 ft.); 450 ft. (5 minutes) extant. Produced by Charles Chaplin. With Chaplin. Unreleased.

The young Chaplin spent his last days of employment at the Essanay Studio in Hollywood (1915–16) reputedly planning his first full-length feature five years before he would actually complete one (*The Kid*). He abandoned the project, called *Life*, but some scenes were salvaged for use in Chaplin's last official film for Essanay, entitled *Police* (1916), and in an unauthorized Chaplin release by Essanay entitled *Triple Trouble*. In *Police*, a flophouse sequence survives from the earlier project. In *Triple Trouble*, two fragments survive: One shows Chaplin as a kitchen boy working with a downtrodden servant who is scrubbing the floors. The other depicts a loudmouthed drunk who cannot be quieted except by a bottle smashed over his head.

The Professor is the one film in Chaplin's directorial output that remains a mystery.

He began production in 1919, and in 1922 sent a telegram to his brother Sydney and a potential distributor: "Now OK for you . . . to deliver two reels Professor in accordance with contracts." But Chaplin never actually released the film to anyone, nor did he show it.

In the mid–1970s, a can of film entitled "The Professor" was found by Kevin Brownlow and David Gill, then preparing material for "Unknown Chaplin" to be shown in Britain and the United States. The five-minute fragment they uncovered stars Chaplin as Professor Bosco. The Professor, carrying a small box entitled "Flea Circus," beds down for the night in a flophouse. While he sleeps, a shabby dog upsets the box and the fleas escape. Soon the other flophouse guests—along with the dog—are busily scratching. The professor awakens and frantically—but carefully—gathers up the brood from the neighbor's whiskers. With the fleas back in the box, the Professor departs in chase of the dog.

Chaplin is said to have reviewed this film in preparation for *The Great Dictator* in 1940, perhaps trying to work it into the film, and in 1951 he recreated a flea circus bit in *Limelight*. Today only the snippet preserved by Brownlow and Gill remains.

59. Henri-Georges Clouzot (1907–1977)

Hell (L'Enfer). 1964, 45 min. Photographed in color by Claude Renoir, Armand Thirard, and Andreas Winding. With Serge Reggiani (Marcel Prieur), Romy Schneider (Odette Prieur), and Dany Carrel (Marylou). Unfinished.

It is possible to view the absurd as the key to any film by the French director Henri-Georges Clouzot. When the director probed deeply enough, he always unearthed something sordid, shocking, and violent because he believed man's nature was essentially evil. Clouzot the director was always in control of every aspect of filmmaking, from the script, to the settings, to the acting, so that whatever appeared on the screen reflected his view of life. He made his first film in 1931, a short called *Le Terreur des Batignolles*, and established himself with *Le Corbeau* in 1943. He is most well known for *Les Diaboliques* (1955, starring Vera Clouzot, the director's wife). Two of Clouzot's films have never been shown in the United States, and another is unfinished.

After the death of his wife, Vera, in 1960, Henri-Georges Clouzot sank into a depression and was tempted to suicide. He didn't recover sufficiently until December 1963, when he remarried and wrote a script called "The Bottom of the Night." It would be the basis for *L'Enfer*, or *Hell*, his first film since *The Truth* (1960), which had starred Vera Clouzot.

Interested only in original scenarios, Clouzot would again try to bring to the screen his own obsessions. *Hell* was to be his carefully crafted "story of a delirium of interpretation," in the author's own words. It would be a clinical analysis of jealousy, mistrust, and disenchantment. The director hired three photographers to extend the possibilities of storytelling and explored the cinematic uses of kinetic art, an art form popular in the 1950s and 1960s. He began filming July 2, 1964, and displayed an almost pathological belief in the maxim of kinetics: Movies should move. Shot partially in color, most of *Hell* has either the actors, the camera, or the scenery constantly in motion. Clouzot's intent is to maintain the ambiguity until the very end, so the viewer is never really sure whether what he sees has actually happened or is only a figment of the imagination of the main character.

243

Louis Jouvet portrays a returning POW in the episode "Return of Jean" (from the film Return to Life, *1949), pictured here with Jo Dest, directed by Henri-Georges Clouzot.*

Shortly after the cameras started rolling, however, the French papers began to ask whether the film was "cursed." First, the star, Serge Reggiani, became ill in mid–July, delaying shooting for about 10 days; then the director himself suffered a heart attack July 31.

By late 1964, director Clouzot clearly wished to resume filming his "dearest project," as he called it. An American producer had indicated a willingness to try to save the production. But his health, Clouzot stressed in late 1964, made it "inconceivable for the time being. My doctor advises me to return to normal activity, but the movie is unrealizable precisely under normal conditions." In addition, Clouzot saw that the film, already way over budget, had a chance for success against the growing popularity of television only if it were a real extravaganza. When the film's suspension allowed the production company to receive 500 million in compensation from the insurance companies, Clouzot abandoned *Hell*.

Forty-five minutes of Clouzot's unfinished film now resides in the French Cinémathèque.

The following excerpts from the original synopsis for *Hell* were published in the book *H. G. Clouzot* by Philippe Pilard.*

L'Enfer

Hell [or The Hell]

In the disturbing shadow of a room, a door opens suddenly. A man appears and remains motionless, as if haunted or fascinated by some unbearable spectacle. He has blood on his hands; his pajamas are stained with suspicious spots. In a mirror, his own face scares him.

Stretched out on the bed, a woman. Dead? No, she is still breathing. But, victim of some unknown attack, she has been tied to the headboard of the bed by her wrists.

By whom? And who is she?

Her name: Odette Prieur.

Once, not long ago, maybe even yesterday, she was a happy, pretty woman. She ran a bourgeois hotel with her husband, in a picturesque corner of France, not far from a river where, on Sundays, people came from the city to water ski.

A quiet life, normal, tuned on the comings and goings of the clientele, punctuated by the din of the trains that roar by on the huge iron viaduct, there, above the valley.

Odette took care of the bar, took the orders for the meals, took her son, the little Paolo, for walks.... In short, one of these ordinary young women who are made to age peacefully and to whom nothing should happen. Yet...

...Yet, this night, she is tied to the headboard of the bed, half naked, like a victim readied for a sacrifice. Over her hangs the still, eerie menace of this man who observes her. Had she not fallen unconscious, she would probably be screaming with terror. Had she been told some months ago...

...But some months ago, nobody would have guessed that Odette Prieur was running this mortal danger that is felt at the sight of this bloodied jailer... he is her husband: Marcel Prieur, hotel keeper, forty years old, a quite ordinary man, till now.

It's always the same story: a small lie that you catch, an equivocal gesture... and, behind the one you think you know so well, someone else is taking shape, mysterious, dangerous. Someone it becomes normal, necessary, to watch.

That is what Marcel Prieur had done; from that day on, his torment began.

There was not a man Odette had not led on, not one who had not had the occasion to hide with her in the attic, that evening when the storm broke out and the power failure had plunged the hotel into a darkness propitious to dissipation. Marcel was seeing again the squalid attic, the old, tattered boxspring. Odette had stretched out there, in her accomplice's arms. She took so much pleasure in his struggles, she put so much fury in them that her bracelet fell off to the floor.

Lacerating recollections. Marcel's rage knows no limits anymore, his jealousy has become universal.

...Universal, to the point where this jealousy has become unbelievable for us.

If, after all, Odette was not guilty of anything? If all her dissipations were pure imagination, fantasies, delirious interpretations?.. Impossible not to question oneself about all that.

Then what?

Who is really responsible, the woman tied to the bed or the man who had tied her to prevent her running off and debauching the whole clientele?

Even Marcel has started to doubt himself. His feverish mind, poisoned by alcohol, incoherent and lucid, full of fury and pity, goes over fifty details of their life in one moment, looking desperately for the proof of Odette's innocence or her guilt in these images.

Marcel is alone with his doubts.

And we, who have assisted at this hellish struggle between a man and himself, we are at the same point he is.

And yet, hesitation is not allowed.

This very morning, Arnoux, the good doctor, the honest man, had recognized that Odette was a nymphomaniac. He had decided that in one hour, at dawn, Marcel would take her to the hospital in Clermont.

Therefore, Odette is guilty.

Yes, but...

What if it was not Odette who was being sent to Clermont? What if it was himself?

What if he was insane, really insane?

My God! Marcel wanders through the hotel, in his pajamas stained with blood. He talks to himself, answers himself, terrorized by his own ghosts, and suddenly, he finds himself face to face with the exact memories of his hallucinations.

Of course, he is insane.

Therefore, Odette is innocent.

Marcel picks her up, gets her on her feet. He wants to leave, right away. Go get himself treated. To be cured.

Untied, Odette falls in his arm: it's a blessing, it's peace.

It is also the hour when, on the great iron viaduct that spans the valley, the roar of the first train resounds.

Driven by the metallic racket that has always been associated with Marcel's worst suspicions, the cruel images file past his eyes one last time.

The blood spurts and speckels the walls of the bathroom... Marcel is still holding his razor in his hand.

But, maybe, all this story of sound and fury, has only unfolded in a man's head?

Maybe this hallucinatory inquiry, this nocturnal rambling, this woman who howls, these flashes of a razor, are they yet only lying images, only the obsession of a jealous mind?

Has Marcel slit Odette's throat? Maybe. But then, how do you explain that she is still well and alive, her wrists tied to the headboard of the bed?

Other Lost Films

"The Return of Jean" (episode in *Return to Life*). 1949, 26 min. Produced by Constantin Geftman. Script by Clouzot and Jean Ferry. Photographed by Louis

Page. Design by Max Douy. With Louis Jouvet (Girard), Noel Roquevert, Jean Brochart, Jeanne Perez, Germaine Stainval, Cecile Dylma, and Jo Dest (the German). Unreleased in U.S.

The Spies (Les Espions). 1958, 120 min. A Filmsoner–Vera Film production. Script by Clouzot and Jerome Geronimi. Based on the novel *Midnight Patient* by Egon Hostowsky. Photographed by Christian Matras. With Curt Jurgens, Vera Clouzot, Peter Ustinoff, Sam Jaffe, Gerard Sety, O. E. Hasse, Paul Carpenter, and Martita Hunt. Unreleased in U.S.

Return to Life, made in 1949, is a 120-minute compilation of four directors' ironic stories about displaced persons and returning prisoners of war after World War II. Shown at Cannes, but not in the United States, the film is of interest because of Clouzot's involvement. Clouzot's episode, the third, is the caustic "Return of Jean," about a handicapped, bitter veteran (Louis Jouvet) who has come back from a Nazi prison. He finds himself recovering in a boardinghouse of a family one of whose members was a Gestapo agent. In keeping with Clouzot's feelings about violence in life, both protagonists receive the director's blasts. The only outcome can be death.

Clouzot's Kafkaesque 1958 film *The Spies* is about the unreal. Clouzot said, "For several years I have wanted to do a book by Kafka . . . but I have never been able to find a solution. . . . [The] antilogical strain in Kafka attracts me enormously. Nightmares follow me in real life."

The setting is a sanitorium—Clouzot himself had spent four years as a patient in one in the 1930s—where chief psychologist Malic (Gerard Sety) has accepted money from an American officer (Sam Jaffe) to hide a top visiting scientist (Curt Jurgens) working on a secret mission. Malic's staff is gradually infiltrated by one foreign spy, then another, all after the scientist because he has devised a superatomic bomb. Malic can't comprehend what is happening: he becomes embroiled in a world of violence, one in which it is difficult to distinguish the inmates from the unwelcome visitors.

60. Maya Deren (1908–1961)

The Witch's Cradle. 1944, 10 min. Produced, scripted, and photographed by Deren. With Marcel Duchamp and Pajarito Matta. Distributed by London Film-Makers' Cooperative. Unfinished.

The American Maya Deren, "the mother of the underground film," made seven films in the years 1943–59. Between her famous *Meshes of the Afternoon* (1943) and *At Land* (1945) she filmed *The Witch's Cradle,* but never completed it, perhaps because she couldn't find the "image juste" to express her ideas.

Deren said this 16mm film "was inspired by the architectural structure . . . paintings and objects" of a 1942 surrealist exhibition, "Art of This Century," in a New York gallery. The focus of the film is artist Marcel Duchamp and one of his creations, a string "installation" and wheel, which impressed her as "the cabalistic symbols of the 20th century." She calls the surrealists "feudal magicians and witches" because they defy notions of time and space—a theme in all of her films. To her, this defiance enabled them to face "real and underlying events."

The Witch's Cradle, her attempt to "delineate this form of magic," was released unfinished in 1961, the year Deren died of a stroke.

61. Germaine Dulac (1882–1942)

Werther. 1922. Produced by Films D. H. Script by Dulac. Adapted from the novel *The Sorrows of Werther* by Goethe. Photographed by Belval. With Gabriel de Gravonne (Werther), Denise Lorys (Charlotte), and J-David Evremond (Albert). Unfinished.

Germaine Dulac (born Charlotte-Elisabeth-Germaine Saisset Schneider) was a feminist, writer, cinematographer, and director who won acclaim as "the outstanding example . . . among women movie-makers," according to the publication *American Cinematographer*, by the early 1930s. She was elected a Chevalier of the Legion of Honor in 1931. Like Carl Th. Dreyer and René Clair, she entered films after a career in journalism. She developed an "axiom of the cinema," stressing the visual component of films over all other elements. She also helped introduce such talents as Joris Ivens into motion pictures.

Germaine Dulac had this to say about films: "To my mind . . . film has only two values: market and research. . . . The director can seek, forever seek. The cinema has not yet arrived at the zenith which permits creation in repose. Yesterday prepares today, today prepares tomorrow."

In 1922, seven years after she entered the cinema, Germaine Dulac attempted to bring to the screen Goethe's great romantic novel, *The Sorrows of Werther* (1774).

In Dulac's adaptation, called simply *Werther*, the title character is a young man in love with the beautiful Charlotte. Unaware that she is engaged to his friend Albert, he makes advances to her. When Albert is called away, she submits. Not until later does she confess to Werther the nature of her relationship to Albert. When Albert returns, Werther commits suicide.

Dulac was not the first filmmaker to try to capture Werther's story on screen. In 1910 the French directors André Calmettes and Henri Pouctal filmed the story for Pathé Films. However, Dulac's effort to complete her film would prove unsuccessful. The reasons are not entirely clear, but in her case, a more pressing project may have intervened. Before this happened, though, Dulac would use *Werther* to explore several innovative and experimental film techniques.

Dulac's partner in making *Werther* was poet-novelist, screenwriter, and producer Irene Hillel-Erlanger, who had written *Les Soeurs Ennemies* (1915), *Géo-le-Mystérieux* (1916), *Vénus Victrix* (1916), and *Dans l'Ouragan* (1916), Dulac's first four films.

Dulac's insistence that she exercise virtually total control over her film projects had led the two to form their own production company, dubbed Films D. H. (for Dulac/Hillel-Erlanger), in 1917. The move was meant to break Dulac's dependence on producers, most of whom would allow her only the freedom to choose a theme, which she stressed was no freedom at all. The story in her films, Dulac said, was merely a starting point. She futher reasoned that a French director had to be responsible for every step of the film or it would not completely achieve his or her vision; she did not feel that the French had yet arrived at the point where "collective filming" produced desirable results.

Dulac's film *Werther* bore a number of her personal stamps. Prisms distorted and multiplied images, meant to represent the characters' mental states. Objects moved, and the camera moved with them—novel effects in films at the time.

Dulac's next film, *The Smiling Madame Beudet* (*La Souriante Madame Beudet*, 1923), established her reputation as a leading avant-garde filmmaker. *Madame Beudet*, she said, "permitted me to work toward the evolution of the matographic art." Dulac's films, in fact, would go on to capture the different phases that the avant-garde filmmakers explored over the years: impressionism, dadaism, surrealism, and abstraction (accompanied by music by Debussy and Chopin).

Of the dozen or so films Dulac directed between 1915 and 1929—most of them shorts—only *Madame Beudet* and *The Sea Shell and the Clergyman* (written by Artaud, 1927) have been released in America.

A modern film adaptation of Goethe's *The Sorrows of Werther* would wait years more. In 1938 Max Ophuls filmed the first sound version of the novel, in France. In 1949 director Karl Heinz Stroux made a German version.

62. Buster Keaton (1895–1966)

Ten Girls Ago. 1962, 72 min. Produced by Edward A. Gollin. Directed by Harold Daniels. Script by Peter Farrow and Diane Lampert. Photographed by Lee Garmes and Jackson M. Samuels. With Keaton, Bert Lahr, Eddie Foy, Jr., Dion, Austin Willis, Jan Miner, Jennifer Billingsley, and Risella Bain. Unfinished.

Buster Keaton's appearances in the Cirque Medrano in Paris after World War II signaled his rediscovery after a 20-year period of decline. In the last two decades of his life the comedian appeared in more than 20 films. Of these films, one is unfinished, one has never been released, and three—one each from Mexico, France, and Italy—have never been shown in the United States.

In 1962, Keaton was north of the border. He participated in the making of a Canadian film called *Ten Girls Ago*. Here he joined forces with two old friends from the 1930s: Bert Lahr and Eddie Foy, Jr. The three were offered, according to Keaton, three weeks of guaranteed work at a very high salary.

The film started out as a black and white, rock 'n' roll comedy. An old-time comedian, played by Bert Lahr, is facing stiff competition from another television network's star: a dog. He plans to do something special. Lahr is going to put on a show in a deli so as to recapture his former glory.

In making the film, which made use of only two sets (the deli for the comedy, and a park for the music), the comedians discussed approaches to take. They would improvise, if necessary, to upgrade the comedy in the film. At one point, Lahr told Keaton to do the "hanger bit . . . you know, the one where you get mixed up with the paper and glue everything."

The film had its share of problems from the start. Director Harold Daniels was not hired until just before shooting was slated to start. Shortly after the black and white filming began, the producer attempted to expand the production beyond the intended teenager market (Dion was in it). He had the script rewritten, and then hired Lee Garmes, the photographer of *Gone with the Wind* (1939), to shoot the film in color and wide screen.

The film was shot in Toronto in 1962. After six weeks instead of three, filming was still not complete. By 1963, with 72 minutes of edited footage,

Ten Girls Ago still required another 20 minutes—three more weeks of filming.

Keaton and the other two comedians departed the set when they were not paid in full. They were never paid for their last week's work, and the film remained unfinished.

Other Lost Films

The Modern Bluebeard/Boom on the Moon (El Moderno Barba Azul). 1946, 90 min. Mexico. Directed by Jaime Salvador. Produced by Alexander Salkind. Script by Victor Trivas. Photographed by Augustin Jimenez. With Keaton, Angel Garasa, Virginia Serret, Jorge Mondragon, and Luis G. Barreiro. Unreleased in U.S.

Duel to the Death (Un Duel à Mort). 1948, short. Produced by Films Azur. Directed by Pierre Blondy. Script by Keaton and Blondy. With Keaton and Antonin Berval.

Paradise for Buster. 1952, 39 min. Produced by Wilding Pictures. Directed by Del Lord. Script by J. P. Prindle, John Grey, and Hal Goodwin. With Keaton. Unreleased.

Velvet Legs (Pattes de Velours/L'Incantevole nemica). 1953, 86 min. Directed by Claudio Gora. Produced by Lambar Film (Paris) and Orso Film (Rome). With Keaton, Silvana Pampanini, Robert Lamoureux, and Raymond Bussieres. Unreleased in U.S.

In 1946, Keaton was south of the border. He made his only Mexican feature in a film career that lasted nearly 50 years. Called the *Modern Bluebeard*, the film was written by Victor Trivas, the German (Russian-born) screenwriter and director. Trivas had collaborated on the 1944 Hollywood film *Song of Russia* and would win an Oscar for his script of Orson Welles's *The Stranger* (1946). Trivas was asked by the producers of *The Modern Bluebeard* to provide a script that would appropriately mark the debut of Keaton in a Latin American production.

Trivas developed a tale in which Keaton plays a shipwrecked American soldier who mistakes Mexico for Japan. On land, he immediately runs into trouble. The color of his facial hair allows an ambitious public official to make a name for himself: He accuses Keaton of being Bluebeard and throws him in jail. Behind bars, Keaton meets another jailbird. They both are asked to choose between the firing squad or a planned rocket trip to the moon.

The craft is to be piloted by a professor (Barreiro), who is accompanied by his daughter (Serret). Of course, Keaton and his new friend accept the free ride. On the trip they all don tunics and pointed, starred helmets. When the rocketship finally crash-lands, Keaton and the others believe they have reached their destination—but they have actually landed on the Mexican volcano Xochimilco. This film was never released in the United States.

In 1948 Keaton was in Paris. There he made the short film *Duel to the Death*. Never shown in the United States, the film provides a look at some material Keaton performed at the Cirque Medrano four years earlier, which helped him return to worldwide popularity.

Back in the United States in 1952, Keaton made another short: He appeared in the film *Paradise for Buster*. Keaton is the sole performer in this pantomime about a man who inherits a farm and makes a fortune fishing. This odd production was made for private showings only. It has not been released anywhere.

Then it was back to Europe. (That same year, Keaton worked for the first and only time with Chaplin. That film was the famous *Limelight*.)

In Italy in 1953 Keaton had a minor role in the French-Italian production called *Velvet Legs*. In this comedy about love and work, Keaton gave a "weighty, comical, burlesque" sketch, according to a French reviewer, when he actually had little to work with. Joined by the comedian Raymond Bussieres, Keaton is said to have turned in a "substantial" comedic routine. This foreign production, too, has not been seen in the United States.

63. Yasujiro Ozu (1903–1963)

Tokyo Is a Nice Place (Tokyo Yoi Toko). 1935, silent. Script by Ozu (under the name James Maki). Unfinished.

In a film career that spanned the years 1927–62, the Japanese film giant Yasujiro Ozu became well known for his stationary camera, which he explained this way: "The reason is that we don't have good camera installation. My camera angle is very low and we don't have a camera which can move at such a low angle. I don't want the audience to be aware of the camera moving."

Ozu made 54 films in his career. Twenty-one of them—all silent—have never been shown in the United States. They are presumed lost. In addition, one of his last silent films is unfinished.

By 1935, Yasujiro Ozu had already directed 32 films. But he had yet to make a sound film. He was waiting until his longtime collaborator, cameraman Hideo Shigehara, had perfected his sound equipment. Ozu hesitated to use the new technology, he said, "because of a promise" to Shigehara. This also put Ozu in a difficult position with his studio. One observer noted that Ozu would "go on making silents when the company was howling for talkies." But to Ozu there was a further element: "If I can't keep promises ... then the best thing would be to give up being a director—which would be all right, too."

So Ozu continued making silent films in the mid–1930s. He began *Tokyo Is a Nice Place*, which centers on a woman raising a child by herself. She spares no effort to see that he gets the best in life. She also makes sure that he goes to college. When he marries, however, he forgets about his mother—but spends a great deal of time with his only child, a girl.

Ozu never finished this film. Instead, he finally made his first sound film the next year, called *The Only Son* (1936). Years later, he commented on the relationship between these two works, saying that *The Only Son* was a rewritten version of *Tokyo Is a Nice Place*. He claimed he could not remember why he had stopped shooting the latter.

The Only Son has been labeled "one of Ozu's darkest," the director's statement on the transitory nature of love, the elusiveness of understanding others (or ourselves), and the sense of aloneness we feel in the world. This film can be found in the Museum of Modern Art in New York and in the Cinémathèque Française.

It appears that Ozu's promise had been kept. His cameraman was ready, the studio was more than eager to introduce sound, and Ozu could proceed with a clear conscience. Yet in making his first sound film, the director indicated in an interview that the film "had the style of a silent," in spite of any attempt he made in any other direction.

Other Lost Films

Over the next 26 years, Ozu made 18 films. All of these have been released in the United States. But out of 34 silent films he directed, 21 have not. Now lost, these films are titled:

The Sword of Penitence (Zange no Yaiba). 1927, 70 min.

The Dreams of Youth (Wakoudo no Yume). 1928, 50 min.

Wife Lost (Nyobo Funshitsu). 1928, 50 min.

Pumpkin (Kabocha). 1928, 60 min.

A Couple on the Move (Hikkoshi Fufu). 1928, 60 min.

Body Beautiful (Nikutaibi). 1928, 60 min.

Treasure Mountain (Takara no Yama). 1929, 100 min.

Fighting Friends—Japanese Style (Wasei Kenka Tomodachi). 1929, 100 min.

I Graduated, but... (Daigaku wa Deta Keredo). 1929, 100 min.

The Life of an Office Worker (Kaishain Seikatsu). 1929, 85 min.

A Straightforward Boy (Tokkan Kozo). 1929, 57 min.

An Introduction to Marriage (Kekkon Gaku Nyomon). 1930, 107 min.

The Revengeful Spirit of Eros (Erogami no Onryo). 1930, 41 min.

Lost Luck (Ashi ni Sawatta Koun). 1930, 60 min.

Young Miss (Ojosan). 1930, 130 min.

Beauty's Sorrows (Bijin Aishu). 1931, 158 min.

Spring Comes from the Ladies (Haru wa Gofujin Kara). 1932, 94 min.

Until the Day We Meet (Mata Au Hi Made). 1932, 110 min.

A Mother Should Be Loved (Haha o Kawazuya). 1934, 93 min.

An Innocent Maid (Hakoiri Musume). 1935, 87 min.

College Is a Nice Place (Daigaku Yoi Toko). 1936.

64. Bernhard Wicki (1919–   )

Transit. 1965, 1 reel. Produced by Peter and Martin Hellstern and Hanns Eckelkamp. Script by Wicki and Max Frisch, from the novels *Mein Name Sei Gantenbein* and *Stiller* by Frisch. Photographed by Sven Nykvist. With Ernst Schroder (Theo Ehrismann), Agnes Fink, Christina Schollin, Blanche Aubry, Richard Munch, and Rudolf Rhomberg. Unfinished.

The Swiss director Bernhard Wicki gained international attention in 1959 with his first full-length feature, *The Bridge* (*Die Brücke*), an account of German youths called to fight in the waning hours of the Third Reich. Acclaimed as one of postwar Germany's best movies, *The Bridge* was a savage indictment of war.

In the years following this success, Wicki tried, as he told the *New York Times* in 1962, to make "small pictures . . . in budget and narrow in scope." He believed audiences were "looking for answers," and his purpose, if he couldn't give them answers, was at least to "present the questions." One such attempt to "stimulate thought and generate emotions," as he put it, was his involvement in the unfinished film *Transit*, based on work by the Swiss writer Max Frisch.

In Zurich in 1965, author Frisch wanted to take part in the various phases of movie production. Encouraged by several producers, Frisch developed a story with the intention of producing one of the most original experiments of postwar European film. Adapting material from his novels *Mein Name sei Gantenbein* (*A Wilderness of Mirrors*, 1964) and *Stiller* (1954), Frisch made a second try at bringing his work to the screen. A few years earlier, he had begun writing a first draft of a movie script, but he stopped. Frisch never revealed the title of this unfinished first work for a film.

In this new film, Frisch aimed to create "a comedy of alienation." *Transit* would have taken little note of chronology, probability, or verisimilitude, yet remain a film of inaction and "no plot whatsoever," as Frisch's work has been characterized. First titled *I Regret Nothing*, then *The Ashes of a Pipesmoker*, and *Zurich-Transit*, it finally became *Transit*.

At the beginning of October, filming began under the direction of Erwin Leiser, best known for *Mein Kampf* (1960). The director had engaged the actors Ernest Schroder, Viveca Lindfors, and Christina Schollin, and signed on Ingmar Bergman's great cameraman, Sven Nykvist. Within a week, however, the project ran into trouble when Max Frisch made it known that he disagreed with the director over the shooting. Leiser, apparently on the verge of a breakdown, then withdrew from the film.

Transit centers on a narrator-protagonist, an engineer named Ehrismann, who learns, while reading a paper in an airplane, that he was killed in an accident. Arriving home on the day of the funeral, he heads for the cemetery to clear up the mixup. But just when he is about to confront his hypocritical family and friends, he decides to remain in the background. Feeling estranged yet free, no longer bound by middle-class values, Ehrismann imagines himself strolling about the city of Zurich as a "transit-tourist" in a number of disguises or roles before disappearing into the night.

When Bernhard Wicki, for whom this was the first film in his homeland, took over direction, he collaborated with Frisch in further developing the story. *Transit* was intended, apparently, to comprise several sketches that Frisch "associatively" connected with each other; some scenes were to fade in and out, while others, only implied in Frisch's books, were to be acted out. Frisch appended additional scenes to the script—a stay in a museum, Ehrismann's meetings with a foreign worker and a former classmate, and more.

Free of his family, Ehrismann was to imagine himself as an underdog, then an unloved man, finally a man mocked by friends. Ehrismann's superiors, for example, were to be shown carrying a tiny coffin across the factory yard where the engineer finds himself, and a company of soldiers was supposed to laugh over these proceedings; his brothers-in-law were all to grin when Ehrismann capsizes while sailing, then throw him "wreaths for life preservers"; Ehrismann imagines himself the cause of a family misfortune, but in a speech to his wife sets everything right; finally, together with his sailing friends, all celebrate his return to the world of the living.

The question of authentic versus inauthentic existence loomed as a major one in the film; another asked whether people are able to unmask the fictions they create for themselves. *Transit* would also have raised the question whether it is appropriate to judge a man by what he has done, without taking into account what he might have achieved, that is, what remains only a figment of the imagination.

Replacing Viveca Lindfors with his wife, Agnes Fink, in the role of Ehrismann's wife, Wicki began his own shooting in late November. After seven days of filming, which was, unfortunately, interrupted by numerous technical difficulties, Wicki managed to complete one reel of footage. Suffering from the flu, the director suddenly took a turn for the worse, and he was rushed to the hospital. Not too much later, the main actor, Schroder, had to leave the set in order to meet prior commitments in Berlin. However, Frisch, having developed a close friendship with the actor, rejected his substitute. A film that might have been another *Last Year at Marienbad* (1959), but without the surrealistic overtones, collapsed.

BIBLIOGRAPHY

Marc Allégret and Yves Edouard Allégret

Ehrlich, Evelyn. *Cinema of Paradox*. New York: Columbia University Press, 1985.
Film Dope, March 1988.
Leprohon, Pierre. *Présences Contemporaines Cinéma*. Paris: Nouvelles Editions Debresse, 1957.
Lorcey, Jacques. *Marcel Achard*. Paris: Editions France-Empire, 1977.
Peyrusse, Claudette. *Le Cinéma Méridional*. Toulouse, Eche, 1986.
Swindell, Larry. *Charles Boyer*. Garden City, N.Y.: Doubleday, 1983.

Juan Antonio Bardem

L'Avant-Scène du Cinéma, no. 34, 1964.
Bardem, Juan Antonio. *Arte, Politica, Sociedad*. Madrid: Sedmay Ediciones, 1976.
_____. *Calle Mayor*. Xalapa, Mexico: Universidad Veracruzana, 1959.
_____. *J. A. Bardem*. Mexico: Universidad National Autónoma de México Dirección General de Difusión Cultural, 1962.
Filmkritik, December 1966.
Films and Filming, June 1957.
Martínez, Palacio. *Pío Baroja*. Madrid: Taurus, 1974.
Vega, Luis Antonio de. *Pío Baroja*. Madrid: Nuevas Editoriales Unidas, 1965.

Robert Bresson

Jeancolas, Jean-Pierre. *15 Ans d'Années Trente*. Paris: Stock, 1983.
Sloan, Jane. *Robert Bresson*. Boston: G. K. Hall, 1983.

Marcel Carné

American Film, November 1981.
Brunelin, André. *Gabin*. Paris: Robert Laffont, 1987.
Carné, Marcel. *La Vie à Belles Dents*. Paris: J. P. Ollivier, 1975.
Cinématographe, October 1986.
Guillot, Gerard. *Les Prévert*. Paris: Seghers, 1967.
Premier Plan, no. 14, Lyons, 1960.
Prévert, Jacques. *Paroles*. Paris: Bibliothèque des Chefs-d'Oeuvre, 1979.
Queval, Jean. *Marcel Carné*. Paris: Cerf, 1952.

Alberto de Almeida Cavalcanti

Cavalcanti, Alberto. *Filmé e Realidade*. Rio de Janeiro: Editore Artenova, 1977.
Deutsche Filmkunst, August 1956; March 1957.
Documentos Cinematográficos, March 1961.
Films and Filming, December 1956; March 1962.
Jules-Verne, Jean. *Jules Verne*. New York: Taplinger, 1976.
Klaue, Wolfgang. *Alberto Cavalcanti*. Berlin: Staatlichen Filmarchiv der DDR, 1962.
Revue du Cinéma, November 1983.
Sight and Sound, Summer 1970; Autumn 1975.

Charles Chaplin

Robinson, David. *Chaplin*. New York: McGraw-Hill, 1985.

Christian-Jaque

Barbier, Philippe. *Alain Delon*. Paris: Editions PAC, 1982.
Castans, Raymond. *Fernandel M'a Raconté*. Paris: Éditions de Provence, 1976.
Cinématographe, January 1982.
Film Dope, April 1975.
Films and Filming, February 1965.
Leprohon, Pierre. *Présences Contemporaines Cinéma*. Paris: 1957.

Reńe Clair

Dale, R. C. *The Films of René Clair*. Metuchen, N.J.: Scarecrow, 1986.
De la Roche, Catherine. *René Clair—An Index*. British Film Institute, 1958.
René Clair. Cinémathèque Française, 1983.
Sight and Sound, Spring 1951.

Henri-Georges Clouzot

Armes, Roy. *French Cinéma Since 1946, Vol. 1*. San Diego, Calif.: A. S. Barnes, 1966.
L'Avant-Scène du Cinéma, April 1977.
Cahiers du Cinéma, January 1965.
Films and Filming, June 1964.
Pilard, Philippe. *Henri-Georges Clouzot*. Paris: Seghers, 1969.

James Cruze

Moley, Raymond. *Hays Office*. Englewood, N.J.: Ozer, 1971.
Yallop, David. *The Day the Laughter Stopped*. New York: St. Martin's, 1976.

George Cukor

Phillips, Gene. *Cukor*. Boston: G. K. Hall, 1982.
Riese, Randall, and Neal Hitchins. *The Unabridged Marilyn*. New York: Congdon and Weed, 1987.

Michael Curtiz

Filmvilag, March 1966.
Kinnard, Roy, and R. J. Vitone. *American Films of Michael Curtiz*. Metuchen, N.J.: Scarecrow, 1986.
Revue du Cinéma, February 1982.
Rosenzweig, Sidney. *Casablanca and Other Major Films of Michael Curtiz*. Ann Arbor, Mich.: UMI Research Press, 1982.
Viviani, Christian. *Michael Curtiz, 1888–1962*. Paris: *L'Avant-Scène du Cinéma*, 1973.
Whittemore, Don. *Passport to Hollywood: Film Immigrants*. New York: McGraw-Hill, 1976.

Maya Deren

Film Culture, Winter 1965.

Thorold Dickinson

Richards, Jeffrey. *Thorold Dickinson*. London: Croom, Helm, 1986.

Slatan Dudow

Arbeiterbuhne und Film, August 1930.
Film a Doba, March 1975.
Film Dope, January 1978.
Herlinghaus, Hermann. *Slatan Dudow*. Berlin: Henschelverlag, 1965.
Manvell, Roger. *Experiment in the Film*. London, Grey Walls, 1949.

Germaine Dulac

American Cinematographer, January 1932.
Ford, Charles. *Femmes Cinéastes*. Paris: Denoel, 1972.
Lawder, Standish D. *The Cubist Cinema*. New York: New York University Press, 1975.
Wide Angle, no. 1, 1979.

Sergei Mikhailovich Eisenstein

Anthologie du Cinéma, vol. 1, 1966.
Birkos, Alexander S. *Soviet Cinema*. Hamden, Conn.: Archon, 1976.

Cinema Journal, Fall 1977; Spring 1978.
Eisenstein, Sergei. *The Film Sense.* New York: Harcourt, Brace, 1943.
Experimental Cinema, January 1933.
Film Quarterly, Spring 1959.
Ivan the Terrible. New York: Simon and Schuster, 1970.
Leyda, Jay. *Kino.* Princeton, N.J.: Princeton University Press, 1960.
Leyda, Jay, and Zina Voynow. *Eisenstein at Work.* New York: Museum of Modern Art, 1982.
Moussinac, Leon. *Eisenstein.* New York: Crown, 1970.
Que Viva Mexico! London: Visions, 1951.
Seton, Marie. *Sergei M. Eisenstein.* London: Bodley Head, 1952.
Taylor, Richard. *Film Factory.* Cambridge, Mass.: Harvard University Press, 1988.

Luciano Emmer

Sight and Sound, Spring 1947.

Jean Epstein

Catalogue de Films de Fiction de Premier Partie, 1929–39. 1984.
Cinemages. New York: G. Bachman, March 1956.
Leprohon, Pierre. *Jean Epstein.* Paris: Seghers, 1964.
Manvell, Roger. *Experiment in the Film.* 1949.
Sight and Sound, October–December 1953.

Paul Fejos

Dodds, John Wendell. *The Several Lives of Paul Fejos.* Wenner-Gren Foundation, 1973.
Film Dope, September 1978.
Filmkritik, August 1979.
Films in Review, February 1954.
Sight and Sound, Summer 1978.

Robert Flaherty

Cinema Journal, Spring 1985.
Murphy, William T. *Flaherty: A Guide to References and Resources.* Boston: G. K. Hall, 1978.
Quarterly Review of Film Studies, Fall 1980.
Sight and Sound, October–December 1953.

Errol Flynn

Flynn, Errol. *From a Life of Adventure.* Secaucus, N.J.: Citadel, 1980.
Higham, Charles. *Errol Flynn.* Garden City, N.Y.: Doubleday, 1980.
Valenti, Peter. *Errol Flynn.* Westport, Conn.: Greenwood, 1984.

John Ford

Bogdanovich, Peter. *John Ford*. Berkeley: University of California Press, 1978.
Sight and Sound, Autumn 1972.

Abel Gance

Cahiers du Cinéma, January 1965.
Le Cinéma de l'Espagne Franquiste, 1939–75. Les Cahiers de la Cinémathèque, 1984.
Gance, Abel. *Ou le Prométhée Foudroye*. Lausanne: L'Âge D'Homme, 1983.
Kramer, Steven Philip. *Abel Gance*. Boston: Twayne, 1978.
Narbona Gonzalez, Francisco. *Manolete*. Madrid: Ediciones Espejo, 1948.

Jean Grémillon

Agel, Henri. *Jean Grémillon*. Paris: Lherminier, 1984.
Anthologie du Cinéma, vol. 2, Paris, 1967.
L'Avant-Scène du Cinéma, no. 18, September 1962.
Bianco e Nero, October/December 1983.
Bravo Maurice. London: George Allen & Unwin, 1973.
Film Dope, April 1976; October 1980.
Filmkritik, June 1982.
Premier Plan, February 1960.
Le Printemps de la Liberté de Jean Grémillon. Paris: Bibliothèque Française, 1948.

Edmond Gréville

Cahiers du Cinéma, January 1965.
Dossiers du Cinéma—Cinéastes III, 1974.
Regent, Roger. *Cinéma de France sous l'Occupation*. Paris: Éditions d'Aujourd'hui, 1975.

Ruy Guerra

Études Cinématographiques, no 93–96, 1972.
Johnson, Ronald. *Cinema Novo X 5*. Austin: University of Texas Press, 1984.

Henry Hathaway

Higham, Charles. *Marlene*. New York: W. W. Norton, 1977.
Paul, William. *Ernst Lubitsch's American Comedy*. New York: Columbia University Press, 1983.
Tuska, Jon. *Close Up: The Contract Director*. Metuchen, N.J.: Scarecrow, 1976.
Walker, Alex. *Dietrich*. New York: Harper and Row, 1984.

Alfred Hitchcock

Durgnat, Raymond. *The Strange Case of Alfred Hitchcock*. Cambridge, Mass.: MIT Press, 1974.
LaValley, Albert J. *Focus on Hitchcock*. Englewood Cliffs, N.J.: Prentice Hall, 1972.
Rohmer, Eric. *Hitchcock, the First Forty-Four Films*. New York: F. Ungar, 1979.
Taylor, John Russell. *Hitch*. New York: Pantheon, 1978.
Truffaut, François. *Hitchcock*. New York: Simon and Schuster, 1984.
Villien, Bruno. *Hitchcock*. Paris: Éditions Colona, 1982.

Kon Ichikawa

Allyn, John. *Kon Ichikawa: A Guide to References and Resources*. Boston: G. K. Hall, 1985.
Sight and Sound, Spring 1966.
Solmi, Angelo. *Ichikawa*. Firenze: La Nuova Italia, 1975.

Joris Ivens

Boker, Carlos. *Joris Ivens, Filmmaker*. Ann Arbor, Mich.: UMI Research Press, 1981.
Delmar, Rosalind. *Joris Ivens*. BFI, 1979.
20 Jahre DEFA—Spielfilm. Berlin: Henschelverlag, 1968.
Viertel, Salka. *The Kindness of Strangers*. New York: Holt, Rinehart, and Winston, 1969.
Wegner, Hans. *Joris Ivens*. Berlin: Henschel, 1965.

Emil Jannings

Bordier, Philipe. *Pierre Louÿs et le Cinéma*. Muizon: Éditions à l'Écart S. 1, 1986.
Engel, Erich. *Schriften über Theater und Film*. Berlin: Henschelverlag, 1971.
Film Dope, July 1983.
Jannings, Emil. *Theatre/Film*. Berchtesgaden: Verlag Zimmer, 1951.
Sight and Sound, Winter 1962.

Mikhail Kalatozov

Leyda, Jay. *Kino: A History of the Russian and Soviet Film*. Princeton, N.J.: Princeton University Press, 1983.

Buster Keaton

Dardis, Tom. *Keaton*. New York: Scribner's, 1979.
Historia Documental del Cine Mexicano, Vol. 3. Editiones Era, 1969.
Lahr, John. *Notes on a Cowardly Lion*. New York: Alfred A. Knopf, 1969.
Morris, Peter. *Canadian Feature Films 1914–64*. Ottawa: Canadian Film Institute, 1965.

Lev Kuleshov

Beitrage zur Film und Fernsehwissenschaft, April 1986.
Film Culture, Spring 1967.
Film Journal, Fall-Winter 1972.
Sight and Sound, Spring 1971.
Taylor, Richard. *The Film Factory*. Cambridge, Mass.: Harvard University Press, 1988.

Pare Lorentz

Pare Lorentz and the University of Wisconsin–Oshkosh. University of Wisconsin brochure, 1972.
Snyder, Robert L. *Pare Lorentz*. Norman: University of Oklahoma Press, 1968.

Lewis Milestone

Films and Filming, June 1957; June 1961.
Higham, Charles. *The Celluloid Muse*. Lake Bluff, Ill.: Regnery, 1971.
Hollywood Reporter, January 9, 1957.
Lacourbe, Roland. *Kirk Douglas*. Paris: PAC, 1980.
McBride, J. *Kirk Douglas*. Moonachie, N.J.: Pyramid, 1976.
Millichamp, Joseph R. *Lewis Milestone*. Boston: Twayne, 1981.
Sight and Sound, Spring 1955.
Tuska, Jon. *Close Up: The Contract Director*. Metuchen, N.J.: Scarecrow, 1976.

Gaston Modot

Catalogue de Films de Fiction de Premier Partie, 1929–39, 1984.
Conroy, William Thomas. *Villiers de l'Isle-Adam*. Boston: Twayne, 1978.
Lacassin, Francis. *Pour un Contre-Histoire du Cinéma*. Paris: Union Générale d'Éditions, 1972.
Spaak, Janine. *Charles Spaak, Mon Mari*. Paris: France-Empire, 1977.

Max Ophuls

Anthologie du Cinéma, vol. 1. L'Avant-Scène du Cinéma, 1966.
Benson, Renate. *Erich Kastner*. Bonn: Bouvier, 1973.
Berriau, Simone. *Simone Est Comme Ça*. Paris: Robert Lafont, 1973.
Beylie, Claude. *Max Ophuls*. Paris: Seghers, 1963, 1984.
Cinématographe, April 1986.
Colette. *Colette at the Movies*. New York: Frederick Ungar, 1980.
Cowie, Peter. *Dutch Cinema*. London: Tantivy, 1979.
Filmkritik, November 1977.
Films in Review, January 1978.
Ozeray, Madelaine. *A Toujours Monsieur Jouvet*. Buchet/Chastel, 1966.
Roud, Richard. *Max Ophuls—An Index*. British Film Institute, 1958.

Yasujiro Ozu

Cinema, no. 1, 1970.
Ozu. British Film Institute, 1976.
Richie, Donald. *Ozu*. Berkeley: University of California Press, 1974.

G. W. Pabst

Atwell, Lee. *G. W. Pabst*. Boston: Twayne, 1977.
Cahiers du Cinéma, September 1967.
Welch, David. *Propaganda and German Cinema*. Oxford: Clarendon 1987.

Marcel Pagnol

Beylie, Claude. *Marcel Pagnol*. Paris: Seghers, 1974.
————. ————. Paris: Éditions Atlas Lherminier, 1986.

Pier Paolo Pasolini

Pasolini. Madrid: Filmoteca National, 1975.
Pier Paolo Pasolini. British Film Institute, 1977.
Snyder, Stephen. *Pier Paolo Pasolini*. Boston: Twayne, 1980.

Vsevolod I. Pudovkin

Dart, Peter. *Pudovkin's Films and Film Theory*. Arno, 1974.
Leyda, Jay. *Kino: A History of the Russian and Soviet Film*. Princeton, N.J.: Princeton University Press, 1983.
Sight and Sound, Spring 1953.

Laszlo Ranody

Hungarian Film Directors, 1948–83. Hungarofilm Bulletin, 1984.
Nemeskurty, I. *Word and Image—History of Hungarian Cinema*. Hungary: Coruna, 1968.

Alain Resnais

L'Avant-Scène du Cinéma, July 1966.
Bounoure, Gaston. *Resnais*. Paris: Seghers, 1974.
Lacassin, Francis. *Pour une Contre-Histoire du Cinéma*. Paris: Union Générale d'Éditions, 1972.
Predal, René. *Alain Resnais*. Paris: Lettres Modernes, 1968.

Hans Richter

Experimental Cinema, 1934.
Film und Volk, October 1929.
Hammond, Paul. *Marvellous Méliès.* London: Gordon Fraser, 1974.
Richter, Hans. *Dada, Kunst, und Antikunst.* Koln: M. DuMont Schauberg, 1964.
————. *Filmgegner von Heute—Filmfreunde von Morgen.* Zurich: H. Rohr, 1968.
————. *Hans Richter.* New York: Holt, Rinehart and Winston, 1971.
————. *The Struggle for the Film.* New York: St. Martin's, 1986.
Seton, Marie. *Sergei M. Eisenstein.* London: Bodley Head, 1952.

Leni Riefenstahl

Cahiers du Cinéma, September 1965.
Hinton, David B. *Films of Leni Riefenstahl.* Metuchen, N.J.: Scarecrow, 1978.
Riefenstahl, Leni. *Memoiren.* Munich: Albrecht Knaus, 1987.

Jacques Rivette

Rosenbaum, J. *Rivette—Texts and Interviews.* BFI, 1977.

Eric Rohmer

Crisp, C. G. *Eric Rohmer.* Bloomington: Indiana University Press, 1988.
Film Quarterly, Summer 1971.
Magny, Joel. *Eric Rohmer.* Paris: Rivages, 1986.
Sight and Sound, Winter 1969.

Roberto Rossellini

Brunette, Peter. *Rossellini.* New York: Oxford University Press, 1987.
Guarner, José Luis. *Roberto Rossellini.* New York: Praeger, 1970.

Franklin J. Schaffner

Film Comment, September 1972.
Films and Filming, October 1964.
Kim, Erwin. *Franklin J. Schaffner.* Metuchen, N.J.: Scarecrow, 1985.
Newsweek, November 8, 1976.

Victor Sjöström and Mauritz Stiller

Bainbridge, J. *Garbo.* New York: Galahad, 1970.
Corliss, Richard. *Greta Garbo.* Pyramid, 1974.
Gronowicz, Antoni. *Garbo.* New York: Simon and Schuster, 1990.

Pensel, Hans. *Seastrom and Stiller in Hollywood*. Vantage, 1969.
Werner, Gösta. *Mauritz Stiller och Hans Filmer 1912–1916*. Stockholm: 1971.
_____. *Svensk Filmforskning*. Stockholm: Norstedt, 1982.

Wolfgang Staudte

Film Dope, January 1978.
Films and Filming, June 1957; June 1958.
20 Jahre DEFA—Spielfilm. Lektorat Seydel, 1968.
Zur Retrospektive Wolfgang Staudte. Berlin: Stiftung Deutsche Kinemathek, 1974.

Jacques Tati

Maddock, Brent. *Films of Jacques Tati*. Metuchen, N.J.: Scarecrow, 1977.
Sight and Sound, Spring 1983.

King Vidor

Durgnat, Raymond, and Scott Simmon. *King Vidor, American*. Berkeley: University of California Press, 1988.

Josef von Sternberg

Callow, Simon. *Charles Laughton: A Difficult Actor*. London: 1987.
Kulik, Karol. *Alexander Korda*. New York: Arlington, 1975.
Sarris, Andrew. *Films of Josef von Sternberg*. New York: Museum of Modern Art, 1966.
Tabori, Paul. *Korda*. Livingston, 1966.
von Sternberg, Josef. *Fun in a Chinese Laundry*. New York: Macmillan, 1965.

Erich von Stroheim

Bessy, Maurice. *Erich Von Stroheim*. Paris: Pygmalion, 1984.
Curtiss, Thomas Quinn. *Von Stroheim*. New York: Farrar, Straus, and Giroux, 1971.
Finler, Joel. *Stroheim*. Berkeley: University of California Press, 1968.
Koszarski, Richard. *The Man You Love to Hate*. New York: Oxford University Press, 1983.
Lennig, Arthur. *The Silent Voice* W. Snyder, 1969.
Weinberg, Herman. *The Complete Wedding March*. Boston: Little, Brown, 1974.
_____. *An Index to the Creative Work of Erich von Stroheim*. 1947.
Wollner, Alexandre. *Homenagem a Erich von Stroheim*. São Paulo: 1954.

Orson Welles

Cahiers du Cinéma, May 1986; October 1986.
Cowie, Peter. *A Ribbon of Dreams*. San Diego, Calif.: A. S. Barnes, 1973.
Higham, Charles. *Orson Welles*. New York: St. Martin's, 1985.
Leaming, Barbara. *Orson Welles: A Biography*. New York: Viking, 1985.
Sight and Sound, Autumn 1966; Winter 1969/70.

James Whale

Curtis, James. *James Whale*. Metuchen, N.J.: Scarecrow, 1983.
Films in Review, May 1962.

Bernhard Wicki

Bauche, Freddy. *Le Cinéma Suisse*. Lausanne: L'Âge d'Homme, 1974.
Pender, Malcolm. *Max Frisch, His Work and Its Swiss Background*. Stuttgart: Akademischer Verlag Heinz, 1979.
Petersen, Carol. *Max Frisch*. Berlin: Colloquium-Verlag, 1976.
Stephen, Alexander. *Max Frisch*. Munich: C. H. Beck, 1983.
Weisstein, Ulrich. *Max Frisch*. Boston: Twayne, 1967.

Sergei Yutkevich

Cinema in Revolution. New York: Hill and Wang, 1973.
De Jonge, Alex. *Stalin*. New York: William Morrow, 1987.
Dickinson, Thorold. *Soviet Cinema*. London: Falcon, 1948.
Film und Fernsehen, April 1979.
Leyda, Jay. *Kino: A History of the Russian and Soviet Film*. Princeton, N.J.: Princeton University Press, 1983.
Penguin Film Review, August 1947.
Schnitzer, Luda and Jean. *Youtkevitch*. Paris: L'Âge d'Homme, 1976.

General Works

Bauer, Alfred. *Deutscher Spielfilm Almanach, 1929–50*. Berlin: Filmblatter-Verlag, 1976.
Bessy, Maurice, and Raymond Chirat. *Histoire du Cinéma Française*. 2 vols. Paris: Pygmalion, 1986.
Dumont, Herve. *Geschichte des schweitzer Films*. Schweitzer Filmarchiv, 1987.
Ford, Charles, and René Jeanne. *Histoire Encyclopédique du Cinéma*. 5 vols. Paris: SEDE, 1955.
Index de la Cinématographie Française, 1947–1965. Paris: La Cinématographie Française.
International Dictionary of Films and Filmmakers. 5 vols. Chicago: St. James, 1987.
Mitry, Jean. *Filmographie Universelle*. 26 vols. Paris: Centre National de la Cinématograph, 1963–1982.

Nemeskurty, Istvan. *A Magyar Film Tortenete, 1912–63.* Budapest: 1965.
New York Times Encyclopedia of Films. 12 vols. 1984.
Sadoul, Georges. *Histoire du Cinéma Française.* Paris: Flammarion, 1962.
Variety Film Reviews, 1908–1986. 19 vols. New York: Garland, 1985, 1988.
World Film Directors. 2 vols. New York: H. W. Wilson, 1988.

Index